THE BIRTH OF INDEPENDENT AIR POWER

THE BIRTH OF
INDEPENDENT AIR POWER

BRITISH AIR POLICY IN THE FIRST WORLD WAR

MALCOLM COOPER

Downing College, Cambridge

London
ALLEN & UNWIN
Boston   Sydney

Allen & Unwin (Publishers) Ltd,
40 Museum Street, London WC1A 1LU, UK

Allen & Unwin (Publishers) Ltd,
Park Lane, Hemel Hempstead, Herts HP2 4TE, UK

Allen & Unwin, Inc.,
8 Winchester Place, Winchester, Mass. 01890, USA

Allen & Unwin (Australia) Ltd,
8 Napier Street, North Sydney, NSW 2060, Australia

First published in 1986

British Library Cataloguing in Publication Data

Cooper, Malcolm
    The birth of independent air power:
    British air policy in the First World War.
1. Air power 2. Great Britain – Military policy
3. Great Britain – History, Military – 20th century
    I. Title
    358.4'03'0941 UG 635.G7
    ISBN 0–04–942204–9

Library of Congress Cataloging-in-Publication Data

Cooper, Malcolm (Malcolm J. D.)
    The birth of independent air power.
Bibliography: p.
Includes index.
1. World War, 1914–1918 – Aerial operations, British.
2. Great Britain. Royal Air Force – History –
World War, 1914–1918.   I. Title.
D602.C66 1986 940.4'4941 86–3316
ISBN 0–04–942204–9 (alk. paper)

Set in 10 on 12 point Sabon by
Computape (Pickering) Limited, Pickering, North Yorkshire
and printed in Great Britain by
Anchor Brendon Ltd, Tiptree, Essex

Contents

List of Illustrations

Cover illustration: A Sopwith Camel starting up in the snow on the Western Front in the winter of 1917–18 (J. M. Bruce/G. S. Leslie Collection)

Acknowledgements

No book is entirely the product of one mind, and in writing this one I feel I have been particularly fortunate to have received so much in the way of help, encouragement and ideas from others. My greatest debt is undoubtedly to Professor Michael Howard, who supervised the D. Phil. thesis upon which much of what follows has been based, and who has taken a keen interest in the project from beginning to end. I have also benefitted greatly from discussing my work with Dr Christopher Bowie and Dr Paul Millett, both of whom read and commented upon the entire manuscript, and from testing my ideas in the military history seminars in Oxford, Cambridge and London Universities. Mr Frank Bailey, Lord Blake, Mr Brian Bond, Mr Peter Grosz, Mr Peter Kilduff, Mr Stuart Leslie, Professor Austyn Mair, Dr Kenneth Morgan, Mr Bonar Sykes and Mr George Williams have all helped along the way with information and advice, and I hope they will all forgive what considerations of space can only allow to be a brief expression of gratitude. Finally, I am indebted to the staff at Allen & Unwin for seeing this book into print in such a cheerful and efficient manner, and to the Master and Fellows of Downing College, Cambridge for providing a stimulating and friendly environment in which to work.

The following have kindly given me permission to quote from material to which they own the copyright: Viscount Addison (Addison mss); Mr Mark Bonham Carter (Asquith mss); the Trustees of the Liddell Hart Centre for Military Archives, King's College, London (Montagu of Beaulieu, Capper and Brooke Popham mss); the Earl of Derby and the Record Office, Liverpool City Libraries (Derby mss); Viscount Scarsdale and the India Office Library and Records (Curzon mss); the Warden and Fellows of New College, Oxford (Milner mss); the Science Museum Library (Pearson mss); Lord Simon (Simon mss); the Smuts Archives Trustees (Smuts mss); Mr A. J. P. Taylor and the Trustees of the Beaverbrook Foundation, and the Clerk of the Records of the House of Lords Record Office (Bonar Law and Lloyd George mss); and the Royal Air Force Museum (Henderson, Newall, Salmond, Sykes and Trenchard mss).

William Heinemann Ltd have allowed me to reprint extracts from N. Macmillan (ed.), *Sir Sefton Brancker*.

Crown-copyright material in the Public Record Office appears by permission of the Controller of H. M. Stationery Office.

MALCOLM COOPER

Abbreviations used in the Notes

Asquith Papers	— Asquith Papers, Bodleian Library
BL Papers	— Bonar Law Papers, House of Lords Record Office
Curzon Papers	— Curzon Papers, India Office Records
IWM	— Imperial War Museum
LG Papers	— Lloyd George Papers, House of Lords Record Office
Milner Papers	— Milner Papers, Bodleian Library
Montagu Papers	— Montagu of Beaulieu Papers, Liddell Hart Centre, King's College London
PRO	— Public Record Office
RAF	— Royal Air Force Museum
Trenchard Papers	— Trenchard Papers, Royal Air Force Museum
WIA	— Sir Walter Raleigh and H. A. Jones, *The War in the Air. Being the Story of the Part Played in the Great War by the Royal Air Force*, 6 vols (Oxford: Clarendon Press, 1922–37).

Introduction

Britain's Royal Air Force, created on 1 April 1918 through the amalgamation of the Royal Naval Air Service and the army's Royal Flying Corps, was the first independent air service in the world. By the end of the First World War, the RAF mustered almost 300,000 personnel and 22,000 aircraft. It had undertaken a long-range bombing campaign against Germany which, but for the armistice, would have been extended all the way to Berlin. It controlled a massive home air defence network, including searchlight and gun batteries, barrage balloons, interceptor squadrons and early warning stations. It was carrying out a wide-ranging series of anti-zeppelin and anti-submarine patrols, not only around Britain's coasts, but also far out into the North Sea and the Western Approaches. In every theatre in which the British army was engaged, most notably on the Western Front, it had provided an intensive programme of air support, including artillery observation, photo reconnaissance, tactical bombing and air superiority patrols. Its aircraft had harassed and disrupted the retreating enemy from France and Belgium to northern Italy, the Balkans, Palestine and Mesopotamia.

Considering that Britain had entered the war in 1914 with less than 200 ill-assorted aircraft, the position four years later reflected a considerable achievement. In its postwar synopsis of the air effort, the Air Ministry felt able to claim 'that the results achieved in all theatres of war, as well as in home defence, have more than justified the establishment of the Royal Air Force as an independent fighting force of the Crown'.[1] The modern day student of military affairs, conscious of the aircraft's increasing dominance during the last half century, is unlikely to fault the Air Ministry's logic, or indeed to question the assumption that the early formation of an independent air service should have given Britain a valuable advantage at the dawn of the air age. The experience of the RAF between the wars, however, was such as to negate any such advantage. For much of the period, the Air Ministry was forced to defend its right to independent existence in the face of War Office and Admiralty attempts to regain control of their respective air branches. The emergence both of the modern fighter force which eventually won the Battle of Britain, and of the bomber force which thereafter took the war to the cities of the Third Reich, was hampered, and at times nearly blocked, by the problems surrounding the air force's position in the defence community.

The development of the RAF between the wars has already attracted a good deal of historical attention, but the emphasis has generally been placed on the peacetime pressures which affected its growth rather than on the wartime causes which brought it into being in the first place. To set British air policy in the 1920s and 1930s into context, and indeed to understand the full developmental process leading up to Sir Arthur Harris's nightly mass assaults on Hitler's Germany, it is necessary to explain just how Britain gained an air force and why the act of birth did not produce a healthy and well-adjusted infant.

Historical writing on the beginnings of British air policy has yet to produce a fully rounded account of Britain's first experience of air war. Developments during the First World War have either been seen as an unimportant prelude to the emergence of strategic air thought between the wars, or have been evaluated in terms of the capabilities of the air forces of 1939–45. Sir John Slessor came closest to the truth when he wrote in 1936 that the first air war had been largely an army co-operation war,[2] but the consequences of this for an air service which was created to perform a poorly defined strategic role have not yet been properly understood.

Any final evaluation of Britain's air effort between 1914 and 1918 must begin with an appreciation of the aircraft's role in the war. The flying machines of the First World War were obviously far less potent weapons than those of the Second World War, and one would search in vain to discover instances in which they dramatically affected the course of battle or campaign. Nonetheless, the aircraft did play an important tactical role in the siege warfare of the Western Front, and must be granted at least a small part of the credit for finally bringing about the rupture of the German fortified positions in France and Belgium. As a strategic weapon in its own right, the aircraft was simply too small, too weakly armed and too restricted in range to pose any serious threat to industrial or population targets. Even in this area, however, the aircraft left its mark. Indeed, as far as the British case was concerned, the intermittent enemy attacks on London and the retaliatory strikes on southwest Germany proved of more significance to the long-term development of air policy than the far more intensive campaign fought out in the skies over the trenches. While British air planners became increasingly fixated on the vision of the future first given coherent form in the Smuts Report of 1917, the wealth of tactical experience gained on the Western Front was largely forgotten. In 1939 the RAF went to war with an ill-defined strategic mission built on the first experiences of long-range bombing, but had to learn the craft of supporting its partner fighting services afresh.

For the past half century the six-volume official history *The War in the Air*, published between 1922 and 1937, has presented the standard account of the British air effort during the First World War. The continuing pre-eminence of this work is in many ways a fair reflection of its merits. The first volume, written by Sir Walter Raleigh, Professor of English Literature at Oxford University, has not aged particularly well. Its author had no specialized knowledge of his subject, and references such as that to 'the half-witted pedantry of the German doctrine and practice of war, which uses brutality as a protective mask for cowardice', make it clear that his work had not escaped the rhetoric of wartime propaganda.[3] H. A. Jones, a former RAF officer and Air Historical Branch researcher, rescued the project from its inauspicious start. The following five volumes of the history display a high standard of argument and presentation, based on a wide knowledge of the available British material. As a monument to the achievements of the airmen of the Royal Flying Corps, Royal Naval Air Service and Royal Air Force, Jones's work is unlikely ever to be superseded.

Nonetheless, as a study of the development of British air policy before 1919, *The War in the Air* is in many ways dated and unsatisfactory. Much material, particularly from German sources and in the private papers of airmen and politicians, was unavailable at the time of writing. While Jones at least was prepared to be critical of certain aspects of the British air effort, both authors were also hampered by their positions as official historians. When the newly created Air Historical Branch began its task, the Royal Air Force was struggling to establish its right to peacetime existence. This struggle was dominated by the then Chief of the Air Staff, Hugh Trenchard, who influenced the service's view of its past as much as he did its plans for the future. The combination of these factors ensured that *The War in the Air* emerged as an apologia for an independent air force, and as a defence of Trenchard's record as a wartime commander.

The official history rarely hints at the conflicts of policy and personality that divided the air command during the war. It also slights many of the senior officers who left, or were driven from the service as a result of these clashes. Trenchard's own rivals are particularly ill-served: Frederick Sykes, for example, is mentioned only twice by name in the volume covering his time as Chief of the Air Staff in 1918. More seriously, there is no detailed treatment of the political dimension of the air war. Although aviation did not occupy the government nearly as much as it would in the 1930s and 1940s, the breadth of political interest was considerable. Churchill, Derby, Curzon, Balfour and Smuts, to name only the more directly involved, all played an important role in the development of air policy.

Government intervention proved the crucial element in the decision to form an independent air service during the war, a decision taken against the better judgement of most senior airmen. Political air-mindedness, however, had not yet developed to the point where the strategic use of airpower was assumed to be a major part of the normal machinery of war. While occasional German raids on London could produce visions of the aerial future similar to those conjured up by the air prophets of the interwar era, such images quickly disappeared when the enemy threat was removed. Even the bombing campaign against Germany was allowed to languish, serving more as a token to satisfy public demands for reprisals than as a threat to even the tottering German war economy of late 1918.

As in so many other aspects of British strategic planning, the government's air policy initiatives proved to be only partially effective. Two interconnected themes running consistently through the development of British aviation between 1914 and 1918 were the domination of policy by the army and the increasing concentration of resources in support of Haig's armies on the Western Front. While the creation of the Royal Air Force ended formal military control over the largest operational component of the air service, the failure to redirect aircraft and men elsewhere left effective command of the field force in the hands of Haig's headquarters. To the end of the war, the RAF remained a servant of the army, largely commanded by men whose service allegiance and strategical outlook had not been altered by the shedding of khaki for air force blue. With the coming of the armistice, and the disbandment of the mass continental army, the RAF found itself without a clearly defined role and only the weakest notions of a future as a strategic arbiter. Its transition to a peacetime footing was thus rendered difficult from the very start by the lack of a real sense of purpose.

The wartime history of British aviation was also reflective of the general difficulties affecting the war effort in an entirely different sense. With the exception of its shipyards, Britain was poorly prepared to face the industrial demands of twentieth-century warfare. British war production was forced to expand on a narrow base, and even massive expenditure and the advent of the Ministry of Munitions could not compensate for a shortage of plant or a paucity of technological expertise. It is not necessary to embrace theories of British industrial decline to account for this development; the simple fact was that Britain was even less prepared to fight the kind of war that developed after 1914 than were either its major ally France or its major enemy Germany. The British aviation industry, one of the smallest and most poorly integrated components of the arms-producing organization, reaped the problems of this lack of preparation to the full.

Most of the problems which affected the direction of air policy between 1914 and 1918 had their origins in the persistent shortage of airframes and aero engines. The antagonism between the military and naval air services, which eventually led to the disappearance of both, arose simply because material resources were insufficient to underwrite their respective policies and needs. Similarly, the independent strategic force, conceived as the striking arm of the Royal Air Force, failed to achieve full strength because industry could not supply sufficient machines to equip both it and the existing tactical formations assigned to support the army in the field. The aircraft industry did experience considerable growth during the war years – by the second half of 1918 it was producing over 2,000 machines a month, appreciably more than its German counterpart. By the same token, it never quite caught up with the needs of the service it was intended to supply. In the first half of the war the foundations for growth had been lacking; in the second, when the air industry was finally integrated into the national war effort under the control of the Ministry of Munitions, Britain's overall manufacturing capacity was severely stretched, leaving insufficient slack to be taken up for the expansion of aircraft production.

The air force with which Britain ended the First World War in 1918 was actually larger than that with which it entered the Second World War in 1939. At the time of the armistice, however, the RAF's independence was unsupported by either administrative tradition or doctrinal coherence, while the service itself functioned first and foremost as an ancillary to the army and navy. During the interwar period the Air Ministry had to struggle hard to give substance to the legislative identity so lightly granted it in 1917–18. This process drove the RAF away from the other services, launching it on a strategic course which assumed a direction and momentum of its own. The result was an air force which operated separately from the remainder of the defence community. In this sense at least, Harris's Bomber Command was at once the antithesis and the product of the air organization which helped Haig break the Hindenburg Line in 1918.

Notes

1 Synopsis of British air effort throughout the war, 1 January 1919, Sykes Papers, RAF, MFC 77/13/62.
2 J. C. Slessor, *Air Power and Armies* (Oxford: Oxford University Press, 1936), p. 1.
3 *WIA*, Vol. 1, p. 387.

[1]

Uncertain Beginnings

In a lecture given at the Staff College in 1913, Colonel J. E. Capper, Commandant of the School of Military Engineering, Chatham, painted a dismal picture of the British air arm: 'Looking at our present numbers of aeroplanes and airships and the number of really trained officers and men we possess, I can only say that we have in England hardly sufficient for a very minor campaign against a savage enemy or against some petty European power.'[1] Capper, who had played a prominent part in the development of military aviation in the preceding decade, was not alone in taking a gloomy view of the situation. Indeed, alarmist sentiments about Britain's lack of aerial preparedness had first surfaced even before Blériot's portentous flight across the English Channel in July 1909. Concern at the German Zeppelin construction programme, fired by the appearance of H. G. Wells's futuristic novel *The War in the Air* (1908), had resulted in a shortlived airship scare in the spring of 1909. Thereafter clandestine visits from Zeppelins had joined hosts of German spies and secret stockpiles of Mausers in the centre of London in the invasion-conscious public imagination.[2] The government's apparent sloth in applying itself to this dangerous military innovation provoked the press, most notably Northcliffe's *Daily Mail*, and the newly formed backbench Parliamentary Aerial Defence Committee into a series of attacks continuing intermittently right up to the outbreak of war.[3] Many observers, it was clear, would have sympathized with Howard Flanders, a pioneer aircraft manufacturer forced out of business due to lack of official support, who complained to the Aeronautical Society: 'Is it not strange that a country of this importance and wealth can do nothing for those who have spent all their time and money in studying the science of aeronautics?'[4]

The government's critics were quite correct in asserting that Britain had fallen a long way behind its continental rivals in official sponsorship of aeronautics.[5] What is surprising is that they should have thought this lapse so dangerous. There was little in the first fumbling attempts at the

1

military application of aviation technology to suggest that ruin from the air was an immediate possibility. Britain, however, was prone to periodic invasion scares throughout the decade before the First World War. With aviation having caught the public imagination and large crowds gathering to observe this most exciting manifestation of progress, it was natural that the large sums of money being expended on aeroplanes and airships in France and Germany should have aroused concern. In that sense, the popular response to Wellsian visions of airborne disaster was of a piece with the reaction to the invasion tales of Sir George Chesney, Erskine Childers and William Le Queux.[6] What made the Zeppelin in particular so threatening was the implied negation of Britain's inviolability as an island. Secure for so long in the knowledge that the Royal Navy would keep any potential foe from bringing war to its doorstep, the British public reacted far more keenly than its European counterparts to the possible threat from the air. As Lord Montagu, a pioneer of the automobile and one of the most vociferous advocates of its winged cousin, told the Aldershot Military Society in February 1910,

> The day is not far distant when England will have to be something besides nominal mistress of the seas. She will have to be at least equal to her neighbours in the matter of aerial defence and offence, and it is our business and the duty of the nation at large to see that the authorities are wakened in time to their responsibilities in this direction.[7]

The authorities were not entirely insensitive to the supposed air menace, and their appreciation of the situation was in many ways more realistic than that of their critics. The report of the Aerial Navigation Sub-Committee of the Committee of Imperial Defence (CID), dated 28 January 1909, took the view that large-scale attack from the air was not an immediate danger but that some experimentation with airships and aeroplanes was necessary to gain an adequate appreciation of any more distant threat.[8] This wait-and-see attitude, motivated by the belief that Britain 'stood to gain nothing by forcing a means of warfare which tended to reduce the value of our insular position and the protection of our sea power', characterized air policy for most of the prewar period.[9] The underdeveloped state of the science of aeronautics justified this attitude to some extent, but it did allow the continental powers an advantage over Britain which proved a serious handicap during the war.

In tracing the prewar evolution of British air policy, there is no need to dwell too long on nineteenth-century military experiments with bal-looning. The army made some use of balloons, manned by the Royal Engineers, in its colonial campaigns, but apart from establishing that regiment as the parent unit of aeronautics and convincing a minority of senior officers that such devices were of some use for observation purposes, this experience was of little relevance to the later development of powered flight.[10] A Balloon Section had first been authorized in the Army Estimates of 1890 and the Balloon Factory at Aldershot had gained its first superintendent in Major J. L. B. Templar seven years later, but it was only with the first flights of the Wright brothers in the United States and Santos-Dumont in France, and the appearance of Zeppelin's first airships in Germany in the early years of the twentieth century, that the question of official participation became important.

The British government has been criticized for failing to interest itself early enough in the experiments of the Wright brothers.[11] Contact had been established with the Wrights in 1904 with the visit of Templar's successor, Colonel J. E. Capper, to America, but R. B. Haldane, the Liberal Secretary of State for War, had eventually declined to commit himself to their support. It is fair to point out, however, that the War Office was at that time supporting the project of a native aviation pioneer, J. W. Dunne, and although the Wright aircraft was eventually to prove a success and its Dunne rival a failure, this was by no means clear before Wilbur Wright made the first of his dramatic demonstration flights in France in 1908.[12] For almost a decade after the Wrights first took to the air in 1903, powered flight remained a poorly understood and highly experimental discipline, and only the experience of war really made the need for massive government intervention clear.

Having said all this, it remains true that British aviation was notably less successful in its early years than its continental equivalents. Neither Dunne's experiments at Blair Atholl, nor those of the American expatriate S. F. Cody at Farnborough, produced an efficient flying machine. The government, while showing some signs of concern at overseas developments, was clearly not to be rushed into active intervention. The CID Sub-Committee on Aerial Navigation, appointed by Asquith in October 1908 to decide how Britain ought to respond to increasing expenditure on aeronautics abroad, recommended that the navy ought to be allowed £35,000 in the estimates to build an experimental airship, but saw 'no necessity for the Government to continue experiments in aeroplanes, provided that advantage is taken of private enterprise in this form of aviation'.[13] As a result, Dunne and Cody were abandoned and the army was left only with its own small airship construction programme.

The Balloon Factory, renamed the Royal Aircraft Factory in 1911, emerged under its new superintendent, Mervyn O'Gorman, first and foremost as an experimental institution, and British air policy came to revolve around state-controlled investigation of the science of aeronautics, at the expense of the subsidization of private entrepreneurs. Denied the official support often granted aviators in other countries, Britain's air pioneers continued to operate on a small scale. While the Short Brothers, the first British concern to establish an aircraft factory, had 16 aeroplanes on order in 1910, the Frenchman Blériot had more than 50. British aeronautics suffered as a result of low output. Manufacturers were too concerned with the struggle for financial survival to devote much time to practical research or technical innovation.[14]

Aviation in Britain, as elsewhere, owed its early development to the activities of a small group of pioneers who were at once pilots, designers and manufacturers. Britain possessed in men such as T. O. M. Sopwith and A. V. Roe innovators as talented as any working abroad, but their efforts to build their small concerns into full-scale aircraft factories were crippled from the start by the scarcity of large government contracts.[15] Initial hesitation need not necessarily have proved damaging: the German government, soon to sponsor one of the most active aircraft procurement policies in the world, began by neglecting the aeroplane in favour of the much more expensive rigid airship, only purchasing twenty-eight of the former in 1911.[16] The serious damage to Britain's aviation industry was done between 1912 and 1914. While such damage was due in part to general limitations on British defence spending, it was also related to specific shortcomings in the newly evolved aircraft procurement policy.

In France and Germany the rapid growth of aviation was concomitant with official support of private aircraft manufacturers. Britain's air industry received only intermittent assistance of this nature. The Admiralty, under the enthusiastic direction of Churchill, actively sought the best aircraft private concerns had to offer. Possessed of its own design facilities in the Royal Aircraft Factory, the army proved reluctant to depend upon designs other than those developed by its own employees. The War Office was justifiably concerned with the standards of construction and promptness of delivery of private manufacturers. Early experience seemed to confirm that civilian companies could not be depended upon and some thought was even given to having the Royal Aircraft Factory undertake all military aircraft construction.[17] The Factory, however, remained largely an experimental and repair centre, building only forty-eight aeroplanes between 1911 and 1914.[18] By and large the army got by depending on its own designs and some of French origin, ordering machines in small batches from private concerns to minimize the effects of any individual contractor's delinquency.

A brief glance at the Military Wing's order sheet in June 1914 illustrates the limitations of this policy. At that time there were 24 contracts extant for 122 aeroplanes, of which 89 remained undelivered. Only four orders involved more than six machines and of these, the largest, for 24, involved the entire year's output of the Royal Aircraft Factory. A mere 25 of the contracted aircraft were of private British design. Of the rest, 16 were French models, while 81 originated with the army's own designers at Farnborough. Apart from the Factory contract, the largest orders were with the big armament firms involved in other forms of arms production:

the Coventry Ordnance Factory with 17 machines and Vickers with 13. Another arms firm, Armstrong, had been given contracts for eight, while the French company Blériot had just delivered five more. Eight small British firms, representing the bulk of the pioneer private manufacturers, held 12 contracts for the remaining 55 machines.[19]

The niggardly size of contracts had the effect of perpetuating those very faults of which the army had been so critical. Unable to anticipate orders large enough to allow the maintenance of proper manufacturing facilities or work forces, the private contractors could not hope to achieve the efficiency required of them. Large orders were dependent on high standards and punctuality, but neither could be achieved if such orders were not forthcoming in the first place. Such an impasse was common to the development of aircraft manufacture in at least one other country. Until 1912 the German army had taken a similar attitude to aircraft procurement, with the same unfortunate results. In 1913, however, five German firms all received orders for more then 30 military aircraft. Next year the two largest, Albatros and Rumpler, produced 338 and 110 machines respectively.[20]

It is of course important to recognize that British aircraft procurement operated within an entirely different economic and strategic framework from its continental equivalents. Even in the tense international atmosphere so pervasive before the war, the Asquith government's commitment to the expansion of the armed forces was hardly whole-hearted. The service ministers were expected by many of their cabinet colleagues to save money rather than spend it in larger and larger amounts. Flying machines, no less than artillery or dreadnoughts, had to be justified to a party largely composed of men whose first commitment remained to liberal ideas of social reform and welfare spending. In this context it is not surprising to find even the aircraft-minded Churchill making arrangements in December 1913 for the 'compression of the Air Service Vote'.[21] The shortcomings of early air policy were to a certain extent only a reflection of that general failure to plan in depth for a European war which lay at the root of so many of Britain's difficulties in 1914–15.[22]

The army's belief that aircraft design and construction should remain firmly in military hands was, however, a mistake in its own right. Apart from denying the Military Wing the products of some of Britain's most gifted aircraft designers, War Office policy drove most of the small aircraft firms into the arms of the navy. While the Admiralty took up a large part of the available production capacity, its peacetime needs were not great enough to stimulate significant growth in the industry. When war broke out, the army found little scope for the quick expansion of its own procurement programme and was forced to turn to the Admiralty for relief. This set underway a struggle for resources between the two services which cast a shadow over the air effort for much of the war and contributed in the end to the formation of the Royal Air Force.

Service air rivalry had more complicated origins than a simple competition for machines. The prewar debate over British strategy in the event of Britain's involvement in a European conflict is now well-charted territory. It is sufficient to note here that the Admiralty's traditional exposition of blockade and amphibious operations, and the War Office's increasing fixation with the continental commitment, were echoed in each department's approach to the new air weapon. The Admiralty, whose political head, Churchill, was perhaps the most influential convert to airpower before the war, adopted a policy which was as wide-ranging as it was ill-defined. Apart from a predictable interest in airships, whose long range gave obvious advantages over sea, the navy looked at all types of aeroplanes, not only as a possible defence against enemy airships, but also for potential uses as widespread as anti-submarine patrol and offensive action against enemy bases.[23] The War Office, on the other hand, viewed the aircraft largely as a reconnaissance vehicle for use in support of the expeditionary force it would send to the continent on the outbreak of war. Indeed, it intended to dispatch the entire operational section of the Military Wing overseas with the British Expeditionary Force (BEF).[24]

Given this difference of outlook, and remembering the distrust and rivalry extant between the two departments at the time, it was hardly surprising that Churchill at least thought that their air arms were bound to develop along divergent lines.[25] What is perhaps more surprising is that the government should ever have attempted to orchestrate close co-operation.

The watching brief suggested by the Aerial Navigation Sub-Committee in January 1909 soon became obsolete. The continuing progress of Germany's airship programme, the increased use of aeroplanes in French army manoeuvres, and the disquieting confusion of opinions thrown up by the abortive 1910 International Conference on Aerial Navigation raised fears that Britain could no longer afford to stand aside.[26]

The services themselves were beginning to take a more positive attitude. When Capper had handed over the Balloon School to his successor Major Sir A. Bannerman in October 1910, the unit had only one aeroplane, donated by the Hon. C. S. Rolls, on charge and two more on order, both in France.[27] The following spring the Balloon School was reorganized as the Air Battalion, and although the latter remained an experimental cadre attached to the Royal Engineers, it had at least acquired thirteen aeroplanes and three small airships by November.[28] The Admiralty for its part had sent four officers to Eastchurch in early 1911 in response to an offer of free training facilities from the Royal Aero Club, and had completed its own airship, which unfortunately broke its back before ever flying. The new First Lord of the Admiralty, Winston Churchill, took a keen interest

6

in aviation from the start and by the end of the year was talking in terms of a 'new Corps of Airmen'.[29]

The government's response to increasing pressure for decisive action was to charge the Standing Sub-Committee of the CID, chaired by Haldane, 'to consider the future development of aerial navigation for naval and military purposes, and the measures which might be taken to secure to this country an efficient aerial service'.[30] The Sub-Committee responded by recommending the creation of a Royal Flying Corps, consisting of a Military Wing, a Naval Wing and a Central Flying School.[31] The report, considered by the prime minister as a matter of some 'urgency', was approved in April 1912 and an Air Committee of the CID established under Haldane to preside over the experiment in inter-service co-operation.[32]

The Air Committee was given no executive power, its functions being entirely consultative and advisory. The official historian spoke of it fading away 'like the Ghost in Hamlet' having fulfilled its task of prompting the army and navy into action.[33] It is crucial to any understanding of early British air policy to realize that the prewar organization of the Flying Corps was not in any way a blueprint for the Royal Air Force. While there already existed a vocal minority, both inside Parliament and without, arguing for a stronger air organization, the bulk of official opinion was concerned merely to put aviation on a sound footing within the existing two-service structure. The sharing of ideas and facilities, when both were in their formative stages, presented obvious advantages to all the participants. Such an arrangement was also very much in accord with the non-interventionist ethos of the Committee of Imperial Defence. Asquith's government in particular could not be expected to impinge on existing departmental responsibilities by attempting the creation of a new service, and Asquith himself was not inclined to interfere when the two wings of the new Flying Corps started to drift apart. The two annual reports produced by the Air Committee in 1913 and 1914 gave evidence of sufficient progress in military and naval aviation to defuse official concern about Britain's comparative aerial position. Indeed, it was clear that, far from disapproving of the desire of the two wings to stand on their own, the committee was convinced that the need for co-ordination was progressively diminished by the overall growth of aviation.[34]

It would be wrong to portray one service or the other as the major villain of the demise of the prewar Flying Corps. The navy gave the more dramatic signal of independence by adopting the title Royal Naval Air Service (RNAS), while the army retained Royal Flying Corps (RFC), simply allowing the appended Military Wing to fade out of use; thus the navy has traditionally been assigned the burden of guilt.[35] Despite the appointment of a naval commandant, the Admiralty certainly did make an adequate contribution to the Central Flying School at Upavon, maintaining all along its own training station at Eastchurch. As Churchill made plain to Asquith in July 1914, the navy had complaints of its own about the returns it received from inter-service co-operation.[36] With different outlooks not only on how aircraft were to be used, but also on how they were to be designed, ordered and built, no amount of goodwill could have kept the two air arms together without intervention from above, a move for which the government could perceive no clear need.

The division of British aviation into two distinct services was further advanced by the natural desire of the Admiralty and War Office to put the administration of aviation on a regular departmental footing and to bring their air services into organizational contact with the forces they were intended to support in time of war. Captain M. F. Sueter was appointed Director of the Air Department at the Admiralty in 1912, and by the summer of 1914 the naval air service had been organized along lines which, as Captain Roskill has suggested, were at least implicitly separatist as far as the concept of a united Flying Corps was concerned.[37] Sueter, however, was not responsible to any particular member of the Board, and this relative freedom allowed the RNAS to follow its own head for the first year of the war, gaining a degree of autonomy which eventually produced an institutional backlash.

The Military Wing, as befitted its perceived role as an ancillary reconnaissance arm of the expeditionary force, was organized along far tighter lines. Initially its administration was left to an informal sub-group of the Air Committee under the leadership of Brigadier-General David Henderson, the Director of Military Training and himself a qualified pilot, and then passed to a new section within Henderson's directorate.[38] The realization that it was insufficient 'merely to carve some niche in the military organization in which to fit inventions'[39] soon produced a separate Directorate of Military Aeronautics. In 1913 Henderson was transferred from his old post to become Director-General of Military Aeronautics (DGMA) and the administrative responsibilities until that time vested in the commander of the Military Wing, Major Frederick Sykes, were transferred to the War Office, despite Sykes's objection that the Wing ought to remain self-contained in anticipation of its move overseas.[40]

The equanimity with which the effective separation of the two wings of the Flying Corps was generally viewed was due in part to satisfaction with the progress of British aviation. The total number of aircraft available to the Flying Corps had increased from 12 in May 1912 to 150 in May 1913 and 269 in May 1914. The number of pilots who had received the Royal Aero Club certificate increased over the same period from 34 to 218 and finally to 340.[41] While these figures did reflect undoubted progress, they unfortunately did not tell the full story. A brief study of the two British flying services' response to mobilization in August 1914 will provide adequate proof that Britain had yet to achieve anything like parity with France or Germany in the air.

The Royal Flying Corps sent four squadrons, mustering 50 aircraft, to France with the BEF. Almost half of the aeroplanes had not been designed in Britain, while every one of the engines was of French origin. Of the 75 aircraft left behind only half were even fit for flying.[42] On 2 August the Royal Naval Air Service order of battle showed 50 aircraft and one airship assigned to 11 different stations with another 50 aircraft in various states of unserviceability. These naval machines were an exceptionally hetero-geneous collection, the 14 serviceable aircraft at Eastchurch, for example, came from eight different manufacturers, one of them German.[43]

By way of comparison, the 24 *escadrilles* initially mobilized by the French *Aéronautique Militaire* took the field with 120 aeroplanes, while the 33 *Feldflieger–Abteilungen* of Germany's *Fliegertruppe* deployed nearly 200.[44] All told, Prussian army aircraft procurement alone had totalled 628 between 1911 and 1913. In 1914 German aircraft factories were to deliver 1,348 machines.[45] To reveal the true state of British aeronautics at the war's onset, these figures need only be set against a remark by Major W. S. Brancker, Henderson's deputy at the Directorate of Military Aeronautics, to the effect that outside of the Royal Aircraft Factory, there was not 'a single organized aircraft factory in England'.[46] No European nation was really prepared for the four-year struggle that followed, but British aviation, like so many other sections of the country's war machine, was far less likely to adapt quickly to the demands of a war of attrition than its continental equivalents.

Britain was equally backward in the development of the airship. While such craft were to prove an expensive disappointment to the Germans, who alone among the European powers had seriously fostered their growth, they did represent the only means available in 1914 for carrying large bombloads over long distances. When Zeppelins first began to visit British cities by night in 1915, prewar paranoia about these menacing giants found expression in a barrage of criticism of the government's air policy which seriously interfered with the air effort in all other fields of activity.

Both army and navy had dabbled with airship construction in the decade before the war, but neither had fully made up its mind as to the airship's usefulness. Churchill had overcome opposition from within his department to maintain the navy's airship programme.[47] In 1914 the navy took over total responsibility for airships, but at the beginning of the war could still only muster seven serviceable units, four of them small and obsolete ex-army machines. Every one of them was of non-rigid construc-tion and no match in size, range or payload for the large rigid airships on order in Germany. As the American historian Robin Higham has con-cluded, Britain had largely frittered away the prewar years as far as airship development was concerned, and its lack of even one modern rigid airship left the Germans enjoying 'a psychological advantage out of all proportion to their abilities.'[48]

In attempting any final verdict on British prewar air policy, it must always be borne in mind that with aviation in such an early stage of development, mistakes in procurement and hesitation as to the aeroplane's place in a future war were inevitable. Much of the contemporary criticism levelled at the early Flying Corps was even more uninformed than the opinions of those responsible for making the decisions. Nonetheless, the shortcomings of prewar planning were to set the tone for much of what was to follow. The air industry, underdeveloped in comparison to its French or German counterparts, did not possess adequate research or production facilities to allow for rapid expansion. The two air services were proceeding about their business without reference to each other and were already showing signs of coming into conflict over areas of responsibility and allocation of resources. Finally, the fear of aerial attack had established a toehold in the popular imagination and was becoming the source of outside pressure on the formulation of aerial priorities. It would take the experience of war, most notably the explosion of German bombs, to set Britain firmly on the road to the creation of the world's first independent air force, but voices were already to be heard prophesying the need for just such a step.

Notes

1 Capper Papers, Liddell Hart Centre, III/2/2b.
2 A. M. Gollin, 'England is no longer an island. The phantom airship scare of 1909', *Albion*, vol. 13, no. 1 (1981), pp. 43–57; C. F. Snowden Gamble, *The Air Weapon* (Oxford: Oxford University Press, 1931), pp. 205–6.
3 The Parliamentary Aerial Defence Committee was formed on 25 April 1909, its first chairman being the Conservative MP Arthur Lee.
4 As quoted in H. Penrose, *British Aviation. The Pioneer Years, 1903–1914* (London: Putnam, 1967), p. 454.
5 C. H. Gibbs-Smith, *The Rebirth of European Aviation* (London: HMSO, 1974), pp. 139, 209; R. Pound and G. Harmsworth, *Northcliffe* (London: Cassell, 1959), pp. 300–1, 352–4, 363; L. Troubridge and A. Marshall, *John Lord Montagu of Beaulieu. A Memoir* (London: Macmillan, 1930), pp. 223–7.
6 For a brief but trenchant discussion of futurist war literature see J. Gooch, 'Attitudes to war in late Victorian and Edwardian England', in J. Gooch (ed.), *The Prospect of War. Studies in British Defence Policy, 1847–1942* (London: Cass, 1981), pp. 35–51.
7 Montagu Papers, V/A/X.
8 Report of the Aerial Navigation Sub-Committee of the CID, 28 January 1909, PRO, CAB 38/15/3.
9 Report of the Technical Sub-Committee of the CID on Aerial Navigation, 30 July 1912, PRO, CAB 38/22/32.

10 For the history of early military ballooning see Gamble, *The Air Weapon*, pp. 25–89; P. W. L. Broke-Smith, *The History of Early British Military Aeronautics* (Bath: Library Association, 1968), pp. 1–29.

11 For an exhaustive discussion of Britain's dealings with the Wrights see A. M. Gollin, *No Longer an Island. Britain and the Wright Brothers, 1902–1909* (London: Heinemann, 1984), *passim*.

12 A. M. Gollin, 'The Wright brothers and the British authorities, 1902–1909', *English Historical Review*, vol. 95, no. 375 (1980), pp. 293–320; A. M. Gollin, 'The mystery of Lord Haldane and early British aviation', *Albion*, vol. 11, no. 1 (1979), pp. 46–65.

13 Report of the Aerial Navigation Sub-Committee of the CID, 28 January 1909, PRO, CAB 38/15/3.

14 Penrose, *The Pioneer Years*, p. 206.

15 For Roe's comments on the problems of aircraft manufacture before the war see PRO, AIR 1/2310/218/1.

16 J. H. Morrow, Jr, *Building German Airpower, 1909–1914* (Knoxville, Tenn.: University of Tennessee Press, 1976), p. 85.

17 Minutes of the 4th meeting of the Air Committee of the CID, 3 December 1912, PRO, CAB 14/1.

18 PRO, AIR 1/686/21/13/2245.

19 PRO, AIR 1/764/204/4/199.

20 Morrow, *Building German Airpower*, pp. 14–47, 84.

21 Churchill to Fourth Sea Lord, Director Air Department and Director of Contracts, 21 December 1913, PRO, ADM 1/8621.

22 For a reassessment of British preparations for the First World War see D. French, *British Economic and Strategic Planning, 1905–1915* (London: Allen & Unwin, 1982), *passim*.

23 Admiralty memorandum on aerial navigation, 9 June 1913, PRO, CAB 37/115/35.

24 Notes on Royal Flying Corps organization, 10 November 1913, PRO, AIR 1/780/204/4/477.

25 Minutes of the 121st meeting of the CID, 7 January 1913, PRO, CAB 38/23/2.

26 Proceedings of the CID with reference to the international conference on aerial navigation, December 1911, PRO, CAB 38/19/60; Esher memorandum on aerial navigation, 6 October 1910, PRO, CAB 38/16/18.

27 Penrose, *The Pioneer Years*, p. 248.

28 List of existing army aeroplanes, November 1911, Brooke-Popham papers, Liddell Hart Centre, IX/4/4.

29 Churchill minute, 9 December 1911, PRO, ADM 116/1278.

30 Asquith minute, 18 November 1911, PRO, CAB 38/20/1.

31 Report of the Technical Sub-Committee of the Standing Sub-Committee of the CID on Aerial Navigation, 28 February 1912, PRO, CAB 38/20/1.

32 Minutes of the 116th meeting of the CID, 25 April 1912, PRO, CAB 38/20/9.

33 *WIA*, Vol. 1, p. 212.

34 First Annual Report of the Air Committee on the Progress of the Royal Flying Corps, 7 June 1913, PRO, CAB 38/24/21; Second Annual Report of the Air Committee on the Progress of the Royal Flying Corps, 9 May 1914, PRO, CAB 38/27/22.

35 See for example G. Norris, *The Royal Flying Corps. A History* (London: Muller, 1965), pp. 46–7; S. Roskill, *Hankey. Man of Secrets*, Vol. 1 (London: Collins, 1970), pp. 185–6.

36 Churchill to Asquith, July 1914, Asquith Papers, 13/177–85.

37 S. Roskill (ed.), *Documents Relating to the Naval Air Service 1908–1918* (London: Navy Records Society, 1969), p. 156.

38 First Annual Report of the Air Committee, 7 June 1913, PRO, CAB 38/24/21.

39 Sykes memorandum, Notes on questions of policy in military aeronautics, 8 September 1913, PRO, AIR 1/757/204/4/100.

40 War Office memorandum, Formation of Military Aeronautics Directorate, 28 August 1913, PRO, AIR 1/520/16/10/1; Brancker to Sykes, 10 November 1913, Sykes to Henderson, 17 November and 16 December 1913, PRO, AIR 1/780/204/4/477.

41 First Annual Report of the Air Committee, 7 June 1913, PRO, CAB 38/24/21; Second Annual Report of the Air Committee, 9 May 1914, PRO, CAB 38/27/22.

42 PRO, AIR 1/118/15/40/39; AIR 1/750/204/4/2.

43 M. Goodhall, 'Royal Naval Air Service. Order of Battle, Aug. 2, 1914', *Cross and Cockade Great Britain Journal*, vol. 3, no. 4 (1972), pp. 137–46.

44 PRO, AIR 1/686/21/13/2248; H. J. Nowarra, *Eisernes Kreuz und Balkenkreuz* (Mainz: Verlag Dieter Hoffmann, 1968), pp. 32–4.

45 J. H. Morrow, Jr, *German Air Power in World War I* (Lincoln, Nebr.: University of Nebraska Press, 1982), p. 202.

46 N. Macmillan (ed.), *Sir Sefton Brancker* (London: Heinemann, 1935), pp. 54–5.

47 Minutes of the 120th meeting of the CID, 6 December 1912, PRO, CAB 38/22/42; minutes of the 122nd meeting of the CID, 6 February 1913, PRO, CAB 38/23/9.

48 R. Higham, *The British Rigid Airship, 1908–1931. A Study in Weapons Policy* (London: Foulis, 1961), p. 73.

[2]

Aviation Goes to War

Most of Europe went to war in August 1914 in the belief that victory would come in months if not even weeks. The British air forces, in common with their parent services, took the field on the assumption that 'the correct policy was undoubtedly to throw every man and machine into the field at the threatened point ... to stave off annihilation at the very outset of the campaign'.[1] In so doing they did themselves damage which took months to repair. The Royal Flying Corps in particular paid a heavy price for laying waste its flimsy administrative and logistic base in the rush to participate in the decisive engagement.

More significantly, the RFC and RNAS went to war independent of any co-ordinated plan of development. During the first year and a half of hostilities, British aviation expanded without direction from above. The failure of the expected aerial menace to materialize effectively reduced pressure on the government to address itself to the question of national air policy. As a result, the army and navy air services were allowed to adapt themselves to the increasing aerial possibilities thrown up by the war without reference to each other, or to the country's potential needs and resources. With each force pursuing a different vision of the aircraft's wartime role, the course was set for an inevitable clash over both strategy and procurement.

The shadow of the Zeppelin exerted an influence over Britain's preparations for the air war out of all proportion to the real threat. Prewar fears of aerial bombardment were given early focus by intermittent raids on continental towns and by the successes of British propaganda in exposing the 'frightfulness' of the Teutonic war machine. Official attention to aviation centred almost entirely around home air defence, with Churchill arguing as early as September for reprisals in the wake of raids on open towns.[2] Despite supposed sightings and occasional rumours of impending mass attacks, summed up accurately enough by one senior airman as 'Zeppelinitis',[3] the first airship did not appear over England until early 1915. British intelligence had in fact heavily overestimated the preparedness of the enemy airship force, and the Germans themselves had yet to plan any cross Channel attacks. Nonetheless, measures taken in anticipation of such hostile visits in the first weeks of the war proved of lasting significance to future air policy.

Until the outbreak of war, the conduct of aerial operations over the British Isles had been interpreted by the army as part of its general responsibility for home defence. A right jealously guarded in peacetime, however, rapidly became an unwanted burden in war. With military attention centred almost entirely on the Expeditionary Force, the War Office was soon keen to be relieved of the 'impossible task of preventing London being bombarded from the air'.[4] After maintaining an erratic system of coastal patrols for several weeks, the army asked the navy to take over. The RNAS, by virtue at least of its lack of other commitments, was certainly better equipped to handle home air defence. Nonetheless, the Admiralty also retained serious reservations concerning the feasibility of the task. Sueter was at some pains to establish that means for intercepting and destroying raiders were painfully rudimentary, while Churchill, aware of the likelihood of successful penetrations of British air space, underlined 'the obvious limits to our responsibility'. Subsequent accusations that the Admiralty's assumption of home defence duties was motivated primarily by departmental ambition can hardly be substantiated. Churchill continued to make it clear that the navy was 'quite powerless' to prevent loss of lives to Zeppelin bombs. The First Sea Lord Fisher even went as far as to attempt to resign 'because the Admiralty under present arrangements will be responsible for the massacre coming suddenly upon and unprepared for by [*sic*] the public.'[5]

Naval doubts about the viability of defence measures were to be proven accurate when the Zeppelin did eventually make its appearance. Hesitation to accept responsibility for home air defence, however, had deeper roots than reservations about equipment or techniques. The relatively equal division of aerial resources between the army and navy, without co-ordination from above, rendered air defence an unwanted burden liable to be seen as a hindrance to military or naval operations elsewhere. As such, attacks by German airships and aircraft, or the threat thereof, were to prove a persistent source of demands for a separate air force as the war went on. Although the army was quickly drawn back into defensive operations at home, the sharing of the burden produced neither departmental harmony nor a consistently efficient protective umbrella. While the Germans never launched an all-out offensive against British cities, the manifest distaste of either the Admiralty or the War Office for facing the consequences of such attacks as did occur fatally weakened their case for retaining control of their own air services.[6]

The naval assumption of home defence responsibilities placed strain on the organization of the air effort in another, more immediate fashion.

Even before the war, Churchill had become convinced that the 'best antidote' to air attack was not passive defence. Believing that Zeppelins were far more vulnerable to bombing attack in their sheds than to the rudimentary weaponry which might be brought against them in the air, he interpreted his new brief as requiring the dispatch of naval aircraft to the continent to attack Zeppelin bases. In order to keep the enemy away from bases near the Channel coast, he intended to maintain 'an aerial control over the area approximately 100 miles radius from Dunkirk'.[7]

The resulting naval campaign did score some impressive successes. Defending the record of the RNAS after his departure from the Admiralty, Churchill could claim that his pilots had done more damage to the enemy's airship arm than all other allied air services together.[8] The free-ranging activities of the navy's air service, however, soon attracted criticism from the BEF. Churchill was partially correct in interpreting Sir John French's claim that naval activities in his zone of operations constituted an unwelcome hindrance as a revival of prewar 'inter-departmental friction'.[9] Short of aircraft itself, the army was becoming increasingly convinced that the naval pursuit of operations unrelated to maritime concerns was unfairly interfering with its own air programme.

The army concentrated its resources on the provision of air support for the BEF. Four squadrons flew across the Channel in August, to be joined by a fifth in October. The strain of operations, particularly as a result of almost daily changes of base during the retreat to the Marne, rapidly depleted the RFC's thin reserves. By the end of the first week in October, forty machines, almost as many as had come overseas in the first instance, had been struck off the strength of the field contingent.[10] Despite stripping the home establishment of aircraft and pilots, the RFC in the Field could still only muster sixty-one aircraft at the end of the year.[11]

The root of the problem, of course, lay in the enfeebled state of the aviation industry. In 1914, 18 British contractors produced 193 aeroplanes, of which no fewer than 60 were experimental types. In 1915 the situation improved substantially, with 34 manufacturers building 1,680 machines, 710 of them the standard Royal Aircraft Factory designed B.E.2c. Even this level of production was still only slightly in excess of German output for the previous year. Only five British firms were responsible for more than 100 machines. Only one, British and Colonial (Bristol) with 335, came close to equalling the previous year's output of the largest German firm (Albatros with 338).[12] Britain's aviation industry fell down most seriously in the production of engines. British designers were slow to find the proper combination of power, weight and reliability, and the services remained dependent on French designs. While French engine output in the last five months of 1914 totalled 894, the British produced only 99. Over the whole of 1915 the respective figures were 7,096 and 1,721. To the end of that year, the French supplied approximately one third of the RFC's engines. The largest French engine firm, Gnôme et Rhône, produced 1,800 engines, all of its own design, in 1914. One year later, the largest British supplier, Daimler, produced only 801, a quarter of them licence-built Gnôme rotaries.[13]

Barely 1,000 men had been employed in the entire British aviation industry in August 1914. By contrast, Gnôme et Rhône had employed 800 workers in one French factory alone, while the German firm Albatros had employed 745.[14] British dependence on foreign suppliers caused particularly severe problems in the supply of engine components. The German firm Bosch, for example, had held a near monopoly on the production of magnetos, and when the war cut off supplies the British were forced to depend on existing stocks until British factories could improve upon the crude copies they had previously manufactured.[15] The overall reliability of engines built in Britain, even licence-built foreign models, compared poorly with French products.[16] Prewar manufacturing facilities might be better characterized as workshops than as factories, and with neither the plant nor the workforce to undertake mass production, they could not respond quickly to the stimulus of large wartime orders. Suffering from a variety of material shortages, technologically backward in several vital areas, and too small to expand or diversify quickly, British aircraft firms faced a difficult future.

Recent historical scholarship has gone some way towards rescuing the reputations of the British soldiers responsible for arms procurement at the outbreak of the war. The most commonly identified villains of the failure of the British aircraft industry were Mervyn O'Gorman, the Superintendent of the Royal Aircraft Factory, and Major (later Brigadier-General) D. S. MacInnes, eventually Director of Air Equipment at the War Office. In reality, these men were no more culpable than the unfortunate Master-General of Ordnance, Sir Stanley von Donop, so effectively blamed by Lloyd George for the early war munitions crisis.[17] The army policy of depending on a standard aircraft, developed by government technicians at Farnborough, proved shortsighted, but the general failure of the aviation industry to accelerate production quickly enough under wartime conditions was at least partially a product of the low level of funding in peace for which the soldiers themselves were hardly to blame. Aircraft production, like most other parts of the munitions programme, was in too parlous a state of development in August 1914 to permit of rapid expansion even with the best of management or the most massive injection of capital.[18]

This said, the air effort did suffer from poor management at home, simply because so much of its small pool of administrative talent joined in the scramble to get to France before the expected early end to hostilities. The most egregious case was the departure of the Director-General of Military Aeronautics, Sir David Henderson, who assumed direct command of the field force and took the former commander of the Military Wing, Frederick Sykes, overseas with him as his chief of staff. The Directorate itself was placed under a junior lieutenant-colonel, W. Sefton Brancker, who along with Major H. M. Trenchard, left in charge of the remnants of the Military Wing at Farnborough, was expected to do little more than push the remaining military air resources overseas as quickly as possible. Brancker found himself left with 'the humble total of three officers, two civil servants, and at the most nine clerks' and Trenchard with nothing more than a collection of unserviceable machines and half-trained pilots. With so little at their disposal, there was not much these officers could do but patch together the ruins of a gutted organization and resist as best they could the attempts of their superiors to dig even deeper into their shallow reserves.[19]

Such problems were common in Britain in the autumn of 1914. The General Staff lost all of its senior and many of its junior officers to the BEF, while the Admiralty was 'manned principally by retired officers, the hurt and the maimed'.[20] Britain, the one major European power uncommitted by geographical position to a large continental war, paid a heavy price in administrative dislocation upon becoming involved. Whatever the miscalculations of the military air command, the problems of the RFC remained inextricably linked with those of the military system to which it belonged.

Confronted with such problems, the army was forced to turn to the navy for assistance. Home air defence was handed over at the beginning of September. Three months later, Brancker, still in charge at the Directorate of Military Aeronautics, wrote to his opposite number at the Admiralty requesting further aid:

> The aeroplane squadrons with the British forces in the field are very seriously short of aeroplanes and complaints of a shortage of flying officers are also being received.
>
> This deficiency is such that it may seriously affect the operations of the Field Army. The causes are:
>
> (i)   The impossibility of obtaining the requisite number of efficient aeroplanes at present to keep up the strength of squadrons abroad.
> (ii) The impossibility of obtaining sufficient training aeroplanes and experienced personnel for the training of a large number of pilots.
>
> Both these causes arise from the immaturity and smallness of the British aeroplane trade...
> Can you help us?[21]

By the time Brancker made his request the Admiralty had already ordered an additional 418 aircraft, 300 of them land-based types, since

The Birth of Independent Air Power

the beginning of the war.[22] There was, however, little chance of the navy lending more than token assistance. Naval air policy, as Churchill made clear to the War Council in April 1915, was progressing beyond 'daring exploits' against Zeppelin bases. The First Lord spoke of 'attacking with bombs on the largest possible scale of military points on enemy territory' and of every effort being made 'to reach 1,000 aeroplanes and 300 seaplanes as early as possible before the end of the present year'.[23] With such objects in mind, and naval air strength building up on both sides of the Channel, the RNAS was hardly likely to serve merely as a supply conduit for the army.

The full commitment of the naval air service to bombing operations on the continent was interrupted in the middle of 1915 by Churchill's departure from the Admiralty and Sueter's subsequent subordination within the Air Department to an officer of more conservative outlook. The seeds of inter-service disagreement had nonetheless been firmly planted. The navy was groping towards a strategic use of airpower not directly related to purely maritime operations, and towards the prosecution of a bombing campaign which the army, still struggling to meet the tactical needs of the BEF, had yet seriously to consider. With insufficient aircraft emerging from British factories to supply both services, and the military command already taking the view that everything must be subordinated to the campaign on the Western Front, the course was set for an inevitable collision.

The army's campaign in France and Belgium proved the focal point of British strategy during the entire war. Debate over allocation of resources, organization of effort and direction of operations hinged on the presence of hundreds of thousands of fighting men in the trenches between Picardy and the sea. From the outset, the air wing of the BEF occupied a similar position in the evolution of aviation policy. The need to supply aircraft and pilots for the RFC in the Field overshadowed the navy's search for a strategic role for its air forces, and eventually emasculated the long-distance bombing force brought into being as a result of the redirection of air policy in 1917–18. The air contingent of the BEF, like the Expeditionary Force itself, resisted all efforts to limit its demands on the country or place restrictions on its position within the overall war effort.

From the start, the RFC occupied a more tightly defined subordinate role in relation to its parent service than its naval counterpart. In the first great campaign of August–September 1914, army aviation was seen almost entirely as a reconnaissance force in the manner of a sort of airborne cavalry. There is little justification for believing that the air arm 'had saved the army' at Mons, or 'directly led to the victory of the Marne'.[24] Technical difficulties exposed by the test of war, the hesitancy of many senior officers to accept RFC reports without corroboration from more traditional sources of intelligence, and the small number of available aircraft placed severe limitations on air reconnaissance. The armies manoeuvring across Belgium and northeast France, compared so aptly to dinosaurs by Correlli Barnett, can only have been aided slightly in their clumsy progress by their new powers of sight.[25]

The end of mobile warfare, however, opened up new possibilities for the aircraft. The siege conditions created by the construction of trench defences along the front led to efforts to improve upon experiments in the use of the camera in the air, wireless communication and techniques for registering and observing artillery fire. Senior army officers were showing interest in these developments before the year ended, but the aircraft's incorporation into the routine of trench warfare was a gradual process.[26] Nonetheless, the relative lull in activity on the Western Front between the First Battle of Ypres in October 1914 and the spring offensives of 1915 was of vital importance in allowing the RFC to develop its ideas and experiments into at least the rudiments of a system of ground–air co-operation.[27]

The groundwork for operations of a more offensive nature was also laid during the war's first winter. In August 1914 the means for attacking land targets from the air were all but non-existent. The small bombs available were dismissed even then as 'little better than fireworks'.[28] Apart from these, the only available weapons were flechettes, no more than heavy darts which, although they enjoyed a certain vogue up to the spring of 1915, could have had little more than nuisance value against a limited range of targets. By 1915, with larger bombs becoming available, Sykes at RFC Headquarters was arguing that 'bomb dropping carried out on carefully considered and systematic lines against a particular target will be of much value'. While the pressure of other work precluded training all aircrew in bombing, it was decided on 15 February to order one flight per squadron to specialize in such work in addition to its normal duties.[29]

Ideas of attacking the enemy in the air itself were also taking shape. Most early air engagements were fought out ineffectually with carbines and pistols. Attempts at using machine-guns under operational conditions often ended with comic-opera results because the underpowered aeroplanes could not carry the extra weight.[30] Nonetheless, the RFC command was aware of the potential of the machine-gun-armed fighting aircraft much earlier than it is often given credit for, and even in the war's second month was searching for a suitable aircraft. It also began to develop that offensive ethos which characterized its fighter operations later in the war. While a clearly defined policy awaited the arrival of a new commander and more effective tools for air fighting, the spirit behind it was manifest in the summary of winter operations compiled by Sykes in February 1915: 'The principle of attacking hostile aircraft whenever and wherever seen ... has been adhered to and has resulted in the moral fact that enemy machines invariably beat immediate retreat when chased'.[31]

Even in these experiments in offensive warfare, the RFC had a more limited horizon than its naval counterpart. While naval airmen shifted their attention from distant Zeppelin bases to dockyards and factories, army airmen remained entirely concerned with the battlefield. Plans for the 1915 offensives reached as far as communications targets immediately behind the German lines, and no further. The RFC's first war expansion schemes reflected this close association with the field force. Army air requirements were calculated on the basis of the size of the BEF, and aimed first and foremost at providing Sir John French's expanding command with the requisite proportion of aircraft to men.

The RFC was no quicker than most other combatant forces in adjusting itself to the demands of a long campaign. Even when the trenches put an end to the war of movement, the feeling persisted that the enemy would soon collapse.[32] Under these conditions it was hardly surprising that the initial plans for expansion were unsystematic. The original estimates for 1914–15 required an increase from one combined airship and kite squadron and five aeroplane squadrons to eight aeroplane squadrons.[33] Of the five original squadrons, one was not ready at mobilization. While the RFC in Britain was attempting to get this unit ready and convert the airship squadron to aeroplanes, it found itself set more and more grandiose objectives by the War Office.

Brancker received instructions from the new Secretary of State for War, Lord Kitchener, to raise an additional five squadrons as early as 10 August.[34] It was not until December that an effort was made to draw up a blue-print for comprehensive expansion. On the 8th of that month Brancker wrote to the Chief of the Imperial General Staff (CIGS), Sir James Wolfe Murray: 'We have been living hand to mouth so far, but I think that the time has now come for a more or less definite statement of policy for the future development of the RFC.' He suggested that there should be one squadron for each army headquarters and each corps at the front, and at least another six squadrons attached directly to RFC Headquarters. With Kitchener proposing to field six armies of three corps each, this meant a minimum force of 30 squadrons, for which Brancker estimated another five squadrons would provide a sufficient reserve. This programme was tentatively approved by Wolfe Murray, but on 21 December Kitchener apparently decided that Brancker's figures were too conservative and arbitrarily doubled the entire programme.[35]

The manner in which army air expansion was implemented was typical of the state of British war organization in 1914–15. Kitchener's intervention to double the expansion programme was very much in keeping with his grandiose plans to create a mass volunteer army. Sadly, his vision of the future with regard to the RFC took no more account of the logistic and administrative problems of growth than did his call for hundreds of thousands of recruits for the Expeditionary Force. The RFC, in pursuit of his expanded programme of development, outgrew its own strength almost immediately. That a relatively junior officer like Brancker should have been responsible for framing the programme in the first place was itself a reflection of both the widespread shortage of competent senior staff at the War Office and the unbalanced relationship between the Directorate of Military Aeronautics and the RFC in the Field. In the first year of the war, while the chief of the Flying Corps and most of his senior subordinates remained in France, the Directorate operated very much as the handmaiden of the field force. Those officers responsible for the provision of pilots and aircraft for the BEF, the very men who might have been expected to appreciate best the limitations on available resources, were generally left entirely in the hands of their colleagues across the Channel, who calculated policy not in terms of what might be provided but in line with what the BEF seemed to require.

The resulting problems were compounded by personal disagreements within the military air command. Many of Britain's early airmen were possessed of strong, not to say headstrong personalities. As perhaps befits their position as pioneers within essentially conservative institutions, they did not work easily within the established service hierarchy. They were often suspected by their superiors, particularly when the possibility of a separate air force became stronger in the later years of the war. It is reflective of the atmosphere in which Britain's early air leaders worked that only one of them, Hugh Trenchard, was left to assume the mantle of 'Father of the Royal Air Force' in the interwar period. Within a year of the armistice, Henderson, Brancker, Sykes and Sueter had all left the field of service aviation for good.

Captain Murray Sueter, the Director of the Air Department of the Admiralty in 1914, might well be described as the quintessential early airman. His innovative turn of mind and strong belief in the possibilities of the aircraft were crucial to the early progress of the RNAS. On the other hand, he was a complete egotist and persistently displayed a scant regard for accepted conventions of service practice. While Churchill controlled the Admiralty, Sueter remained within the fold, but when the Balfour–Jackson regime attempted to reform the RNAS in 1915–16, largely to bring an errant department under tighter and more conservative control, Sueter became an early casualty. His departure to the Mediterranean in late 1916 was to mark the end of his air career. It also proved symptomatic of that enervation of RNAS administration which hamstrung eventual naval participation in the formation of the Royal Air Force and so limited the development of naval aviation in the interwar years.[36]

It was more than coincidental that two of Sueter's army counterparts, Frederick Sykes and Sefton Brancker, were also to spend part of the war in

21

semi-disgrace in the Mediterranean. Tightly bound to the Expeditionary Force, the RFC did not prove a benevolent environment for those whose ideas of aerial warfare transcended the limited horizons of the army command. Indeed, it was largely those officers who were closely associated with the field force for most of the war who emerged as the postwar leaders of the RAF. Those who spent much of their time in administrative posts in London tended to become the object of official suspicion and found their services dispensed with either during or immediately after the war.

Sir David Henderson, the nominal chief of the RFC from its inception in 1912, enjoyed a high reputation as a soldier at the outbreak of war. Asquith, in fact, even considered him a candidate for Chief of Staff.[37] His early career, which took him to the War Office as Director of Military Training in the heady days of prewar army reform, was distinguished by any standards. He was not happy with his appointment as DGMA, which he saw as ruining his chances of further promotion within the army as a whole.[38] The official historian has painted him as a simple and honest character, not at his ease in the world of civil–military relations in which he was to spend most of his wartime career.[39] Although his remaining papers provide little material to substantiate a more sophisticated analysis, Raleigh's view would seem somewhat wide of the mark. Exposed repeatedly to the inadequacies of the existing arrangement of the air effort, Henderson, who was certainly more adept at handling politicians than most of his colleagues, became convinced of the necessity of a separate air service and thus alienated himself from both his colleagues on the Army Council and Haig's field command. Henderson's exercise of his duties as DGMA proved a recurrent source of frustration to his immediate subordinates. His shortcomings as an administrator, however, were not the result of a weak character, but rather of his own dissatisfaction with the situation in which a lack of strong central direction in the national air effort and the domination of the BEF over the army's own air service placed him. Unfortunately, Henderson's gradual collapse under the weight of an uncongenial position only exacerbated the problems of co-ordination which he himself found so trying.[40]

Henderson's deputy at the outbreak of war, Frederick Sykes, had a far more mercurial career. Feeling that the field command had been usurped by Henderson, he was anxious to see the latter return to the War Office.[41] Assuming temporary command of the RFC in the Field while Henderson was absent on sick leave in early 1915, Sykes managed so to offend his superior as to be sent home days after the latter's return to duty in May. No firm evidence exists to show just what Sykes had done, but later allegations of 'awful intrigue', and the intense dislike subsequently displayed by the normally forgiving Henderson, make it likely that Sykes had campaigned to retain the elusive field command on a permanent basis.[42] In the wake of his dismissal he was seconded to the Royal Marines and sent to command the naval air detachment in the eastern Mediterranean.

Unlike most of his contemporaries in the air command, Sykes had come from a fashionable regiment (15th Hussars) and was politically well-connected, eventually marrying Bonar Law's daughter. While the RFC held no future for him as long as Henderson remained in command, his efforts to find employment in it after his return from the Dardanelles were supported by an impressive array of testimonials from the highly-placed and the powerful.[43] In 1918 Sykes emerged temporarily as the head of the new air force. For most of the war, however, he exercised neither authority nor influence.

W. Sefton Brancker, who had passed out as 'Top Gunner' in his year at Woolwich and later graduated with distinction from the Staff College at Quetta, was the only member of the early war inner circle of military airmen never to hold supreme command. Hard-working, loyal and gregarious, Brancker virtually ran the Directorate of Military Aeronautics until 1917 without ever being vested with formal authority. Unfortunately, his overt frankness served him ill with his superiors, and like Henderson he was to become tainted in military eyes through involvement in the debate over the supreme direction of the air effort, even though he was not himself a convert to the concept of separating aviation from military control. Brancker ended the war with considerably less influence than he had wielded through most of it. He left the service after the war, like Sykes before him, for the barren fields of the directorship of civil aviation, eventually dying in the R.101 disaster.[44]

The least powerful of the four in 1914, and arguably the least gifted with natural intellect, was Hugh Trenchard, left in command at Farnborough in the wake of the field force's departure for France. Trenchard had overcome wounds and sickness to rescue an unpromising career through sheer hard work and force of personality. All but incoherent both verbally and on paper, this difficult man eventually exercised a virtual monopoly over strategic thought within the air service. The free hand he was later allowed by Haig while commanding the RFC in France unfortunately accentuated his single-minded outlook on the exercise of authority. While no other man contributed so much to the establishment of aviation as an important part of the British war machine, his relations with his political masters and professional colleagues, during the war at least, were distinguished by his lack of tact and a persistent refusal to tolerate what he too easily perceived as interference. Trenchard's eventual elevation to the command of the entire air service quickly resulted in the most severe crisis of the war in the air organization, in the process almost ending his own career.[45]

Recent historiography has tended to portray Sykes and Trenchard as personal rivals whose battle for the control of air policy dominated the early history of British aviation.[46] There is a certain degree of truth in this, although it was in fact Henderson and not Trenchard who blocked Sykes's reacceptance into the RFC between 1915 and 1918. Trenchard and Sykes represented two divergent schools of thought with regard to the application of air power. Whatever his later record as the defender of the RAF's independence and the apostle of the bomber, Trenchard remained during the war first and foremost a soldier, wedded to the belief that the aircraft was the servant of the field army. It was Sykes who came far closer to believing in an independent strategic role for airpower, a stance which made him popular with the political exponents of the Royal Air Force in 1918. The careers of the two men during the war mirrored the course of British air policy, with Trenchard exercising a pervasive influence through 1916 and 1917, and Sykes failing to overcome the resulting military domination of aviation, despite the exercise of supreme office as Chief of the Air Staff in 1918.

Notes

1   Sir F. Sykes, *From Many Angles. An Autobiography* (London: Harrap, 1942), pp. 123–4.
2   Churchill to Grey, 25 September 1914, M. Gilbert (ed.) *Winston S. Churchill*, Companion Vol. 3, pt 1 (London: Heinemann, 1972), p. 140.
3   Brancker to Henderson, 3 September 1914, PRO, AIR 1/776/204/4/387.
4   ibid.
5   Sueter memorandum, Report on the defence of London against aerial attack, 16 October 1914, PRO, CAB 37/121/125; Churchill memorandum, Aerial defence, 22 October 1914, PRO, CAB 37/121/133; Churchill memorandum, Imminent Zeppelin attacks on London, 1 January 1915; Fisher to Churchill, 4 January 1915, M. Gilbert, *Winston S. Churchill*, Companion Vol. 3, pt 1, pp. 373–4
6   For a detailed description of the services' response to home air defence problems see C. Cole and E. F. Cheesman, *The Air Defence of Britain, 1914–1918* (London: Putnam, 1984), *passim.*
7   Minutes of the 122nd meeting of the CID, 6 February 1913, PRO, CAB 38/23/9; Churchill to Battenberg and Sueter, 5 September 1914, M. Gilbert, *Winston S. Churchill*, Companion Vol. 3, pt 1, p. 88.
8   Churchill memorandum, 25 October 1914, M. Gilbert, *Winston S. Churchill*, Companion Vol. 3, pt 2, pp. 1238–41.
9   Churchill to French, 15 November 1914, ibid., pt 1, pp. 264–5.
10 PRO, AIR 1/812/204/4/1253.
11 PRO, AIR 1/141/15/40/308.
12 PRO, AIR 1/2302/215/10; Morrow, *Building German Airpower*, p. 84.
13 PRO, AIR 1/2302/215/12; J. M. Laux, 'Gnôme et Rhône – an aviation engine firm in the First World War', *Aerospace Historian*, vol. 27, no. 1 (1980), p. 20.
14 H. Penrose, *British Aviation. The Great War and Armistice, 1915–1919* (London: Putnam, 1969), p. 9; Laux, 'Gnôme et Rhône', p. 20; Morrow, *Building German Airpower*, p. 84.

15 Ministry of Munitions, *History of the Ministry of Munitions*, Vol. 7, pt 1 (London: HMSO, 1922), p. 103.
16 PRO, AIR 1/835/204/5/248.
17 D. Lloyd George, *War Memoirs of David Lloyd George*, Vol. 1 (London: Nicholson & Watson, 1933), pp. 125–213; S. Bidwell and D. Graham, *Fire-Power. British Army Weapons and Theories of War, 1904–1945* (London: Allen & Unwin, 1982), pp. 48, 94–6.
18 French, *British Economic and Strategic Planning*, pp. 134–5, 151–67.
19 Henderson to Brancker, 9 September 1914, and Brancker to Henderson, 10 September 1914, PRO, AIR 1/118/15/40/36; Sykes to Trenchard, 13 September 1914, PRO, AIR 1/762/204/4/161; Brancker to Henderson, 20 August 1914, PRO, AIR 1/876/204/5/574; Macmillan (ed.), *Sefton Brancker*, p. 58.
20 Maj.-Gen. Sir C. E. Callwell, *Experiences of a Dug-Out* (London: Constable, 1920), p. 28; J. Gooch, *The Plans of War. The General Staff and British Military Strategy, c. 1900–1916* (London: Routledge & Kegan Paul, 1974), p. 302; A. J. Marder, *From the Dreadnought to Scapa Flow. The Royal Navy in the Fisher Era, 1904–1919*, Vol. 4 (Oxford: Oxford University Press, 1969), p. 60.
21 Brancker to Sueter, 2 December 1914, PRO, AIR 1/2561.
22 Admiralty memorandum, Additions to the shipbuilding and aircraft programme since the beginning of the war, 9 December 1914, PRO CAB 37/122/187.
23 Churchill minute to War Council, 3 April 1915, Milner Papers, 122/129.
24 Sykes, *From Many Angles*, p. 138.
25 C. Barnett, *The Swordbearers. Studies in Supreme Command in the First World War* (London: Eyre & Spottiswoode, 1963), p. 77.
26 Rawlinson to Kitchener, 25 November 1914, PRO, PRO 30/57/51 (Kitchener Papers), WB 7.
27 For a succinct account of this process see P. Mead, *The Eye in the Air. History of Air Observation and Reconnaissance for the Army, 1785–1945* (London: HMSO, 1983), pp. 65–71.
28 Brancker to Henderson, 3 September 1914, PRO, AIR 1/776/204/4/387.
29 Sykes memorandum, Bomb dropping attacks, 15 February 1915, PRO, AIR 1/921/204/5/889.
30 PRO, AIR 1/118/15/40/36; IWM, Sound Records, 000024/17; L. A. Strange, *Recollections of an Airman* (London: Hamilton, 1933), p. 42.
31 RFC War Diary, February 1915, PRO, AIR 1/1176/204/5/2595.
32 Strange, *Recollections of an Airman*, p. 79.
33 PRO, AIR 1/502/16/1.
34 Macmillan (ed.), *Sefton Brancker*, p. 67.
35 Brancker to Wolfe Murray, 8 December 1914 and attached Wolfe Murray and Kitchener minutes, PRO, AIR 1/2413/303/11.
36 Roskill, *Documents Relating to the Naval Air Services*, pp. 56–8; G. Till, *Air Power and the Royal Navy, 1914–1945. A Historical Survey* (London: Jane's, 1979), pp. 111–17; Rear-Admiral M. F. Sueter, *Airmen or Noahs* (New York: Putnam, 1928), *passim*.
37 Asquith to Stanley, 22 January 1915, M. and E. Brock (eds), *H. H. Asquith. Letters to Venetia Stanley* (Oxford: Oxford University Press, 1982), pp. 390–1.
38 Minutes of the Committee on the Administration and Command of the RFC, 3 and 5 July 1916, PRO, AIR 1/518/16/7/17 and 19.
39 *WIA*, Vol. 1, p. 445.
40 For a brief account of Henderson's wartime career see H. A. Jones, 'Sir David

Henderson, father of the Royal Air Force', *The Journal of the Royal Air Force College*, vol. 11, no. 1 (1931), pp. 6–12. Other valuable sources regarding the character of this retiring officer are Macmillan (ed.), *Sefton Brancker*, and Henderson's correspondence with Trenchard, Trenchard Papers, MFC 76/1/76. Henderson's own papers, see Henderson Papers, RAF, AC 71/2 and 4, are fragmentary.

41 Sykes, *From Many Angles*, pp. 94–5, 122.

42 Brancker to Trenchard, 13 and 16 March 1916, Trenchard to Brancker, 14 March 1916, Trenchard Papers, MFC 76/1/5.

43 Duchess of Marlborough to Curzon, 28 April 1916 and Caillard to Curzon, 15 May 1916, Curzon Papers, Eur.F.112/170.

44 Macmillan (ed.) *Sefton Brancker* is in fact autobiographical for the wartime period and as such constitutes an invaluable guide to Brancker's character and ideas. So too does his long correspondence with Trenchard in 1916–17, for which see Trenchard Papers, MFC 76/1/5–17.

45 The only biography of Trenchard is highly partisan. See A. Boyle, *Trenchard* (London: Collins, 1962), *passim*. Trenchard's own autobiographical notes do provide an interesting insight into his stormy early career. See Trenchard Papers, MFC 76/1/61.

46 See for example R. Higham, *The Military Intellectuals in Britain, 1918–1939* (New Brunswick, NJ: Rutgers University Press, 1966), pp. 119–58.

[3]

The Problems of Growth

The year 1915 witnessed the gradual growth and consolidation of European airpower and its first participation in the set-piece offensives which characterized warfare for the rest of the conflict. The introduction of the armed fighting aircraft towards the end of the year made aerial combat itself a feasible proposition, accelerating the development of the air war into a struggle of attrition. This process placed added demands on industries already stretched by the necessity of providing an extended range of ancillary services for their respective siege machineries. The British air forces, like the army they supported, had a great deal of ground to make up on their continental counterparts, and even at the end of the year could not be said to have matched the French or Germans in size or in administrative and technological efficiency.

British flying operations on the Western Front were as much a disappointment to the apostles of airpower within the RFC and RNAS as the offensives from Neuve Chapelle to Loos, the missed opportunity at Gallipoli and the lack of decisive action in the North Sea were to the nation as a whole. Trenchard's verdict on RFC participation at Aubers Ridge in May, 'that we did not have enough Air to make it widely felt in the battle, and we did not know how to use it enough',[1] might well have served as a general epitaph for a year of betrayed hopes. The British services and the government behind them had as yet to understand or adjust to the demands of the war into which they were being ever more deeply drawn.

Lack of adequate numbers was undoubtedly the foremost factor inhibiting British aviation's performance during Sir John French's 1915 offensives. Henderson commanded seven aircraft squadrons at Aubers Ridge. His successor could still muster only twelve in support of the attack on Loos in late September.[2] As the Flying Corps was now divided into wings of approximately equal strength, attached on a one-to-one basis to each army, and as the British attacks of 1915 were carried out on frontages narrow by First World War standards, only a portion of the available units were ever directly engaged. The actual number of machines deployed was almost ludicrously small. On 31 March there were 112 army aeroplanes in France, including 19 at the Aircraft Park (reserve depot for the repair and distribution of machines). By 30 June the number had risen to 144, of which 38 were at the Aircraft Park. Finally on 30 September, 185 aeroplanes were available, 32 of them in reserve.[3]

The effectiveness of these small numbers was further limited by constraints on the use of machines and personnel. Even Sykes's prewar prediction that 'no aeroplanes or engines, and few pilots and observers, will stand the strain of more than three months' active service without relief',[4] proved in some senses too optimistic. In the summer of 1915 the commander of the RFC's Second Wing, Lt. Col. C. J. Burke, explained the limits on the use of pilots to his army headquarters: 'Though a pilot may fly for four hours on one day, it cannot be expected that he can fly for 28 hours in a week; this is the same, but expressed differently, as saying that though infantry can march 25 miles in one day, they cannot be expected to cover 175 miles in a week.' In the light of the high rate of attrition that would result from having pilots fly too much, he concluded that approximately 25 hours in the air per month was all that could be asked of a pilot.[5] In a report sent to RFC Headquarters on 31 July, Burke calculated the average amount of flying done by each serviceable aeroplane under his command as just under one hour per day.[6] When one considers that Second Wing, with a mean daily strength of 32 operational machines, was responsible for approximately 15 to 20 miles of the front, the weakness of the air contingent becomes readily apparent.

Efforts to bring this small air strength into play were obstructed as much by a limited appreciation among army officers of the aeroplane's potential as by the technical difficulties of ground–air communication. Battery commanders ignored the reports of fall of shot relayed by artillery observation machines, while infantry officers seldom bothered to mark forward positions for friendly air identification or to do enough to ensure that their men fired only at hostile machines. To the average soldier in 1915, the aeroplane remained an occasional alien intruder in an environment already different enough from that which he had been trained to expect. Among the high command there was little attempt to integrate air operations with general attack plans. Trenchard as commander of the RFC in France attended the planning conference for the Loos offensive, but was never consulted, or even spoken to, by the others present.[7] The development of proper co-ordination at the tactical level was largely a matter of familiarization between Flying Corps and field army which would progress in time of its own accord. Understanding, or at least receptiveness, at GHQ would increase tenfold when Trenchard converted Haig to the virtues of airpower in the months before the

Somme. In 1915, however, the RFC, if not quite an abandoned child, was certainly a neglected one as far as tactical planning was concerned.

Technical difficulties such as the accurate observation and transmission of the fall of artillery shells were worked out through trial and error at the front, not at experimental institutions at home. By the winter of 1915–16, the techniques of tactical co-operation had been developed, if not yet put to full test.[8] Two more overtly offensive functions, bombing and aerial combat, remained in a more uncertain state of growth.

Considerable hope was held out for bombing attacks on German lines of communication during the 1915 offensives. Low-level attacks on such targets as railway stations and junctions commenced during the Neuve Chapelle operation. Despite increasing casualties due to enemy ground fire, these attacks were continued, often by single aircraft. The results, unfortunately, were commensurate with neither risks nor expectations. An army survey showed that between 1 March and 20 June, the allied air services carried out 483 attacks in which 4,062 bombs were dropped. With the exception of isolated attacks on Zeppelins, results were negligible. Of 35 attacks on ammunition dumps, factories, power stations and shipyards, only four were adjudged to have been effective. For attacks on railway junctions and stations, by far the most important part of the joint bombing offensive, the success rate was even lower. Altogether, 141 attacks were carried out, but only three had been successful.[9]

Changes in method of attack, especially on railways, brought some results at Loos. During the period 23–28 September, approximately five and a half tons of bombs were dropped. Five or six trains were thought to have been destroyed, and RFC Headquarters concluded: 'Although no great damage was done, considerable interference was undoubtedly caused to the German railway organization, as is shown by the fact that they have apparently withdrawn the majority of their anti-aircraft guns from the front, and placed them at railway junctions and stations.'[10] As long as raids continued to be carried out by small numbers of unsuitable machines with light bombs, such attacks would continue to be primarily of nuisance value.

The emergence of a proper air fighting capability was equally hesitant. The machine-gun gradually became more common as the main form of air armament during 1915. The performance of the aeroplanes themselves remained persistently poor and the methods of mounting weapons crude. With only a handful of machines available for purely offensive duties, encounters remained infrequent and generally indecisive. In August 1915, for example, RFC Headquarters recorded sixteen aerial combats, of which only four were decisively successful.[11] The Germans introduced the prototype of the modern fighter when they started to bring the Fokker *Eindecker* to the front in the late summer of 1915. The new monoplane fighter, however, was slow to appear in any numbers, and the experience of one pilot with No. 5 Squadron, who did not see a single Fokker before his departure for home service in early 1916, can hardly have been exceptional.[12]

No single innovation had as decisive an impact on the air war as the machine-gun-armed German fighter. As far as Britain was concerned, this was largely because the appearance of an effectively armed opponent inevitably increased casualties. British personnel losses up to June 1915 had totalled less than 100, almost entirely as a result of accidents or fire from the ground.[13] One product of the low casualty rate was an abnormal sensitivity in the RFC to even slight increases in losses. Concern over losses to German anti-aircraft guns was so great in July 1915 that the Directorate of Military Aeronautics had to circulate a list of casualties to show how few men had actually been killed by the enemy.[14]

It has long been realized that the moral effect of the Fokker was 'far greater than its actual success justified'.[15] The *Eindecker* was an aircraft of unexceptional performance which achieved prominence simply through its monopoly of effective armament, in the form of a fixed machine-gun on the engine cowling, synchronized to fire forward through the propellor arc along the line of flight. Demoralized British pilots usually reported themselves to have been completely outflown by the monoplanes they met. In fact, only a handful of skilled enemy pilots were capable of getting enough out of their mediocre mounts to make them a real danger.

The Fokker scored its first success on the British sector on 1 August 1915. Despite a promising start, the Fokker did not enter large-scale production until the winter.[16] By 14 October VI *Armee*, holding a 50-mile stretch of the front opposite the British, listed only seven Fokkers on its strength.[17] Between August and October only 15 British aircraft were lost behind enemy lines.[18] That the Fokker had not yet achieved the omnipotence it was later to assume in the British airman's imagination is demonstrated by the experience of one officer, who reported having economized on machine-gun ammunition in late September by engaging an attacking monoplane with a rifle.[19] Three months later such an action would have been inconceivable. Indeed, as early as 25 October Trenchard was writing to the War Office: 'In view of the fact that the number of combats in the air is constantly on the increase, it is suggested that pilots and observers under instruction at home should be trained as far as possible in fighting in the air.'[20]

From November 1915 through January 1916 flying operations were frequently interrupted by poor weather. Seven aircraft were lost in November, eleven in December and ten in January. Low though they were, these losses were sufficient to tie down a disproportionate percentage of British air strength on escort duties. On 14 January, RFC Headquarters was compelled to make the provision of a heavy escort a matter of established doctrine.[21] Even in the spring, when the first generation of British fighters was arriving at the front, the Fokker continued to hold sway over the air command. In March Trenchard was still afraid of 'getting badly left by the German' in the production of up-to-date aircraft. A report to Henderson, dated 3 April, demonstrates how dramatically the Fokker was still cutting into the normal level of operations: 'I have cut down the work, in my opinion enormously. I have dropped bombing, no long distance reconnaissances are done, and jolly few short ones, and these are only just over the line.'[22]

By the summer of 1916, the Fokker had been all but hunted from the skies, leaving the British fighter force in almost uncontested control over the Somme battlefield. The experience of the so-called Fokker Scourge, however, had profoundly affected British perceptions of fighter warfare. Full discussion of the RFC's tactical response to the Fokker must be postponed until a later chapter. For the present, it is sufficient to observe that the arrival of the fighter considerably broadened the scope of action necessary to provide the tactical support for the army which remained the RFC's sole *raison d'être*. In so doing, it greatly complicated the expansion programme undertaken in response to earlier demands on the air service.

The autumn of 1915 witnessed an important reshuffling of the military air command in response to the belated realization that the RFC required a more satisfactory administrative structure than that left in the wake of the rush to France the year before. This involved Henderson's departure from the front to assume his long neglected duties as DGMA at the War Office, and his replacement by Hugh Trenchard. Henderson had been under increasing pressure to return to London from the beginning of 1915. Brancker had soldiered on as Deputy-Director since the previous August with ever deepening responsibilities but no real extension of authority. In a forceful letter written to Henderson on 28 July 1915, Brancker underlined the shortcomings of the existing arrangements:

> We must wake up in the senior officer line or get left.
> The drawback to the situation is that you are our only really senior officer. I do not feel that I fill this place properly. If it requires a Major-General to command the R.F.C. in the Field, it certainly wants one here, where instead of being a valuable asset, the R.F.C. is still an expensive and precocious innovation. The fact that you come home occasionally does not help; rather the reverse, for it makes my position much weaker – the innate but, I presume, unconscious obstruction, financial and otherwise, will not treat me seriously, and they use the desire to treat with *you* and not me as a means of avoiding action.

Henderson was not easily convinced that his place was anywhere else but the front. In August Brancker wrote again:

31

The Director-General of Military Aeronautics must be a Major-General at least, have a loud voice in the War Office, and if possible, be on terms of equality with the Army Council. It is obviously the appointment for you, and if you hold it, it would also imply the command of the whole Flying Corps.[23]

Finally convinced of the need for at least a temporary return to the War Office, Henderson gave up his place at RFC Headquarters and went home. Trenchard was promoted Brigadier-General and appointed in his place.

There was never any real question of anyone else but Trenchard taking over the field command. Since coming to France in late 1914, he had far outdistanced all his peers. As commander of First Wing, Trenchard had been directly responsible for the air support of the offensives carried out by the First Army at Neuve Chapelle, Aubers Ridge and Festubert. He had already established a special rapport with that army's commander, Sir Douglas Haig. Haig, said Trenchard in describing their first meeting, 'believed in the air though he did not understand very much about it, but he accepted what I had said'.[24] Under the circumstances, Trenchard succeeding Henderson seemed as natural a process as Haig replacing French several months later.

Henderson's intended task on returning home was to inject fresh vigour into the army's air expansion programme. The British army which fought the battles of 1915 had been built around the professional BEF of 1914. The arrival of Kitchener's volunteers in large numbers, and the reforming of Haig's command into four and eventually five armies, changed the complexion of the Expeditionary Force to that of a mass army in a quasi-continental mould. As this massive military edifice began its preparations for a full-scale offensive, the RFC had to undertake its own programme of growth in order to provide a proportionate degree of air support. The advent of serious fighting in the air itself, consequent on the appearance of the Fokker, produced a need for specialist fighter squadrons, and hence for an even greater increase in numbers.

On 23 November 1915 Henderson wrote a detailed memorandum for the CIGS Sir Archibald Murray concerning the future development of the air service. He noted that the authorized establishment of the RFC stood at 60 service squadrons, 20 reserve squadrons and 4 aircraft parks. At the time, there were 18 service squadrons abroad (14 of them in France) and a further 13 in various stages of organization at home. Half of the reserve squadrons had also been formed. Henderson predicted that 36 service squadrons would be operational by 1 April 1916, and that if the strength of these units remained at 12 aeroplanes and 12 pilots, the rest could be turned out at a rate of one a week. As the air command was unanimous that the strength of squadrons should be increased to 18 aeroplanes and pilots as soon as possible, he thought that 'the full 60 squadrons at this increased strength would not probably be completed much before the end of 1916, at the present rate of expansion'.[25]

A new command structure for the additional squadrons was provided for in two Army Council letters of 25 August and 10 December 1915. The RFC in the Field, currently divided into three wings, each attached to an army headquarters, was to be reconstituted as a brigade. As fresh units became available, new brigades were to be formed until there was one for each of the BEF's armies. It was originally planned that each brigade would comprise three wings, but in the event there were only two until the middle of 1918. One, designated the Corps Wing, was for general co-operation duties; the other, designated the Army Wing, was for army reconnaissance, bombing and air fighting duties.[26] On 1 January 1916, the RFC order of battle still listed three autonomous wings, but by the middle of February the first three brigades had been formed. An extra brigade for Rawlinson's newly organized Fourth Army was operational by the beginning of April. Finally, a Headquarters Wing, attached directly to GHQ, was created just before the Somme offensive began, and when a Fifth Army went into the line in the middle of the battle, squadrons were redeployed to form yet one more brigade.[27]

Between Loos and the Somme the RFC in France more than doubled in size. Henderson's prediction that the relatively slow rate of growth in the first year of the war would allow rapid expansion thereafter nonetheless proved over-optimistic. By March 1916, Brancker was complaining that 'we have rushed the brigade system and the new squadrons too fast'. Trenchard considered 27 squadrons with 12 pilots the indispensable minimum requirement for the spring, but as another communication from Brancker made clear, even this total was now slipping out of reach:

Not only is it impossible to let you have five more new squadrons during April, but it has proved absolutely necessary to postpone the departure of the last three due to join you before March 31. This will be extremely inconvenient and annoying for everyone, but I was forced to advise it, as I find that the pilot situation is really very serious, and unless we take a pull and get level with your demands and those of the various organizations at home at once, we shall land into most awful trouble. I reckon that at the moment we are actually about 100 pilots short of what we require to be on a really sound basis both at home and abroad. This shortage is partly due to weather, partly due to optimistic estimates, and partly to sending out new squadrons too early.[28]

The shortage of trained pilots was in fact only one symptom of a deeper crisis of expansion affecting the air effort at all levels. The administrative system in Britain, still entirely the responsibility of an understaffed War

33

Office directorate, could not yet co-ordinate the spiralling needs of the field service with the productive capacity of the aircraft factories and flying schools. Monthly aircraft deliveries in the spring of 1916 had reached the 200 level, but this was insufficient to meet both the requirements of growth and the rising attrition rate at the front.[29] There were also disturbing signs that the aircraft themselves were becoming outdated.[30]

The mainspring of the army building programme was the two-seat B.E.2c, essentially a modified version of the standard military aircraft designed by the Royal Aircraft Factory before the war. During 1915, 710 of 1,680 aircraft delivered were of this type.[31] This dependence on a machine which, although workmanlike and effective, was approaching obsolescence in mid-1916, was a product first of the army's prewar attitude to aircraft procurement and second of the damage done to private manufacturers by this policy. The attractions of a standardized and relatively simple design were irresistible at a time of rapid expansion. A price had to be paid, however, in a lack of flexibility in the face of rapid wartime technological change. A manufacturing system built around a group of new and technically inexperienced firms, producing a heavily sub-contracted, standard machine, simply could not be redirected without severe dislocation. As a result, B.E.2 variants were still arriving at the front in the spring of 1917.

The sluggishness of the army's aircraft procurement system pushed it into conflict with the navy, whose air service generally enjoyed better equipment. Other factors were also conspiring to remove military aviation from the vacuum in which it had operated since the war began. Through the first year of the war the RFC had actually turned down a large number of applications for commissions on the grounds that its waiting list was already long enough.[32] When this surplus was swallowed up, the service was slow to adapt to the changing manpower situation. Although the French and Germans made heavy use of NCO pilots from the start, the RFC would not be shaken from its belief that only officers could make good military aviators. It persisted in depending upon the traditional source of such men, the educated middle and upper classes, despite the severe depletion of the limited supply due to the high demand for infantry subalterns from a similar background on the Western Front. On 30 June 1916 Brancker provided a disturbing insight into the future: 'Our waiting list in England is growing perilously short, and heavy casualties in other arms will make officers increasingly difficult to obtain.'[33]

The supply of pilots was only one side of the RFC's personnel problem. As the service grew so did the need for skilled technicians. The number of specialists necessary to keep contemporary aircraft flying was quite staggering considering the relative simplicity of the machines themselves.

The return of strength by trades for First Wing corporals and air mechanics on 2 April 1915, for example, showed 1 acetylene welder, 27 batmen, 8 blacksmiths, 22 carpenters, 3 coppersmiths, 12 clerks, 11 cooks, 84 m.t. drivers, 9 electricians, 76 fitters and turners, 8 instrument repairers, 29 motor cyclists, 24 wireless operators, 48 riggers, 12 sailmakers, 4 storemen, 2 vulcanizers and 6 photographers – a total of 396.[34] These were the very same men whose services were most in demand in the war industries. Through the first year of the war the RFC managed to meet its needs through transfers from the army at large. Towards the end of 1915 it became obvious that this arrangement would no longer serve. Unfortunately for the air service, the proposed increase in establishment coincided with the tightening of Ministry of Munitions restrictions on the enlistment of skilled labour and the first signs of army opposition to transfers of soldiers with specialized skills from frontline units.[35] The difficult task of expanding the corps was thus complicated by the need to train a large number of unskilled recruits in the various aviation trades. Shortages were inevitable, and in the first week of the Somme offensive, Trenchard's command was still 150 engine fitters under establishment.[36]

As a result first of its own size and second of the general lack of co-ordination of the war effort, British aviation went through the first year of hostilities without any real supervision from on high. Expansion brought the air services into contact with the various official agencies around them for the first time in the winter of 1915–16. Airmen at the front, frustrated by the sluggishness of their support organizations, began to realize that 'the battle of the air will be won or lost at home'.[37] Their colleagues in Britain, along with the government, the press and the public, also began to view aviation as part of the overall problem of winning the war. This realization in turn produced a reorganization of the air effort aimed at bringing the army and navy air arms more closely into line with their respective departments' practices and interests.

Henderson's return to the War Office had initially been intended as a temporary measure. Indeed, only a bout of illness prevented him from returning to France before the end of 1915. In January 1916 the Army Council decided that Henderson should go back to France on 12 February and that Trenchard should come home in his place. With Henderson remaining effective commander of the whole corps, the Directorate of Military Aeronautics would be firmly subordinated to the field command. Official word of this decision did not reach France until 1 February, and while Henderson certainly remained enthusiastic about the proposed change, the Army Council was apparently experiencing doubts. Trenchard had actually returned to Britain, and Brancker, Henderson's designate chief of staff, gone overseas, when a War Office telegram postponed the new arrangement. After several weeks of confusion, the Army Council finally cancelled the proposed move altogether and solidified the old arrangement by appointing Henderson himself as a member.[38]

In March and April the reform of the Directorate of Military Aeronautics was taken one step further with the expansion of its existing departments into subordinate directorates with greater authority. Brancker, as Director of Air Organization, became responsible for all general staff and adjutant-general's work. Brig.-Gen. D. S. MacInnes, the new Director of Air Equipment, was charged with the design, supply and maintenance of aircraft. The Finance Directorate remained under the control of two senior civil servants, A. E. Turner and F. R. Stapely, who had been with the old contracts department (MA3) since before the war.[39]

There is little doubt that these changes were motivated by more than administrative expediency. Henderson's retention in particular was a response to increasing pressure on the air service from without. Discussions of air defence in the War Committee after a serious increase in Zeppelin activity over the winter had revealed for the first time the full dimensions of the breakdown between the RFC and RNAS. Criticism of the army air service itself had been mounting in response to the casualties inflicted by the German Fokkers in France, and was to be given sharp focus by the victory of the independent 'First Air Member' Noel Pemberton Billing over a Unionist opponent in the East Hertfordshire by-election on 9 March.[40] The decision to form Lord Derby's Joint War Air Committee, taken on 15 February, was probably sufficient to persuade the War Office that Henderson, easily its most senior airman, must be kept at home. His elevation to the Army Council ensured that departmental interests would best be served in the anticipated struggle against both the navy and public opinion.

Henceforth Henderson was to be occupied by the 'frivolities' of air politics on an almost full-time basis.[41] Although nominally invested with ultimate authority as DGMA, he exerted a diminishing influence over the corps itself, leaving the RFC in the Field under Trenchard to dominate and ultimately dictate military air policy. Henderson's involvement in the political debate over the future of the air service aroused the distrust of his air colleagues, who, as Brancker pungently opined, found him 'a damned useless type of fellow to be under' as far as the defence of their particular vision of the air war was concerned.[42] The groundwork was thus established for that split in the army air command which eventually resulted in Henderson drawing up the blueprint for an independent air service without reference to the tenets of military air policy and against the wishes of that policy's guardians in France.

By the time the public storm broke over the air effort in early 1916, the navy had also reshaped its air command in a manner which was ultimately to aid in the formation of the Royal Air Force. The RNAS was very much the personal creation of Churchill, whose personal enthusiasm for the aircraft had enabled the service to expand in a manner which entrenched departmental conservatism would otherwise have made most difficult. The Balfour-Jackson regime which took over at the Admiralty after Churchill's fall in mid-1915 looked on the freedom allowed the RNAS by the former First Lord with traditionalist disapproval. Jackson himself found discipline bad, expenditure enormous and wasteful, and the service as a whole unwieldy and inefficient.[43] Career officers with little or no experience of aviation were drafted into senior administrative posts to bring the errant child back into line. The unconventional Sueter was himself placed under a new Director of Air Services, Rear-Admiral C. L. Vaughan-Lee, another non-flying officer.

Modern historians have not been kind to Vaughan-Lee, finding little in his actions to suggest a deep understanding of aviation and its possibilities.[44] He was, however, only the servant of an administration concerned first and foremost with maintaining the RNAS as the obedient servant of greater naval interests. Vaughan-Lee and his colleagues proved zealous defenders of naval prerogatives in the inter-service debates carried out under the auspices of the Derby Air Committee and the Curzon Air Board. Unfortunately for the long-term future of maritime aviation, their efforts were to prove counterproductive, naval obstructionism being one of the most decisive factors in proving the case for an independent air service. In the short term, the conservative backlash against Churchill's enthusiasm for aviation divided the RNAS itself, convincing many airmen that aviation was not likely to progress 'under such maladministration'.[45] Frustrated aspirations transformed many into advocates of a separate air service, prepared even to ghost articles in the press and pass confidential information to such advocates of an imperial air service as Montagu of Beaulieu.[46] Shipborne aviation became one of the most conspicuous postwar casualties of the formation of the Royal Air Force, but in one sense at least the Admiralty was the early architect of its own misfortunes. Naval airmen, confined within the institutional strait-jacket placed on them in 1915–16, turned their backs on naval careers and when the opportunity arose left for the Royal Air Force in large numbers.

With the reorganization of the military and naval air commands in late 1915 and early 1916, the lines were drawn for the inter-service confrontation which dominated British air policy in the last nine months of the Asquith government. While it is important to realize that forces were already emerging within the air services pushing in the direction of an integration of aviation within a single organization, the political campaign of 1916 was to be fought largely as a battle between the two administrations which each adhered to concepts of airpower best described as ancillary to the operations of the senior services involved. Both the Admiralty and the War Office were determined to maintain their air arms primarily as servants of their own interests, either in the North

Sea or on the Western Front. The histories of the Joint War Air Committee and the Air Board revealed that these interests could not be reconciled within the limits imposed by available resources of men and machines. In the final analysis, however, the debates and controversies of 1916 merely proved that the government itself did not yet see a case for intervention.

As was revealed by the Zeppelin scares of 1914, the government's main concern with regard to aviation was home defence. It was largely content to allow aerial matters not directly related to the aerial protection of Britain to remain in the hands of the service experts. This disinclination to interfere was strengthened by the general lack of any sort of technical knowledge of the subject. Churchill alone could be described as having some awareness of what aircraft were, or were not, capable of achieving. For the rest, occasional flickers of interest, such as that aroused in September 1915 by a plan to burn or blight Germany's harvest from the air, gave evidence only of the depths of their ignorance.[47]

As in so many other fields of war administration, the government remained firmly wedded to the forms of peacetime organization. Following his departure from the Admiralty, Churchill submitted a memorandum calling for the formation of a combined air department 'to make the British Air Service indisputably the largest, most efficient, and most enterprising of any belligerent power'. It was dismissed merely 'as a scheme for providing Winston with something to do', but the comments of the prime minister's private secretary Maurice Bonham Carter, endorsed by Maurice Hankey (secretary successively of the War Council, the Dardanelles Committee and the War Committee), provide an accurate summation of the existing consensus on air policy:

> The military wing is a success largely because it has been developed and trained as a branch of the army and with military objects strictly in view. The naval wing is a failure because it has not been designed for naval objects with the result that it has degenerated into a crowd of highly skilled but ill-disciplined privateersmen. What is wanted is to make the naval wing more 'naval' not more 'aerial'.[48]

Only the explosion of German bombs on British soil could break down this adherence to the status quo. Early raids were isolated and light affairs, and it was not until the night of 31 May/1 June when a German army airship left seven dead in east London that the first bombs actually fell on the capital. By the end of the year, Zeppelins had dropped just over 36 tons of bombs, killing 208 civilians and wounding another 432.[49] It was by no stretch of the imagination the feared apocalypse, but the gradually increasing strength of the raiders seemed to hint at worse. In a sense the German 'baby-killers' stepped into a role already provided for them by official propaganda and public apprehensions. Popular demands for both protective and retaliatory action became the common postscript to each civilian death, and faced with the inability of its defence forces to bring down a single raider on British soil, the War Committee began to intervene directly in the provision at least of guns and searchlights for London's defence.[50]

Naval arrangements for defending Britain single-handed had been shown inadequate as soon as they had been put to the test. At the end of 1915 the protection of Britain from air attack was a dual army and navy responsibility, although neither service was equipped in any way even to discourage raiding Zeppelins. The obvious bias of both air arms towards the needs of their own services focused public attention on the existing organization of aviation as the crucial element in the problem. Beneath the cries for reprisals there lay a discernible belief that only a change in institutions, be it either 'the appointment of an Air Minister who will work hand in hand with the Navy and Army, or the actual creation of an imperial air service'[51] could bring an end to the Zeppelin menace. On the night of 31 January/1 February, nine German navy airships launched the largest raid on England to date, thereby forcing a formal government response. The course of air politics over the remainder of the year, however, demonstrated that neither the War Committee nor the services subscribed to the vision of the future being promulgated with increasing fervour by their critics.

Notes

1 Autobiographical notes, Trenchard Papers, MFC 76/1/61.
2 PRO, AIR 1/676/21/13/1880; AIR 1/823/204/5/248.
3 PRO, AIR 1/141/15/40/308.
4 First Annual Report of the Air Committee on the Progress of the Royal Flying Corps, 7 June 1913, PRO, CAB 38/24/21.
5 Burke to Second Army HQ, 11 June 1915, PRO, AIR 1/2268/209/70/216.
6 Burke to RFC HQ, 31 July 1915, PRO, AIR 1/920/204/5/884.
7 Autobiographical notes, Trenchard Papers, MFC 76/1/61.
8 *WIA*, Vol. 2, pp. 82–110; Mead, *The Eye in the Air*, pp. 66–7.
9 RFC HQ memorandum, Bomb dropping in the western theatre of war from 1 March to 20 June 1915, July 1915, PRO, AIR 1/921/204/5/889.
10 RFC HQ memorandum, Operations of the Royal Flying Corps from 23 to 28 September 1915, October 1915, PRO, AIR 1/753/204/4/69.
11 PRO, AIR 1/758/204/4/119.
12 IWM, Sound Records, 000086/08.
13 Historical notes on the Royal Flying Corps, August 1914 to June 1915, 10 June 1915, PRO, AIR 1/408/15/231/50.
14 Lt.-Col. C. C. Marindin (Acting DDMA) to Home Establishment Wings, 13 July 1915, PRO, AIR 1/121/15/40/103.
15 *WIA*, Vol. 2, p. 150.
16 Production orders, German Air Service, Bundesarchiv-Militärarchiv, RL2/v.3301; Morrow, *German Air Power in World War I*, pp. 40–2.
17 A. Imrie, *German Fighter Units, 1914–May 1917* (London: Osprey, 1978), p. 8.
18 British casualty returns for the period before July 1916 are fragmentary.

Statistics have been compiled from information in PRO, AIR 1/687/21/20/1–7, AIR 1/688/21/20/8–13, AIR 1/689/21/20/14–20, AIR 1/690/21/20/21–9, AIR 1/758/204/4/119, AIR 1/939/204/5/301, Air 1/1181/204/5/301, AIR 1/1181/204/5/2595 to AIR 1/1184/204/5/2595.

19 RFC War Diary, September 1915, PRO, AIR 1/1182/204/5/2595.
20 Trenchard to DDMA, 25 October 1915, PRO, AIR 1/138/15/40/281.
21 RFC War Diary, November 1915 to May 1916, PRO, AIR 1/1184/204/5/2595.
22 Trenchard to Henderson, 3 April 1916, Trenchard Papers, MFC 76/1/76.
23 Brancker to Henderson, 28 July and August 1915, Macmillan (ed.), *Sefton Brancker*, pp. 106–9.
24 Autobiographical notes, Trenchard Papers, MFC 76/1/61.
25 Henderson to Murray, 23 November 1915, PRO, AIR 1/404/15/231/45.
26 Army Council to French, 25 August and 10 December 1915, PRO, AIR 1/529/16/12/72.
27 PRO, AIR 1/2129/207/83/1.
28 Brancker to Trenchard, 8 and 13 March 1916, Trenchard Papers, MFC 76/1/5.
29 Monthly production figures for 1916 can be found in the weekly Air Board reports sent to the War Cabinet in 1917. For the period February to May 1916 see Air Board reports to the Cabinet, G.T. 306, 24 March 1917, PRO, CAB 24/9; G.T. 468, 14 April 1917, CAB 24/10; G.T. 718, 12 May 1917, CAB 24/13; G.T. 1081, 16 June 1917, CAB 24/16.
30 Brancker to Trenchard, 11 April 1916, Trenchard to Brancker, 17 April 1916, Trenchard Papers, MFC 76/1/5; Trenchard to Brancker, 2 June 1916, MFC 76/1/6.
31 PRO, AIR 1/2302/215/10.
32 Correspondence of Director-General of Military Aeronautics, PRO, AIR 1/361–4.
33 War Office Memorandum, 30 June 1916, PRO, AIR 2/127/B12062.
34 Return of strength by trades, 2 April 1915, PRO, AIR 1/792/204/4/755.
35 Transfers to and re-enlistments into Royal Flying Corps, Brancker Papers, IWM, 73/183/1.
36 Brooke-Popham to Brancker, 9 July 1916, PRO, AIR 1/405/15/231/46.
37 Trenchard to Derby, 19 March 1916, Trenchard Papers, MFC 76/1/81.
38 Henderson to Trenchard, December 1915 and 1 February 1916, Trenchard Papers, MFC 76/1/76; minutes of the 148th meeting of the Army Council, 14 January 1916, PRO, AIR 1/2129/207/98; correspondence between Haig and Army Council, February 1916, PRO, AIR 1/529/16/12/72.
39 Macmillan (ed.), *Sefton Brancker*, p. 114.
40 Pemberton Billing, whose previous attempt to win a seat had failed by 376 votes at Mile End in January, polled 4,950 to the Unionist candidate's 3,559 votes. See B. D. Powers, *Strategy without Slide-Rule. British Air Strategy, 1914–1939* (London: Croom Helm, 1976), pp. 22–4.
41 Brancker to Trenchard, 13 April 1916, Trenchard Papers, MFC 76/1/5.
42 Brancker to Trenchard, 17 August 1916, Trenchard Papers, MFC 76/1/7.
43 Minutes of meeting to discuss Air Department, 3 August 1915, Montagu Papers, V/N/4.
44 Roskill (ed.), *Documents Relating to the Naval Air Service*, p. xi; Till, *Air Power and the Royal Navy*, p. 113.
45 Sladden to Montagu, 28 March 1916, Montagu Papers, I/C/6.
46 Montagu Papers, I/C/6, 18, 19, 22 and 26; Roskill (ed.), *Documents Relating to the Naval Air Service*, pp. xi–xii.

47 Report of a conference on the proposed devastation of the enemy's crops, 28 September 1915, PRO, CAB 42/3/42.
48 Churchill memorandum, Notes on the formation of an air department; Bonham Carter to Hankey, 10 June 1915, Hankey to Asquith, 12 June 1915, Asquith Papers, 27/253–62.
49 PRO, AIR 9/3, Folio 7.
50 Minutes of the 67th meeting of the War Committee, 26 January 1916, PRO, CAB 42/7/13.
51 *Daily Mail*, 4 April 1916; Pemberton Billing memorandum, Air Services – proposals for the creation of an imperial air service and the reorganization of the existing services, 12 April 1916, Asquith papers, 30/16–26.

[4]

The Rise of Inter-Service Rivalry

Two major strains of opinion can be discerned behind the awakening of public interest in the air effort during the winter of 1915–16. In the first instance there was a growing concern that the existing arrangements for the direction of the war were not proving adequate to meet the task. Aviation came under a critical eye, already sharpened by the discovery of incompetence elsewhere in the civil–military edifice, which searched out the 'crassly ignorant' with almost inquisitorial fervour.[1] In the second instance, the German air raids aroused deep outrage, not only at the enemy for behaving as he was by then expected to behave, but also at the government for failing to punish him. The *Daily Mail*'s call 'Hit Back! Don't Wait and See!' was typical of a public frustration given no release in either the destruction of the intruders over British soil or the knowledge that the Germans were being paid back in kind.[2]

By the second year of the war a number of public reputations had already been sacrificed to the belief that Britain's apparently pusillanimous conduct of hostilities was the product of incompetence in high places. The accusations freely aired in the press, and by senior soldiers and politicians in pursuit of their own particular vendettas, found an answering chord in a public imagination ready to believe that Britain's fighting men could only have been denied victory by their ineffectual superiors. The resulting witch-hunt tended to obscure the deeper failure of institutions, concentrating instead on the individuals held responsible for sending British servicemen to their deaths without adequate equipment or intelligent object. With his appetite for politico-military scandal already whetted by the shell shortage and the Dardanelles, and the public disgrace of such officers as von Donop and Troubridge, the man in the street was quite ready to believe that the air services were also being mismanaged.

Even before rumours of the 'Fokker Scourge' began to filter through from France, the civilian deaths caused by Zeppelin bombs in London and other cities in the eastern half of the country provided ready fuel for such speculation. The depth of feeling aroused by early airship depredations is difficult to comprehend in the wake of the relative calm with which a later generation tolerated a far worse ordeal at the hands of Hitler's *Luftwaffe*. Yet, in the First World War, the British civilian had not been indoctrinated in the belief that even he might expect to be in the front line of a modern war. Zeppelin attacks, like the occasional bombardments of east coast ports by the High Seas Fleet, seemed a gross perversion of the expected conduct of war. Even when the first airships came down in Britain in 1916–17, there was concern lest their dead crews be treated as anything other than common murderers.[3]

Although Britain's rudimentary home defence network did register some early successes against raiding Zeppelins, no airship was actually destroyed over British soil until September 1916. Most attempts at interception ended merely with a series of crashes on poorly lit airfields and the disappearance of the enemy into the night. Perhaps more annoying to inflamed opinion was the disinclination of the air services to launch retaliatory raids against German cities. Discussions between army and navy authorities only left the impression that neither command was prepared to face the problems of defence and retaliation. Although the War Committee settled on a rough allocation of responsibilities in the wake of the heavy raid of 31 January/1 February – 'the navy to undertake to deal with all hostile aircraft attempting to reach this country, whilst the army undertake to deal with all such aircraft which reach these shores' – the overriding impression remained, as Northcliffe complained to Bonar Law, that the existing administration had no 'time or imagination as to the size of the job'.[4]

Dissatisfaction with the state of British aviation produced two responses: a judicial inquiry into the administration of the RFC, and a committee to co-ordinate the activities of the army and navy air wings. The latter proved of lasting significance to the development of air policy. The former, very much a product of that search for military incompetence commented upon above, was an irrelevance almost from the start and is best dealt with briefly at this point in the discussion.

The Committee on the Administration and Command of the Royal Flying Corps was in many senses the creation of the new MP for East Hertfordshire, Noel Pemberton Billing. Pemberton Billing was not the first publicly to question the conduct of the air war. Parliamentary orators and press pundits had been attacking various aspects of the air effort throughout the winter of 1915–16. Pemberton Billing's charge 'that quite a number of our gallant officers have been rather murdered than killed' provided, however, just that combination of sensationalism and professional expertise (its author having been a pilot in the RNAS) to force the government to act.[5]

The product of Pemberton Billing's accusations was very much of a piece with those other ineffectual tribunals set up by the Asquith government to perform the last rites on the Gallipoli expedition and Townshend's fiasco at Kut. Judge C. W. Bailhache was appointed chairman of a committee 'to inquire into and report upon the administration and command of the Royal Flying Corps with particular reference to the charges made both in Parliament and elsewhere against the officials and officers responsible for that administration and command and to make any recommendations in relation thereto'.[6] The body suffered throughout by its coexistence, first with Derby's Joint War Air Committee, and then with Curzon's Air Board. Energy and attention tended to be diverted to these more important bodies, and Curzon spoke for most of his colleagues in dismissing the inquiry as a 'preposterous and almost criminal farce' wasting valuable resources better expended on his board.[7] Such feelings of waste were reinforced by the fact that most of the accusations which had brought the committee into being in the first place were out of date by the time it began its deliberations in the summer. The charge, for example, that British pilots were labouring under an insuperable disadvantage in their efforts to combat the German Fokker due to 'the flood of obsolete aeroplanes which continue to pour in from the makers', seemed of little relevance when a new generation of fighter aircraft was hunting the same Fokker from the skies over the Somme.[8]

Indeed there was little in the drawn-out deliberations of the inquiry to cast doubt on Brancker's early verdict that it had been 'nicely squared to play up for Government'.[9] Bailhache, an expert in commercial law, and the majority of his colleagues were manifestly out of their depth in the technical discussions which developed around most of the allegations put forward. From the start they showed an inclination to defer to the expertise of Henderson, who was in almost constant attendance. Henderson's presence also had a pronounced deterrent effect on the presentation of evidence. Critics such as Pemberton Billing and C. G. Grey, the editor of the influential periodical *The Aeroplane*, were heavily dependent on informants within the services and aircraft industry, but they found it next to impossible to persuade either airmen or manufacturers to appear in person. Despite honest attempts to encourage them to come forward under offers of anonymity, no service pilots proved willing to take their careers in their hands by testifying against their senior officers. Similarly, private aircraft manufacturers were not willing to risk the loss of contracts by appearing singly before the inquiry.[10]

Opposition to the Royal Aircraft Factory, which provided the basis for many of the allegations made against the army air command, revealed the weakness of the opposition case at its most vulnerable point. The private manufacturers, who had a real grievance against military procurement, were not sufficiently well organized to make a collective appeal.[11]

Without solid evidence of the deleterious effects of overcentralization on private initiative and growth, the committee had little option but to accept Henderson's view that the case against his organization rested insecurely on simple jealousy of the Factory.[12]

Trenchard's outlook was entirely typical of the contempt in which the military air command held the committee. On 25 June he told Henderson: 'I do not know who makes the silliest remarks in the papers. Pemberton Billing thinks everybody is sent up to be killed, and the members of the Enquiry think the war can be conducted without any risk.'[13] Brancker actually refused to appear before Bailhache unless given a direct military order to that effect.[14] They could afford to be dismissive; when Bailhache's final report eventually appeared on 17 November 1916 the inquiry itself had long been an anachronism. Its exoneration of Henderson and his subordinates on all charges of mismanagement aroused scarcely any interest. Perhaps its only real impact on the air effort had been the detrimental effect on its central direction caused by the diversion of so much of the senior army air officer's time and energy into its deliberations.[15]

The Bailhache Inquiry had been pushed outside the mainstream of air policy at the very beginning. The other product of the agitation of early 1916, the Joint War Air Committee (JWAC) was more central; so much so that one recent historian has concluded that the formation of the Royal Air Force 'became inevitable in political terms' from the moment of its failure.[16] While such a verdict is simplistic, the JWAC did represent the first wartime attempt to impose an overall order on Britain's air priorities, and as such pointed the way towards the more drastic remedies of 1917–18.

The naval and military representatives invited to the War Committee meetings after the winter Zeppelin raids treated their civilian masters to an arresting display of rivalry. The exchange of information on home defence was attended by complaints from each of the two air services that the other was interfering with its duties and sources of supply. A memorandum from Henderson, dated 28 January, was typical of the entire argument, both in its tone and in its preoccupation with the supply of aero engines:

> There is only a limited amount of aeronautical material available for both services, particularly with regard to the supply of engines. I do not anticipate serious difficulty in providing aeroplanes of suitable design and in sufficient quantity: but the question of high-powered engines is serious, and is at present chiefly affecting the military service.
>
> ... The Royal Flying Corps is now suffering from a lack of suitable engines for its necessary daily work, while it is understood that the

Admiralty is using a large number of the most suitable engines for land work.

I suggest therefore that the War Council be invited to consider the following points:

1 What are the immediate duties of the R.N.A.S.?
2 What are the immediate duties of the R.F.C.?
3 What is the order of importance of these duties?
4 In view of these decisions, what is the best distribution of available material?[17]

Service complaints forced the government to realize that no agreement on the allocation of air resources and responsibilities either existed or was likely to exist without some change in the organization of the air effort. The war, however, had not jolted Asquith and most of his colleagues out of their proclivity for attempting as much as possible within the framework of peacetime procedure. Isolated voices like those of Churchill and Curzon might echo popular demands for some form of air ministry, but the official consensus remained more in tune with the views of the prime minister himself, who, while professing an open mind on the higher direction of the air effort, was predictably not in favour of the creation of a new department of state.[18]

The War Committee's disinclination to meddle with the existing forms of military and naval organization was reinforced by the advice of its secretary, Maurice Hankey. In his memorandum on Churchill's proposal for an air ministry the year before, Hankey had deprecated such a move as likely to prove very unpopular with the two air services and looked back to the prewar CID Air Committee as the body best suited to sorting out difficulties.[19] Hankey, whose minutes and memoranda generally served as the seminal documents for official policy, advanced a similar solution in response to Henderson's challenge. Arguing that any new ministry would cause too much dislocation among existing institutions, he recommended merely 'the revival of the Air Committee in a modified form'.[20]

On 15 February the War Committee accepted a draft proposal to set up a body along the lines suggested by Hankey.[21] Edward Stanley, 17th Earl of Derby, was named chairman of the new Joint War Air Committee, and Lord Montagu of Beaulieu, the prewar advocate of airpower, was appointed as his deputy. The remainder of the committee was made up of three naval representatives, including the Director of Air Services, Vaughan-Lee, and two military representatives, one of whom was the Director-General of Military Aeronautics, Henderson. The goals set out for the JWAC seemed to augur well for the future of the air effort:

To ensure that the manufacture and supply and distribution of *matériel* required by aircraft are in accordance with the policy of aerial warfare laid down by His Majesty's Government, to avoid clashing or overlapping demands upon the manufacturing resources available, whilst securing the full and harmonious use of the same, and to eliminate correspondence between the Departments upon points which affect more than one.[22]

The obvious weakness of such an arrangement was that there was no 'policy of aerial warfare laid down by His Majesty's Government'. Hankey was later to claim that the JWAC's failure was largely due to the unfortunate choice of civilian personnel. There was obvious justice in this claim. Derby, who in any case was heavily involved in the campaign to introduce conscription, was not strong-willed enough to dominate his fractious companions.[23] Montagu was unpopular with both the military and naval representatives as a result of his open advocacy of an independent air service.[24] He had, in addition, only joined the committee on the understanding that it would assume executive powers. His belief 'that nothing short of the establishment of a proper administrative department under a minister with full powers can remedy the present defects and lay the foundations for improvement' rendered him an inevitable casualty, and incidentally provided the less resolute Derby with an excuse for his own resignation.[25]

In the final analysis, however, the failure of the Joint War Air Committee was due not to the inadequacies of its civilian directors but to the lack of any mechanism for forcing agreement between the service representatives. The army was demanding concessions from the navy – concessions that were considered necessary because the RNAS had, in military eyes, achieved a position of strength out of proportion to its justifiable needs or responsibilities. The navy did not recognize the justice of the army's case, and with the views of the two services thus 'incapable of mutual adjustment', the points at issue had simply to be referred back to the government.[26]

Indeed, Derby's letter of resignation, drafted after the naval representatives had refused to commit themselves to a document requesting the definition of national air policy and the extension of the JWAC's powers, provided an accurate assessment of the real problem. Derby told the prime minister that his lack of executive power had prevented him from getting agreement on anything but minor details. An understanding on 'bigger questions' would remain impossible, he claimed, until a general policy was introduced delineating the respective duties of the two services. Only an amalgamation of the RFC and the RNAS seemed likely to solve aviation's problems, but Derby considered such a step far too complicated an undertaking to attempt in wartime. He concluded that some degree of co-ordination might be achieved through a reconstituted committee with wider powers, but once again could not see how this could be achieved without coming up against the entrenched opposition of the Admiralty and War Office.[27]

The JWAC failed because it was little more than a modified version of the prewar Air Committee. That the latter body should have been so highly thought of by Hankey among others was a result not of any real record of effectiveness, but rather of the different circumstances under which it had operated. British aviation had been so underdeveloped before the war that the Air Committee had served only as a forum for discussion and as a monitoring agency for progress. The gradual divergence of the military and naval wings had been of little significance when the RFC and RNAS were operating on a very small scale without clear demands on their services or properly developed conceptions of their roles. All this had changed by the beginning of 1916. With the Admiralty and War Office in direct competition for resources which could not possibly underwrite the policies of both, and with each wing functioning as the tightly controlled extension of its parent service, there was a clear need for higher control. Denied any executive power, the Joint War Air Committee, as Derby complained to Trenchard after his resignation, 'was simple farce and had no power of any sort or kind'.[28]

The different reactions of the naval and military establishments to the JWAC's formation reflected the fact that only the latter had anything to gain from its existence. The navy, relatively comfortable without the strain of providing for a war of attrition on the Western Front, was never enthusiastic, and A.J. Balfour as First Lord did his best to obstruct the committee's its formation.[29] From the outset the naval representatives were kept on a tight leash, while Sueter, a potential divisive force, was actually ordered to have no contact with Montagu.[30] The army, although no more favourably inclined towards political interference in its affairs, was prepared to co-operate as long as a favourable redefinition of air responsibilities and priorities seemed the most likely result. Trenchard wrote privately to Derby expressing his support, while Henderson sounded an almost triumphant note:

> the establishment of the new Joint War Air Committee is going to give me a lot more work, and I think very useful work as we are now bound to get the Navy more or less into line. Derby is an ideal Chairman and I am sure will do a lot of good.[31]

There was little in the performance of Derby's committee to justify such optimism. Its effective existence barely spanned six weeks. From the start it was clear that the army and navy representatives were not likely to agree, and that Derby had no power either to persuade or to force them to do so. Whatever Derby's own conclusions on the formation of air policy, and there is little evidence to suggest that his ideas on the subject were well thought out, they had limited relevance on their own. No consensus was possible between the services; no executive action was likely on the part of the government. The chairman himself, whose influence in Britain's war councils did not match his status as a senior Conservative peer, could force no one's hand.

If Derby's committee served any purpose, it was simply to produce a clearer expression of the respective views of the naval and military air commands. On 3 March both sides submitted detailed statements of their policies, strengths and future requirements. The RNAS listed five main duties 'such as can best be carried out by personnel with naval training':

1   To attack the enemy's fleets, dockyards, arsenals, factories, air sheds, etc., from the coasts, whether the coasts be the enemy's or our own (i.e. long-distance bombing).
2   To patrol our own coasts to look out for enemy's ships and submarines, and to meet and repel enemy's aircraft. Possibly also to discover minefields.
3   Observation of fire during ships' bombardment of enemy's coasts. Destruction of enemy's coast batteries, means of communication thereto, and material in connection therewith.
4   Scouting for the fleet and reconnaissance work from ships.
5   To assist the Army whenever and wherever required.

For its planned long-range offensive alone, the RNAS estimated its immediate requirements as 50 heavy bombers, 80 light bombers and 50 long-distance fighters. Of this total of 180 aircraft, 140 were already on order. The navy also claimed that it required 228 bomber and fighter aircraft for other duties, of which 77 were in service, and a further 333 (to allow for attrition) on order.[32]

The RFC memorandum, while granting the RNAS the right to purely maritime operations and its contribution to home defence, sought *carte blanche* for military control of all air operations in land theatres, including long-range bombing:

> The first duty of the Royal Flying Corps is to perform efficiently all the services in the air which are required to enable the military forces in the field to overcome the enemy. These services include reconnaissance, artillery observation, fighting in the air, and offensive operations against objectives on the ground. The strength, equipment and armament of the squadrons employed for this purpose may vary according to the type of warfare and the nature of the theatre.
>
> It is considered essential that all air forces working in a theatre of land operations should be entirely under the control of the military commander in that theatre.
>
> The Royal Flying Corps must also be prepared to undertake long-range offensive operations, against military or national objectives. Such operations, if undertaken by land aeroplanes, will almost invariably be based on a theatre occupied or controlled by land

forces, and should therefore be undertaken by the Royal Flying Corps. Forces for this purpose, however, should be separately organized, and the squadrons allotted to this duty should be extra to the establishment provided for normal duty with the forces in the field.

The army went on to claim that naval encroachment in the field of long-range bombing produced wasteful competition, and would result in two weak efforts rather than a single stronger one. It also argued that the navy's plans would interfere with the provision of the 3,350 aircraft necessary to build up the RFC to its required strength. The army memorandum concluded that the alternative to the division of responsibilities it advocated was 'a joint or independent air service, which hardly seems to be within the sphere of practical discussion at the present moment'.[33]

The further proceedings of the JWAC revolved around attempts to reconcile these two memoranda. An interim report, produced on 20 March, made it clear that long-range bombing remained the major point of disagreement. The committee, of course, was in no position to decide whether either service should be granted its claim to responsibility for such operations. Indeed, it could only exhort the RFC and RNAS to co-operate closely on any project 'not of a purely local character', and recommend that 'in the event of there being any vital difference of opinion in regard to the feasibility or extent of the co-operation, the matter shall be referred to the War Committee'.[34]

Its inability to resolve the question of responsibility for different operations left Derby's committee to adjudicate over the allocation of airframes and engines without any criteria as to priorities. Not surprisingly, nothing of significance could be achieved. One small point was won when Derby was able to supervise an agreement whereby the two services would restrict their orders of foreign rotary engines to separate types. Beyond this, the JWAC could do little but canvass the vague possibility of future co-operative action. Unfortunately, there was little in the demeanour of either side to lend credibility to the belief that continued discussion 'should lead to a more systematized coordination and collaboration where supply and distribution of aircraft material are concerned'.[35]

During the two weeks following the appearance of the interim report, the military and naval representatives continued to exchange verbal and written broadsides over Derby's head. The navy complained that the recent agreement over rotary engines left it short of power-plants for up-to-date fighters.[36] The army pressed for preference in the supply of a new generation of powerful water-cooled, inline engines upon which the navy was depending for its planned long-range bombing force.[37] On 23 March the RNAS representatives submitted a note accusing their RFC counterparts of duplicity in negotiations over supply. They argued that the army had made too much of 'overlapping and interference in design, supply, contract work, etc.', and that the RFC's problems were rooted not in naval over-acquisitiveness but in the failure on the Royal Aircraft Factory to fulfil expectations. Vaughan-Lee and his colleagues accused the army of trying to co-opt naval resources instead of making a sincere effort to form an equal partnership.[38] On 1 April Henderson replied for the army, itemizing the cases of interference of which he had earlier complained. These included three cases where 'the Admiralty are depending for engines upon firms developed by us', and the competition for French-built aircraft and engines, where 'at a period when the requirements in the Military Wing were very heavy, and those in the Naval Wing comparatively light, the demands on the Navy were usually in excess of those of the Army'.[39]

In refusing to sign Derby's note of 27 March, the RNAS members questioned whether any real divergence over policy existed outside the issue of long-range bombing, and argued that any attempt to assign exclusive responsibility in this area would be retrograde and restrictive. When the supply of aircraft and engines was assured, both services would be able to launch raids on the enemy's heartland. The general logic behind this Byzantine argument was, of course, that any attempt to force the War Committee to define its air priorities before resources were sufficient to supply both services could only harm the navy, which undoubtedly enjoyed a better proportion of men and material to perceived needs.[40]

The necessity of establishing priorities with regard to air warfare would of course have been less immediate had Britain been able to produce more aircraft. Both the army's pursuit of aerial superiority on the Western Front and the navy's projected assault on German war industry could have been undertaken simultaneously if the supply of modern aero engines had not been so limited. The army was not very interested in strategic bombing in its own right, and only laid claim to jurisdiction over all operations in France when it became obvious that RNAS plans would use up aircraft the RFC felt it needed more.

It was reflective of the parlous state of air procurement that the relatively small number of machines required for the RNAS bombing offensive should have caused the army such discomfiture. Despite military claims that the naval air service was larger than their own, the actual frontline strengths of the RNAS and RFC, as reported to the Derby committee, were 646 and 1,350 aircraft respectively.[41] The few hundred new machines needed for the operations of what was to become No. 3 (Naval) Wing in the late spring of 1916, were of little obvious account compared to the thousands required to support the BEF in France, and the naval authorities had every reason to consider the allowing of military access to naval manufacturers a 'retrograde step'.[42]

Such were the limitations of the British aircraft industry, in fact, that it would have required the complete subordination of all other needs or projects to meet the requirements of the RFC in the Field. The RNAS maintained a sufficiently strong grasp on home-based private manufacturers to leave the RFC insufficient room to expand its own procurement network. Specific military grievances were centred in three main areas: the availability of the Sopwith aircraft which the RNAS was planning to use in the initial phase of its bombing campaign, the development of high-power engines for employment in the next generation of aircraft, and the division of the quota of engines and aircraft made available for British use as a result of the growth of the French aviation industry beyond its own service's needs. The first of these is best discussed in conjunction with the development of the naval bombing wing and can thus be left until the following chapter. The other two, however, were the product of long-term weaknesses in aircraft procurement, and can be dealt with here.

The RFC/RNAS disagreements over high-power engines were complicated by the lack of clear appreciation of future needs on the part of both sides. The situation was further confused by the fact that few designs involved had progressed beyond the experimental stage. Up until 1916, British engine production had been restricted by and large to copies of foreign rotaries of between 80 and 100 horsepower, and heavier, but not appreciably more powerful inline designs of both British and French origin.[43] A few more powerful engines were beginning to enter large-scale production in 1916, but the future quite obviously lay with even more powerful engines – designs which remained at the blueprint stage. The British engine industry had a difficult task ahead of it. In the first case, it had nothing approaching the experience or the resources of its continental rivals, on whom it had been almost completely dependent until the war. In the second, it made things far more difficult for itself by attempting to produce a powerful engine of strong but light construction, and paying a heavy price in loss of reliability and ease of manufacture.[44]

Beyond all this, the basic problem remained that an insufficient manufacturing capacity was being divided in a manner unlikely to satisfy either of the service rivals. In 1915 British contractors had produced 1,720 aero engines; in 1916 the figure increased to 5,363.[45] Even this increase only brought British output up to 69 per cent of the German figure (7,283) for the same period, and 33 per cent of the comparative French total (16,149).[46] The new British designs, of which so much was hoped by both the naval and military authorities, were usually developed by private firms and then ordered from their factories by the respective procurement agencies. Rough rules governing access to these factories had been worked out at the beginning of the war,[47] but with the situation changed out of all recognition, both services tended to seek the best available power-plants with scant regard to informal conventions as regards precedence. This scramble for the latest products of the relatively underdeveloped factories of Rolls Royce, Sunbeam and other companies led directly to the accusations of poaching which so blighted Derby's efforts at achieving a consensus. It also had the effect of souring relations between the producers and the services, convincing at least one prominent engine manufacturer that the army air command was incompetent.[48]

The supply of engines from France caused almost as many problems. France provided Britain with 24 per cent of the latter's engines in 1916, and as late as the spring of 1917 six of the twelve RFC single-seater squadrons stationed on the Western Front were equipped with French fighters.[49] Both services maintained missions in Paris to compete for access to the valuable French surplus. Despite efforts at co-ordination, all that had been achieved by April 1916 was an arrangement to deal with separate French firms. This in itself was largely meaningless, as the two were still in competition for the favours of the French government officials who remained the effective arbiters in any agreement.[50] Attempts to effect further changes to the procurement apparatus in Paris were hindered by the resistance of RFC Headquarters at the front. Trenchard was concerned that any alteration of the existing system would interfere with his own direct supply of French aircraft, arranged without reference to his nominal superior in London.[51] In the final analysis, the difficulty regarding French supplies was as insoluble within the existing framework of the British air organization as were the various problems associated with domestic aviation. With insufficient means available to support both of their programmes simultaneously, the RFC and RNAS were unlikely to agree on a co-ordinated procurement strategy as long as their immediate objectives continued to diverge and their political masters refused to force a system of priorities upon them.

The Joint War Air Committee failed to bring order to the British air effort because it was ultimately only the child of its time. Asquith's regime was not entirely out of tune with the demands of total war, but its response to the challenge of strategic direction was severely restricted by its predisposition to peacetime forms of compromise and continuity. By 1916 British aviation was deeply mired in a crisis of expansion which required as much as anything else co-ordination and direction from above. Lord Derby's committee was in every way typical of the administration's distaste for, and lack of understanding of, the expedients necessary to get the best out of Britain's war potential. Its failure was but one incident in that overall failure to impose control on the war effort which was ultimately to project Asquith into the political wilderness.

Notes

1 Northcliffe to Montagu, 27 March 1916, Montagu Papers, V/H/9.
2 *Daily Mail*, 4 April 1916.

3 R. L. Rimell, *Zeppelin! A Battle for Air Supremacy in World War I* (London: Conway, 1984), pp. 102–4.
4 Minutes of the 69th meeting of the War Committee, 10 February 1916, PRO, CAB 42/8/5; Northcliffe to Bonar Law, BL Papers, 52/2/52.
5 *Hansard*, vol. 81, HC Deb., 5s., 22 March 1916, cols 238–61; 28 March 1916, cols 601–711.
6 Proceedings of the committee on the administration and command of the Royal Flying Corps, 15 June 1916, PRO, AIR 1/516/16/7/1.
7 Curzon to Asquith, July 1916, Asquith Papers, 17/1–6.
8 Proceedings of the committee on the administration and command of the Royal Flying Corps, 23 June 1916, PRO, AIR 1/517/16/7/11.
9 Brancker to Trenchard, 18 May 1916, Trenchard Papers, MFC 76/1/6.
10 Interim report of the committee on the administration and command of the Royal Flying Corps, 3 August 1916, PRO, AIR 1/2405/303/4/5; Cotes-Preedy to Montagu, 2 June 1916.
11 H. Penrose, *The Great War and Armistice*, p. 157.
12 Proceedings of the committee on the administration and command of the Royal Flying Corps, 7 July 1916, PRO, AIR 1/518/16/7/21.
13 Trenchard to Henderson, 25 June 1916, Trenchard Papers, MFC 76/1/76.
14 Macmillan (ed.), *Sefton Brancker*, p. 124.
15 Final report of the committee on the administration and command of the Royal Flying Corps, 17 November 1916, PRO, AIR 1/2405/303/4/5.
16 Sir M. Dean, *The Royal Air Force and Two World Wars* (London: Cassell, 1979), p. 22.
17 Duties of the Royal Naval Air Service and the Royal Flying Corps, 28 January 1916, PRO, CAB 42/8/2.
18 Asquith to Curzon, 23 February and 25 March 1916, Curzon Papers, Eur.F.112/119.
19 Hankey to Asquith, 12 June 1915, Asquith Papers, 27/253–62.
20 Duties of the Royal Naval Air Service and the Royal Flying Corps, 28 January 1916, PRO, CAB 42/8/2.
21 Minutes of the 71st meeting of the War Committee, 15 February 1916, PRO, CAB 42/8/5.
22 Joint War Air Committee, AIR 2, The constitution, functions and procedure of the committee, 25 February 1916, PRO, AIR 1/2319/273/26.
23 Hankey to Asquith, 6 April 1916, Curzon Papers, Eur.F.112/173. For a savage contemporary judgement on Derby see R. Blake (ed.), *The Private Papers of Douglas Haig, 1914–1919* (London: Eyre & Spottiswoode, 1952), p. 279.
24 Brancker to Trenchard, 18 May 1916, Trenchard Papers, MFC 76/1/6; Hankey to Curzon, 4 May 1916, Curzon Papers, Eur.F.112/171.
25 Montagu to Asquith, 15 March and 3 April 1916, Montagu Papers, V/A/12 and V/A/8.
26 Joint War Air Committee, AIR 2, The constitution, functions and procedure of the committee, 25 February 1916, PRO, AIR 1/2319/273/26.
27 Derby to Asquith, 10 April 1916 (actually dictated 27 March), Derby Papers, Liverpool Record Office, 920 DER (17) 26/2ii.
28 Derby to Trenchard, 13 April 1916, Trenchard Papers, MFC 76/1/81.
29 Minutes of the 69th Meeting of the War Committee, 10 February 1916, PRO, CAB 42/8/5.
30 Sueter to Montagu, 7 April 1916, Montagu Papers, V/S/16.
31 Trenchard to Derby, 19 March 1916; Henderson to Trenchard, 25 February 1916, Trenchard Papers, MFC 76/1/81 and 76.

32 Joint War Air Committee, AIR 4, Policy of the RNAS, 3 March 1916, PRO, AIR 1/2319/223/26.
33 Joint War Air Committee, AIR 5, Policy of the Army Council with regard to Royal Flying Corps (Military Wing), 3 March 1916, PRO, AIR 1/2319/223/16.
34 Joint War Air Committee, AIR 11, Interim report of the Joint War Air Committee, 20 March 1916, p. 4, PRO, AIR 1/2319/223/26.
35 ibid., pp. 4, 7.
36 Joint War Air Committee, JWAC 1, Present deficiencies and future requirements of the Royal Naval Air Service, 23 March 1916, PRO, AIR 1/2319/223/26.
37 Joint War Air Committee, JWAC 2, Present deficiencies and future requirements of the Royal Flying Corps, 23 March 1916, PRO, AIR 1/2319/223/26.
38 Joint War Air Committee, JWAC 3, Note by the naval representatives on the Joint War Air Committee, 23 March 1916, PRO, AIR 1/2319/223/26.
39 Joint War Air Committee, JWAC 7, Remarks by Major-General Sir D. Henderson on note by the naval representatives on the Joint War Air Committee, 1 April 1916, PRO, AIR 1/2319/223/27.
40 Joint War Air Committee, JWAC 5, Functions and powers of the committee, 29 March 1916; JWAC 8, Remarks by the naval members of the committee on draft minute JWAC 5, 3 April 1916, PRO, AIR 1/2319/223/26 and 27.
41 Minutes of the 69th meeting of the War Committee, 10 February 1916, PRO CAB 42/8/5; Joint War Air Committee, AIR 3 and AIR 5, PRO, AIR 1/2319/223/26.
42 Sueter to Vaughan-Lee, 3 July 1916, PRO, AIR 1/2642.
43 PRO, AIR 1/2302/215/12.
44 R. Pearsall, 'Aero engines of the First World War', *The Royal Air Force Quarterly*, vol. 12, no. 3 (1972), pp. 199–201.
45 PRO, AIR 1/2302/215/12.
46 Laux, 'Gnôme et Rhône', p. 20; Morrow, *German Air Power in World War I*, p. 210.
47 Brancker to Curzon, 10 June 1916, Curzon Papers, Eur.F.112/173.
48 Johnson to Montagu, 28 March 1916, Montagu Papers, V/J/12.
49 PRO, AIR 1/2302/215/12.
50 PRO, AIR 1/630/17/122/13.
51 Trenchard to Brancker, 25 April and 27 July 1916, Trenchard Papers, MFC 76/1/5 and 7.

[5]

The Curzon Air Board

The Air Board, chaired by Lord Curzon between May and December 1916, has not generally been considered any more effective than its short-lived predecessor, Derby's Joint War Air Committee. Like that body, the Air Board was denied effective executive power. As a result, it appeared to many observers to serve only as a gladiatorial arena in which the army and navy representatives could fight out their fruitless war of words. Curzon's own intervention in favour of the military view of air policy merely polarized the debate into that exchange of discourtesies between Balfour and himself, so engagingly characterized by Hankey as 'an amazing dialectical duel, rapier versus bludgeon'.[1] The 'First Report of the Air Board', produced by Curzon in October, proposed a detailed reshaping of air procurement apparatus, but was so blatantly partisan as to give Balfour every excuse to treat it as nothing more than 'thirty solid pages of abuse of the Admiralty'.[2]

Curzon's report reflected months of frustration at the navy's refusal to consider any alteration to the existing organization of aviation. Its author all but laid the entire blame for air difficulties at the door of the Admiralty:

No expansion of the work of the Air Board, no complete fulfilment of the charge with which it was entrusted, and no adequate provision for the urgent necessities of the future, are, in our opinion, possible, so long as the Admiralty adopts its present attitude towards the Air Board, and so long as the administration of that branch of the Air Service which is in the hands of the Admiralty is conducted on the present lines. It is with no pleasure that my colleagues and I question the administration of a Department possessed of such splendid traditions, and with such a glorious record of service, as the Admiralty. But it is our profound conviction ... that the addition to the Navy of responsibilities for the air – not in itself necessarily impracticable – has, in the manner in which it has been carried out, been attended with results that have been equally unfortunate to the

56

Navy and the Air Service, and, if persisted in, will be incompatible
not merely with the existence of an Air Board, but with the immense
and almost incalculable development that ought to lie before a
properly co-ordinated and conducted Air Service in the future.[3]

Balfour's public response, apart from demonstrating the skill with which
he could wield his dialectical rapier, gave further proof of the intensity and
apparent bankruptcy of the discussion:

I do not suppose that in the whole history of the country any
Government Department has ever indulged so recklessly in the
luxury of inter-departmental criticism. The temptation no doubt has
often existed; but hitherto it has been more or less successfully
resisted. In the case of the Air Board, however, the ardour of youth
and the consciousness of superior abilities have completely broken
through the ordinary barriers of self-control. The Army also is
mentioned, [in Curzon's report] but only for the purpose of artistic
contrast. It is the virtuous apprentice, the lustre of whose shining
merits serves but to darken the shadows in the character of his wicked
rival.[4]

Nonetheless, the recriminations which attended the Air Board throughout its six-month existence should not be allowed to obscure its long-term
significance in the development of air policy. Merely by surviving for as
many months as its predecessor had weeks, the Curzon Board established
a tradition of superior co-ordination which went some way towards
limiting the independence of the services. Despite persistent naval opposition, and only intermittent government interest, Curzon did supply a
blueprint for the supervision of aircraft supply from which his successor,
Lord Cowdray, reaped considerable benefit in 1917. The intervention of
the Ministry of Munitions, in support of the unified control of war
industry, ultimately denied Curzon the degree of authority he had
requested, but the acceptance by the Admiralty of the Munitions plan as
the lesser of two evils was largely the product of Curzon's remorseless
attacks on its independence.

The administrative consequences of the 'First Report of the Air Board'
were delayed by the fall of Asquith's government in December 1916. As
Lord President of Lloyd George's new War Cabinet, Curzon generally
stayed out of the front ranks of the air debate. The draft conclusions
arrived at during the discussion of his recommendations in late November
were, however, adopted almost wholesale following the hiatus caused by
Asquith's fall. The relatively clear road allowed Cowdray's rejuvenated
Air Board thereafter is sufficient cause for reinterpreting Curzon's contribution to the formation of British air policy. The history of the first Air
Board should be seen more as a preliminary stage in the establishment of

political control over the air effort than as the amusing, but essentially fruitless incident, depicted by Lloyd George as part of his indictment of Asquith's administration of the war.[5]

Curzon also presided over the decisive stage in the inter-service rivalry which had first brought the government into the field of air policy. Once again, the delayed effects of his initiatives have tended to disguise his impact on the institutions with which he came into contact. For much of his term at the Air Board, the naval bombing wing charged with long-range operations against Germany served as the symbol of the Admiralty's determination to pursue an independent course in the air. This formation survived into the spring of 1917, but by the time of its disbandment in April, the navy had effectively surrendered its claim to an equal voice in Britain's air councils. The army, supported by Curzon, had already succeeded in enforcing that division of responsibilities bluntly delineated by Trenchard to the effect that 'the Army is responsible for land operations and the Navy only for work with the fleet'.[6] From the end of 1916, the military air service dominated policy to the extent that the air effort was overwhelmingly directed towards the support of Trenchard's war of attrition on the Western Front. In the final analysis, Curzon was one of the architects of that military domination of air policy which was to become far more dangerous to the political direction of airpower than naval obstructionism had ever been.

The key to the performance of the Air Board was the character of its president. Curzon's own inflated opinion of himself should not be allowed to conceal his real ability and influence. As a former Viceroy of India and a leading Conservative peer, he possessed an undoubted wealth of administrative experience. Unlike Derby, he was a sufficiently powerful and ambitious figure to focus existing discontent with the organization of the air effort and give a sense of purpose to the struggle for reform. Aviation critics as far apart in outlook as Churchill, the father of naval airpower, and Montagu of Beaulieu, the sternest critic of the Admiralty's pretensions to an independent air policy, rallied behind him.[7] Curzon undoubtedly saw himself as one of the rising powers in the government's prosecution of the war, and although his aspirations ran far higher, he was anxious to make the creation of some form of air department a stepping stone on his path to the top.

Curzon's energy and influence, however, must be set against his record as the most difficult of partners in any co-operative venture. Trenchard was only exaggerating a well-known character fault in describing Curzon as 'that mountain of conceit'.[8] Hankey, who helped him organize the Air Board, complained in his diary: 'Curzon is an impossible person to do business with – pompous, dictatorial and outrageously conceited.'[9] He was at his worst when thwarted, his assertion that Edwin Montagu was treating him 'as a public enemy' in opposing his scheme for the control of aircraft procurement was typical of his oversensitivity to criticism.[10] Curzon's high-handedness made the task of more subtle opponents like Balfour far easier, while also serving to devalue his opinions in the eyes of non-partisan cabinet colleagues. A supreme egotist, embittered by a severe spinal deformity and the frustration of soaring political ambition, the new president of the Air Board was the last man to steer a careful course between two services notoriously sensitive to anything resembling the usurpation of their privileges.[11]

Nonetheless, Curzon must be granted credit for injecting fresh life into the air debate following the collapse of the Derby Committee. Chafing at his relative lack of involvement as Lord Privy Seal, Curzon settled on the air debate as the ideal field in which to make his mark as a war leader. His first major sally was a memorandum on the political co-ordination of aviation submitted at the time of the formation of the JWAC.[12] Despite being confined to bed as the result of a traffic accident, he continued to badger Asquith with claims that the existing arrangements were 'quite unsound' and required the direct attention of a member of the government. Protesting embarrassment 'at the position I occupy in the greatest crisis of our history', Curzon argued that his administrative skills and freedom from other commitments made him the ideal man to undertake responsibility for aviation, and do more than merely 'keep the peace between the Admiralty and the War Office and prevent them flying at each others' throats'.[13]

Encouraged by the prime minister, who stood in clear need of new ideas on the subject, Curzon submitted another memorandum on 16 April, suggesting terms of reference for a new body.[14] His proposals were intensively debated by the War Committee, with Balfour deploying every argument to block the formation of 'a third fighting department, whose activities will be inextricably entangled with those of the two which already exist'.[15] The pressure for a fresh political initiative, and Curzon's manifest enthusiasm for his self-imposed task were sufficient to overcome naval intransigence. While the new Air Board, formed under Curzon's presidency on 11 May, was to a certain extent the inevitable product of Derby's failure to quiet the troubled waters of RFC/RNAS relations, it nonetheless bore the stamp of its creator. In his April memorandum, Curzon had advanced the opinion that 'unless the Cabinet explicitly regard and treat the Board as a possible preliminary to, and should it be so, as the official precursor of an Air Department in the future, it would be futile to set it up, and no sane man would be found to accept the chair ...'[16] Events were to prove that the cabinet was far from unanimous as to the organizational consequences of its acceptance of Curzon's board, but with him in the chair, even the services began to acknowledge that some form of permanent political control of aviation was in the wind.[17]

In many senses the Air Board was certainly a far stronger creation than the Joint War Air Committee. Curzon received valuable assistance from his two civilian colleagues. Lord Sydenham, who as Sir George Clarke had amassed a wealth of administrative experience as prewar secretary of the Committee of Imperial Defence, lent obvious respectability to any experiment in civil–military relations. Sydenham was in general agreement with his president's vision of aviation's future, even to the extent of believing that 'long distance bombing ought to be taken out of the hands of the Admiralty altogether'.[18] He had, however, seldom exerted the influence that his position might seem to have merited, largely through the lack of those qualities of tact and flexibility which so distinguished the CID's most effective secretary, Hankey. Approaching seventy, he was useful only in a secondary role, and resigned along with Curzon at the end of the year after the intrusion of the Ministry of Munitions into aircraft supply.[19]

Major J. M. Baird, the Air Board representative in the House of Commons, was in the long term a more valuable acquisition. He too shared Curzon's views on air organization, and discharged his brief as parliamentary defender of the board with quiet effectiveness. Unlike most of those associated with the politics of airpower, Baird seems to have been able to deal with senior airmen without offending their overdeveloped professional pride, even earning from one of them the rare accolade of being 'an honest politician'.[20] Close to the Unionist leader Bonar Law, Baird was to prove particularly valuable in regularizing the Air Board's contacts with both the House and the government, and in repairing the damage often done by Curzon's irregular, and sometimes offensive, methods.[21] He was also to provide a strand of continuity in the generally unstable political framework of air administration, serving on with Cowdray's Air Board in 1917 and the new Air Ministry in 1918.

Curzon's insistence on the inclusion of senior representatives from both services on the Air Board was to produce more mixed results. This innovation had been aimed at the navy, whose delegates on the Joint War Air Committee had been able to block effective discussion by claiming lack of authority and referring all matters of policy back to the Admiralty.[22] With the Third Sea Lord, Sir Frederick Tudor, officially representing naval interests on the Air Board, this expedient was no longer practicable. The Admiralty, however, persistently refused Curzon's demands that it appoint an additional Sea Lord with sole responsibility for aviation. It thus allowed itself frequent recourse to the argument that air policy was too tightly intertwined in the existing administrative structure to permit the easy separation of any part of naval authority, particularly the control of procurement which Curzon was so anxious to transfer to the Air Board.[23] In a sense, the Admiralty had destroyed Derby's Committee by proxy, but Curzon's success in bringing the Sea

Lords into the front line of the air debate did nothing to weaken their resolve to undermine any change.

Unlike the JWAC, the Air Board was granted wide enough terms of reference to encompass the discussion of air policy. Curzon put his own gloss on these, telling his colleagues at their first meeting that the Board's functions 'would comprise not only the settlement of points of detail but formulation of policy and the President would ultimately be expected to advise the Government as to the creation of a larger body to deal with questions of the Air and the formation of a separate Air Service'.[24] He was given some encouragement in this belief by statements made in the House by Bonar Law, among others, intimating that the Air Board was indeed intended to expand gradually into the role of a fully-fledged ministry.[25] The government, however, had withheld executive powers from the Board at the time of its formation, and did not show itself very receptive to Curzon's attempts to assume the powers he thought had been promised him at the outset.

While aviation had managed to squeeze on to the wings of the political stage, it was still allowed only brief moments at the centre. Few of those in effective control at Westminster were prepared to be rushed into action on a matter which still seemed of secondary importance. Lloyd George's portrayal of the air debate as a minor issue allowed to take up too much valuable government time, and Bonar Law's noncommital approach to a board to which he had seemed to promise great power six months before, were typical of a general disinclination to meddle with the structure of the existing civil–military organization for the sake of a few hundred aircraft in France.[26]

Curzon, then, was left very much on his own in mediating between the services. By the time the Air Board began its deliberations on 22 May, RFC/RNAS consensus on policy and procurement had slipped even further away. With no effort being spared to provide air support for the approaching Somme offensive, and Trenchard continually complaining that reinforcements were not arriving in sufficient quantity, the army took the view that everything must be subordinated to the supply of the RFC in the Field, and that strategic bombing, as planned by the navy, must be postponed until the air war on the Western front had been won.

Naval plans for just such strategic operations were already well advanced. On 4 April, Vaughan-Lee had submitted a memorandum on 'Defence Against Zeppelin Raids' to the Admiralty. In it he argued that such raids seemed destined to become a matter of routine and that their military value could not be gainsaid. Vaughan-Lee claimed that 'a defensive policy limited to our own shores cannot compare with a vigorous offensive' and that 'an organized and systematic attack on the Germans at home ... will serve two purposes. It will restrict Zeppelin activities, and it will have an immense moral effect on Germany itself.' His conclusion seemed almost calculated to pre-empt military opposition: 'It now appears essential that a definite policy of retaliation be laid down and carried into effect without any further delay. A sustained offensive will have a decided effect in weakening the enemy's activities at the Front by calls for defensive measures.'[27]

The idea of redressing the balance of terror, while simultaneously damaging German war production and drawing German aircraft back to home defence, was to prove an attractive package. The same mixture of objectives was to be advanced again in the second half of 1917 during the debate on the creation of the Royal Air Force. The acceptance of naval control of a campaign to be waged from land bases in the middle of France was an entirely different matter.

The controversy over bombing revolved in the first instance around questions of jurisdiction and practicality. Those charged with mediating between the RFC and RNAS had to decide who was to assume responsibility for long-range operations, and whether such operations could be underwitten by existing manufacturing resources. In brief, the RFC argued that all air operations over land, including any attempt to raid Germany from French bases, should be under its control. Haig spelled this case out clearly in a letter to the War Office in November 1916:

> the employment of bombing machines in France is, I contend, primarily even if not entirely, a military question, and I desire to protest emphatically, in the interests of the Empire, against any interference by the naval authorities with the British land forces in such questions. I desire further to represent strongly that, unless my requirements have first been adequately provided, the provision of flying machines by the naval authorities for work on the fronts of the French or Belgian armies in France amounts to very serious interference with the British Land Forces and may compromise the success of my operations.[28]

The army further claimed that the possible results of long-range bombing operations did not justify the inroads they would make into the more important task of supporting the armies in the field. In a statement delivered to the Air Board in June, Trenchard explained the reasoning behind the army's insistence on the primacy of tactical operations on the Western Front:

> One of the first essentials to tactical success under existing conditions is the development to the utmost of accurate artillery fire, and under the long-range conditions of the present day the possibility of this development depends very greatly on accurate observation from the air. The provision of the means for this observation must be regarded as of primary importance to all bombing operations, and, therefore,

so far as the Flying Corps is concerned, efforts should be devoted to providing observation requirements in the first instance.[29]

Underpinning these statements was the belief, explicitly expressed by Haig in his letter to the War Office, that 'our military policy in aerial, as in other respects, must be based on the principle that a successful end of the war can be brought about only by decisive victory over the enemy's forces in the field'.[30] The navy naturally did not share this fixation, and was not in any case inclined to allow the army to take over either aircraft or manufacturing facilities which it had initially developed on its own.[31] Considering that the case in favour of long-range bombing operations had already been made, if only by German attempts at the same thing, the Admiralty took the view that the utilization of airpower in a strategic role did not fall within the immediate responsibilities of either service, and should best be carried out, in the beginning at least, by the service with the surplus resources to do so.[32]

It has recently been argued that the potential of strategic bombing during the First World War was considerable, and that the navy's attempts to fulfil that potential were thwarted by RFC obstruction rooted in a narrow and essentially incorrect view of airpower as a tactical adjunct to land and sea warfare.[33] The opposing point of view has played down the effectiveness of early bombing aircraft, and has censured the navy for allowing its more visionary air officers to deflect air policy away from the prime requisites of support for the fleet towards a wasteful exercise in strategic one-up-manship quite beyond the resources and responsibilities of the RNAS.[34] These interpretations largely restate the cases put before the Curzon Air Board in 1916 by its naval and military delegates. Any attempt at judgement must proceed from the realization that neither was entirely free from disingenuousness.

Naval opposition to the army and the Air Board was fired as much by departmental pride as by a belief in the importance of strategic airpower. The relative neglect accorded maritime air operations reflects badly on the general airmindedness of the Admiralty, which embarked on the bombing campaign against Germany in a mood of indulgent experimentation and then dug its heels in at what it perceived to be intrusion on its prerogatives by its opponents.[35] On the other side, there is something unconvincing about the army's repeated complaints that the Admiralty's air plans were fatally undermining its own. The actual allocation of aircraft to the naval bombing wing remained low throughout. The RFC's chronic shortage of aircraft was partially the product of military mishandling of procurement, and partially a symptom of the general immaturity of the British air industry. It could scarcely have been cured by the redisposition of a handful of naval bombing machines.

It is certainly true that the results achieved by the naval bombing wing (known as No. 3 Wing) during its six month operational existence (October 1916 to April 1917) were unimpressive. Only 13 raids were launched from its base at Luxeuil near Belfort. The average strength of each attacking formation was a mere fifteen aircraft; the average weight of bombs dropped was just over a ton. The reports of returning pilots indicated serious damage to industrial targets in the Saar basin, but in common with most early bombing reports, these were wildly optimistic, taking little account of the uselessness of the standard 65-pound bomb against the heavily constructed blast furnaces most commonly attacked. German reports do reveal a very slight drop in the output of the factories attacked (four per cent in November and December).[36] There is, however, no evidence to support the claim, made both by the RNAS and its latter-day apologists, that the naval campaign was considered sufficiently threatening by the Germans to cause them to redirect a significant portion of their air resources to home defence.[37] The German *Heimatluftschutz* had been created in response to the erratic French bombing campaign initiated in 1915 and maintained throughout No. 3 Wing's existence. It remained very much the poor cousin of the *Luftstreitkräfte* at the front, and received neither men nor machines otherwise intended for the fighter squadrons in France and Belgium.[38]

It has been argued that the naval bombing campaign was only prevented from realizing its potential by poor weather and military interference with its supply of aircraft.[39] Successful military demands for a proportion of the Sopwith bombers originally intended for No. 3 Wing certainly did weaken the naval campaign. Paradoxically, the navy had allowed the first diversion of resources to pass with little resistance, offering the RFC one third of the machines on order in mid-May in the belief that the deficit would rapidly be made up by increasing output.[40] Production, however, did not live up to expectations. A total of 423 Sopwith 1½ Strutters were built in Britain during 1916. The RFC in France had received 135 of these by the end of December – all but 50 of them in the last four months of the year.[41] During the entire period of its existence, the RNAS strategic bombing force was allocated only 137 – a number insufficient to maintain it at even half its projected strength.[42] Belated naval attempts to inject fresh life into the bombing programme, particularly through large orders of new engines from French sources, foundered at the end of the year on entrenched army and Air Board resistance and, one is driven to suspect, on the growing indifference of the Admiralty itself.

The low operational effectiveness of naval bombing aircraft, however, only supports the case against the raids ever having been attempted in the first place. The average number of combat flights extracted from each machine assigned to Luxeuil was only 1·4, while less than twenty per cent of the station's available strength could actually be deployed after November.[43] It is obvious that the machines themselves could not be depended upon to carry a significant payload to any distant objective on a regular basis. There is, in fact, little in the history of early air bombardment to suggest that the naval campaign, even if waged in the strength originally intended, would have been effective.

None the less, it is insufficient to arrive at a final judgement in terms only of operational results. The German attacks on Britain were no more impressive as regards the damage they caused, but they did appear to point the way towards a more dangerous future. Apart from raising demands for reprisals, the Zeppelins and the Gotha aircraft which followed them convinced the public of the need to prepare for the time when aircraft would come in much larger numbers and drop more lethal cargoes. The Parliamentary Aviation Committee, founded in the summer of 1916 'with the object of creating in Parliament active support for a forward aircraft policy', was the product of a more widespread phenomenon than the belief of a few enthusiasts in the immediate need for an independent air service.[44]

Whatever their real effectiveness, bombing attacks on German cities were becoming a necessary feature of a popular war policy. The timing of the naval campaign was unfortunate in that it coincided with the neutralization of the Zeppelin threat. The destruction of four airships over Britain in September and early October gave public demonstration that the air service had finally developed the technical capability to defeat their old adversaries. Future Zeppelin incursions were infrequent and carried out at such great height, and to so little effect, that the intended victims were seldom even aware of the danger.[45] The demise of the naval bombing wing, therefore, went relatively unremarked.

The recrudescence of the German threat in the summer of 1917, in the more ominous guise of formations of multi-engined bomber aircraft, brought home forcibly to the Lloyd George government its predecessor's mistake in allowing its strategic bombing capability to fall victim to military arguments stressing operational priorities rather than popular expectation. Even this early in the bomber age, public opinion required the means to punish, if not necessarily to deter, enemy air attack. When the new prime minister looked to provide evidence of his administration's will to strike back in kind, he found the nation's air resources were committed overwhelmingly to the support of the army in France. His subsequent creation of the Royal Air Force, as a device for circumventing the military stranglehold on air policy, was thus in a sense forced upon him by the RFC's earlier victory at the expense of the navy's inflated bombing ambitions.

It is on the surface difficult to understand just why the navy eventually surrendered its bombing capability to the army. The replacement of the Balfour–Jackson regime by Carson and Jellicoe, neither of whom evinced any particular interest in attacking industrial targets miles from the sea, was obviously an important factor. The first RNAS squadron, however, was transferred to Trenchard's command in the autumn of 1916. No. 3 Wing itself was starved of resources throughout its existence, and Admiralty attempts to reinvigorate it through large-scale orders of French engines in October were not pursued with the single-mindedness the situation obviously required.[46] Finally, Balfour's acceptance of the Ministry of Munition's entry into the field of aircraft supply was a negation of the established naval case for the maintenance of all aspects of naval air policy within Admiralty control.

In the final analysis, Balfour's critics have not been too wide of the mark in asserting that his resistance to Curzon was conducted 'more as a dialectical exercise than as a firmly felt policy'.[47] Certainly there is little in Balfour's public performance to suggest that either he or his senior advisers were interested in long-range bombing as anything more than a speculative diversion. Naval resistance to the Air Board and the military view of air priorities with which it became associated under Curzon was largely motivated by departmental pride and Curzon's own disregard for polite practice or the finer sensibilities of his opponents. Balfour's behaviour during the Air Board crisis of November makes it clear that he was more concerned to frustrate his personal adversary than to defend the naval commitment to long-range bombing. With Curzon's departure from the air debate, and Air Board pretensions thwarted by the intervention of the Ministry of Munitions, Balfour had won a victory of sorts. His successors, uninterested in maintaining the sickly infant at Luxeuil, handed over the bulk of naval land-based airpower to the RFC in the Field without much thought as to the consequences.[48]

If one important product of Curzon's tenure as President of the Air Board was his partial victory over the Admiralty on the issue of long-range bombing, another was his defeat at the hands of the Minister of Munitions, E. S. Montagu, over responsibility for aircraft production. In a memorandum placed before the War Committee in September, Montagu argued for a simplification of a situation 'under which the supply of aircraft *matériel* is the concern of two bodies – the War Office and the Admiralty – acting under the general supervision of a third – the Air Board – and in constant and inevitable competition with a fourth – the Ministry of Munitions'. Montagu made it clear that the constant expansion of the air effort had given rise to a situation where aircraft production could no longer be considered as independent of the general output of war machinery:

> From the point of view of supply, the essence of the present situation is that the means and materials of production are now becoming more and more limited. Both of labour and of materials there is now not enough to satisfy demands. The problem is therefore one of the

more complete organization of the engineering and allied industries, in order that the best possible use may be made of all the materials, labour, machinery, and experience which are available.[49]

Montagu's claim that it made more sense to incorporate aircraft production under the experienced care of his Ministry than to create a separate department for its supervision was sternly resisted by Curzon. His claim that such a move would cause great dislocation of accumulated expertise was supported by the bulk of the military air command. Only Henderson, already isolated from his colleagues both at home and abroad, supported the Munitions plan.[50] The Ministry of Munitions, however, had more powerful friends on the War Committee, most notably its former head, Lloyd George, now Secretary of State for War. Balfour's conversion to the Munitions plan, tactically inspired though it was, brought both service ministers into line against Curzon and neutralized whatever pressure his repeated threats of resignation might have brought to bear.[51]

The case for the incorporation of aircraft supply within the Munitions brief had much to recommend it. Curzon's belief that the expanded air programme did not require sufficient additional resources to justify the intervention of another department was misguided. Air Board requests for an overall upgrading of priorities for aircraft work, and improvements in the supply of steel, machine tools and skilled labour, had pointed the way towards the future as early as the summer of 1916.[52] The growth of the air effort, combined with the contraction of surplus manufacturing capacity, no longer allowed the aircraft industry to function in a vacuum. Montagu quite rightly pointed out that Curzon's requirement of 7,000 extra workmen could not be met without reference to the needs of other sectors of an overextended war industry.[53] The view that rapid changes in aircraft design made the mass production techniques which Curzon and his supporters associated with Munitions procedures inappropriate was also out of touch with the realities of the war.[54] By the spring of 1917, the RFC in the Field was losing 300 aircraft a month, and the rate of attrition was to continue to rise thereafter. In any event, Trenchard's constant complaints regarding the incompetence of the War Office's Directorate of Air Equipment were eloquent as to the failure of the existing military procurement system to keep abreast of even the qualitative requirements of the air war.[55] The air effort desperately needed both qualitative and quantitative improvement in the supply of aircraft, and with the increasing encroachment of manpower and material shortages throughout the industry, the superior co-ordination offered by the Ministry of Munitions was an obvious necessity.

On the other hand, the separation of supply from operational policy implicit in Montagu's plan posed obvious dangers. While the Air Board in its new guise served as a channel of communication, it proved a weak link. In 1917 the air command lost touch with the procurement apparatus to the extent that its leaders no longer possessed a realistic appreciation of the inventive and productive capacity of the industry behind them. This ignorance was contributed to by the dangerous overoptimism of the new masters of aircraft supply, whose projections of the potential output of British factories revealed an imperfect awareness of the technical difficulties surrounding the design and construction of a complex weapon.

Overall, Curzon's Air Board was very much the unwitting precursor of the Air Ministry. While its president did not believe that a separate air service was a viable proposition as long as the war lasted, it oversaw two changes in air organization which eventually conspired to bring just such a service into being. The destruction of the navy's long-distance bombing capability left Britain with no strategic force to satisfy public demands for a response to a renewed German offensive against London. At the same time it concentrated available resources in the hands of an army so intent on the pursuit of a war of attrition at the front as to require a major organizational change to break its monopolization of policy. The introduction of a new system of aircraft production brought air procurement into the mainstream of British war industry. This eventually produced a situation in which the possibility of a surplus of material persuaded the goverment to embark on a new strategic policy, outside of the constraints placed upon it by the oppressive presence of Haig's mass army in France. These factors will be dealt with sequentially in the following two chapers.

Notes

1   Lord Hankey, *The Supreme Command, 1914–1918*, Vol. 2 (London: Allen & Unwin, 1961), p. 551.
2   Balfour to Curzon, 26 October 1916, Curzon Papers, Eur.F.112/170.
3   First Report of the Air Board, 23 October 1916, PRO, CAB 42/25/10.
4   A Reply to the First Report of the Air Board, 6 November 1916, PRO, CAB 42/25/10.
5   Lloyd George, *War Memoirs*, Vol. 2, pp. 977–8.
6   Trenchard to Henderson, 12 November 1916, Trenchard Papers, MFC 76/1/76.
7   Churchill to Curzon, 26 May 1916, Curzon Papers, Eur.F.112/170; Montagu to Curzon, 31 May 1916, Montagu Papers, V/C/6.
8   Trenchard to Henderson, 21 April 1916, Trenchard Papers, MFC 76/1/76.
9   Roskill, *Man of Secrets*, Vol. 1, p. 271.
10 E. Montagu to Curzon, 23 October 1916, Curzon Papers, Eur.F.112/170.
11 Earl of Ronaldshay, *The Life of Lord Curzon. Being the Authorized Biography of George Nathaniel, Marquess of Kedleston, K.G.*, Vol. 1 (London: Ernest Benn, 1928), *passim*; L. Mosley, *Curzon. The End of an Epoch* (London: Longman, 1960), *passim*.
12 Air Service in War (I), 4 February 1916, PRO, CAB 37/142/37.

13 Curzon to Asquith, 8 and 23 March 1916, Asquith Papers, 16/71–6 and 111–119A.
14 Air Service in War (II), 16 April 1916, PRO, CAB 37/146/6.
15 Questions suggested by the proposal for a new minister of air, 29 April 1916, PRO, CAB 37/146/25; minutes of the 87th meeting of the War Committee, 11 May 1916, PRO, CAB 42/13/7.
16 Air Service in War (II), 16 April 1916, PRO, CAB 37/146/6.
17 Brancker to Trenchard, 18 May 1916, Trenchard Papers, MFC 76/1/6.
18 Sydenham to Curzon, 20 May 1916, Curzon Papers, Eur.F.112/170.
19 J. Gooch, 'Sir George Clarke's career at the Committee of Imperial Defence, 1904–1907', Gooch (ed.), The Prospect of War, pp. 73–91; Sydenham to Curzon, 12 and 26 December 1916, Curzon Papers, Eur.F.112/170.
20 Brancker to Trenchard, 2 July 1916, Trenchard Papers, MFC 76/1/7.
21 Baird to Curzon, 25 October and 12 December 1916, Curzon Papers, Eur.F.112/170; Baird to Bonar Law, 2 November and 27 December 1916, BL Papers, 53/4/14 and 81/1/72.
22 Hankey to Asquith, 6 April 1916, Curzon Papers, Eur.F.112/173.
23 Minutes of the 19th and 22nd meetings of the Air Board, 26 July and 24 August 1916, PRO, AIR 6/2.
24 Minutes of the 1st meeting of the Air Board, 22 May 1916, PRO, AIR 6/1.
25 First Report of the Air Board, 23 October 1916, PRO, CAB 42/25/10.
26 Lloyd George, War Memoirs, Vol. 2, pp. 977–8; Bonar Law to Curzon, 23 and 24 October 1916, Curzon Papers, Eur.F.112/170.
27 Defence against Zeppelin raids, 4 April 1916, PRO, ADM 1/8449/39A.
28 Haig to Army Council, 1 November 1916, PRO, CAB 42/26/1.
29 RFC HQ policy statement, 3 June 1916, PRO, AIR 1/978/204/5/1139.
30 Haig to Army Council, 1 November 1916, PRO, CAB 42/26/1.
31 Sueter to Vaughan-Lee, 3 July 1916, PRO, AIR 1/2642.
32 Defence against Zeppelin raids, 4 April 1916, PRO, ADM 1/8449/39A.
33 N. Jones, The Origins of Strategic Bombing. A Study of the Development of British Air Strategic Thought and Practice up to 1918 (London: Kimber, 1973), passim.
34 Roskill (ed.), Documents Relating to the Naval Air Service, pp. x–xvii, 269–74.
35 ibid.; Till, Air Power and the Royal Navy, pp. 111–17.
36 PRO, AIR 1/361/15/228/18–20; AIR 1/2266/209/70/18.
37 Jones, The Origins of Strategic Bombing, p. 128.
38 PRO, AIR 1/711/27/13/2214; AIR 1/682/21/13/2217–18.
39 Jones, The Origins of Strategic Bombing, pp. 103–29.
40 Vaughan-Lee memorandum, 15 May 1916, PRO, AIR 1/2623.
41 PRO, AIR 1/2302/215/10 and 12.
42 PRO, AIR 1/2266/209/70/18.
43 ibid.
44 Aircraft policy and proposed parliamentary committee Montagu Papers, III/C/35.
45 D. H. Robinson, The Zeppelin in Combat. A History of the German Naval Airship Division, 1912–1918, revised edn (London: Foulis, 1966), pp. 262–83.
46 Order of aero-engines in France, 25 November 1916, PRO, CAB 42/26/1.
47 Mosley, Curzon, p. 157.
48 PRO, AIR 1/513/16/3/71.
49 G.77, Supply of aeroplanes, September 1916, PRO, CAB 42/20/11.
50 Brancker to Trenchard, 18 November 1916, Trenchard Papers, MFC 76/1/8.

51 Minutes of the 140th and 141st meetings of the War Committee, 28 November 1916, PRO, CAB 42/26/1–2.
52 Secretary, Air Board to Secretary, Ministry of Munitions, 19 July 1916, PRO, MUN 4/482.
53 G.77, Supply of aeroplanes, September 1916, PRO, CAB 42/20/11.
54 G.83, Supply of aeroplanes, 12 October 1916, PRO, CAB 42/23/9.
55 Trenchard to Henderson, 29 October 1916, Trenchard Papers, MFC 76/1/76; Trenchard to Brancker, 7 July and 12 November 1916, MFC 76/1/7 and 8.

[6]

A Policy of Relentless and Incessant Offensive

The Battle of the Somme, the British army's first experience of mass attritional warfare on the Western Front, marked the crucial phase in the evolution of military air doctrine and the domination of air policy by the RFC in the Field. Soon after his elevation to command, Trenchard had persuaded Haig that airpower could contribute substantially to the ground war. In the spring of 1916, the air service in France went through a difficult period of expansion in preparation for assuming a wider role in offensive warfare. During the battle itself, the RFC fulfilled its promise as a tactical auxiliary but, as a result both of the quickening pace of air operations and of the increasing impact of efficient fighter aircraft, began to experience an unprecedented level of casualties.

Trenchard's offensive policy, as defined in a staff memorandum in September 1916, brought the army air service solidly into line with Haig's own concept of modern warfare:

> The sound policy, then, which should guide all warfare in the air, would seem to be this: to exploit this moral effect of the aeroplane on the enemy, but not to let him exploit it on ourselves. Now this can only be done by attacking and continuing to attack.[1]

Such a policy, with its tacit acceptance of the doctrine of attrition, produced a call on the nation's air resources which allowed little room for other operations. By the summer of 1917, when the appearance of German bombers over London raised afresh questions of home air defence and retaliatory strikes against enemy cities, Trenchard was in effective control of the bulk of British air strength.

Any discussion of the military domination of aviation must begin with an appreciation of the doctrine behind it. Trenchard's 'policy of relentless and incessant offensive'[2] has been surrounded by controversy since its inception. Its high cost in lives proved a magnet for wartime critics of air

71

policy, particularly those arguing for the reallocation of resources to long-range bombing operations. After the war, the offensive policy became grist to the mill of strategic debate, prophets of airpower such as L. E. O. Charlton, P. R. C. Groves and Trenchard's old rival Frederick Sykes exposing its 'stubborn stupidity' as an indictment of the official attitude to aerial warfare.[3] Indeed it was reflective of the central position occupied by the offensive policy in the early historiography of the first air war that the final volume of the official history, the seminal exposition of Trenchard's vision of the campaign, should have concluded with a lengthy defence of that policy's soundness.[4]

The offensive policy was a product both of its creator's intuitive but unsystematic mind, and of the intellectual climate of an army of which, during the war at least, he was a very typical member. As a theorist of airpower, Trenchard always depended on insight rather than empirical observation. His ideas revolved around abstract principles, which were supported in argument by meaningless statistics with little basis in operational research. Converted into dogma by refraction through his own belief in the aircraft's offensive potential, these ideas became as much a projection of Trenchard's aggressive will as a comprehensive doctrinal code. The contradictions so often implicit in his policy statements were exacerbated by his notoriously weak powers of self-expression. Most of the documents originating in RFC Headquarters during Trenchard's tenure as commander were given literate form by his aide, Maurice Baring, whose undoubted gifts as a man of letters and complete devotion to his chief could not compensate for his lack of aviation expertise.[5]

Trenchard's doctrine of air warfare was constructed around two basic assumptions: that intensive air support was of vital importance to the success of operations on the ground, and that this support could only be provided, and the enemy denied a similar luxury, through the pursuit of a policy of interdiction, or interference with the enemy air force, far behind the German lines. The potential utility of aircraft in the siege conditions of the Western Front was already emerging when Trenchard assumed command of the RFC in the Field in August 1915. Difficulties of artillery observation in terrain where most of the vantage points were in enemy hands, of troop control miles away from senior command positions, and of reconnaissance behind the impenetrable barrier of the trench lines, made the incorporation of aircraft into tactical practice inevitable. While the general conservatism of the army with regard to the utilization of airpower was already breaking down when he arrived, it was Trenchard's conversion of Haig to the doctrine of close air support which finally made the RFC an integral part of the growing war machine at the latter's disposal.

The relationship between Trenchard and Haig was of vital importance to the development of military air policy, and ultimately to the aerial future of the nation. The bond holding them together was almost empathetic, a similarity in outlook and temperament being complemented by Haig's complete dependence on his subordinate's technical expertise and by Trenchard's near hero-worship of his omnipotent chief.[6] Throughout the two years they were together in command at the front, Trenchard and Haig spoke as one on the subject of air policy. Most of GHQ's air policy statements were but lightly rewritten copies of briefs received from Trenchard, while senior air officers all but breathed the doctrine of attrition so central to Haig's vision of the defeat of Germany.

Trenchard's belief that the aircraft was a military instrument which could only be put to use in an offensive role originated during the period of the 'Fokker Scourge'. Convinced that the large escorts necessary to protect army co-operation machines from the attentions of isolated fighters represented a wasteful allocation of resources, he was converted to a policy of interdiction by the early successes of the first true British fighter squadrons, and the similar experiences of the French in the later stages of the air battle over Verdun.[7] With the commencement of the Somme offensive in July 1916, Trenchard put into practice his belief that the best way of ensuring the safety of machines operating in support of Haig's attacking troops was to push his own fighter force as deep as possible into the enemy zone, to engage the enemy on his own ground, regardless of loss or of calls for protection against any hostile machines which might evade its attention.

The total disruption of German air forces in the first few weeks of the Somme solidified Trenchard's ideas. The rebirth of German air strength following reorganization and re-equipment in the autumn, only served to convince Trenchard that the Germans had divined his secret and that the offensive must therefore be pushed all the harder.[8] The pamphlet 'Offence and Defence', produced in September under the shadow of the German revival, amply demonstrates the hardening of his belief in the efficacy of his policy:

> It is sometimes argued that our aeroplanes should be able to prevent hostile aeroplanes from crossing the line, and this idea leads to a demand for defensive measures and a defensive policy. Now is the time to consider whether such a policy would be possible, desirable and successful.
>
> It is the deliberate opinion of all those most competent to judge that this is not so, and that an aeroplane is an offensive and not a defensive weapon. Owing to the unlimited space in the air, the difficulty one machine has in seeing another, the accidents of wind and cloud, it is impossible for aeroplanes, however skilful and vigilant their pilots, however powerful their engines, however mobile their machines, and however numerous their formations, to prevent

hostile aircraft crossing the line if they have the initiative and the determination to do so.

The aeroplane is not a defence against the aeroplane. But the opinion of those most competent to judge is that the aeroplane, as a weapon of attack, cannot be too highly estimated ...

The sound policy would seem to be, if the enemy changes his tactics and pursues a more vigorous offensive, to increase our offensive, to go further afield, and to force the enemy to do what he would gladly have us do now. If on the other hand, we were to adopt a purely defensive policy, or a partially offensive policy, we should be doing what the French have learned by experience to be a failure, and what the rank and file of the enemy, by their own accounts, point to as being one of the main causes of their recent reverses.[9]

The undoubted ascendancy gained over the Germans in the early stages of the Battle of the Somme served thereafter as the ideal which all subsequent air support efforts were aimed to match. Pressure, both from frontline infantry commanders to provide direct air cover, and from airmen themselves to reduce casualties, was successfully resisted with the support of Haig.[10] Wing and squadron leaders who attempted to protect their pilots from the full rigours of the offensive were disciplined if not purged, one early victim being the future hero of the Battle of Britain, Hugh Dowding, who was removed from the command of the Headquarters Wing after bearing the full brunt of the summer fighting on the Somme.[11]

It would be unwise to follow too far in the wake of Trenchard's critics in evaluating the effectiveness of the offensive policy. In the first instance, the offensive itself was not as unremitting, nor as independent of changes in the overall military situation as has often been suggested. One RFC circular, issued in June 1917, specifically cited a shortage of reserves in defence of the plea that 'it is just as impossible for the air forces to fight a continuous offensive as it is for the infantry'.[12] An analysis of British casualty statistics further suggests that the interdiction tactics pursued by the British fighter force often succeeded in their primary objective of protecting army co-operation machines. After a torrid spell in the spring of 1917, when obsolescent equipment seriously reduced the value of the fighting squadrons, losses among the vulnerable two-seaters working in the front line areas rarely exceeded twenty per cent of total aircraft casualties.[13] As regards the secondary goal of wearing down the enemy's air strength, German records do at least make it clear that units operating in the face of the RFC's attritional attacks suffered more severely than those deployed against the French.[14]

Nonetheless, the offensive policy was a very blunt instrument, the effectiveness of which was reduced by the distance between Trenchard's poorly thought-out theories of air warfare and the operational realities of fighting a well-trained enemy, already committed to a posture of flexible defence. There is considerable justice in the claim of one critic, himself a veteran of the campaign, that the official conception of offence was no more complex than the maintenance of an armed presence as far behind the lines as possible.[15] When Fourth Army Headquarters attempted in mid-1917 to substitute large-scale raids on enemy aerodromes for 'feeble patrols all along the front', Trenchard responded that 'all patrols are offensive patrols and they are for the purpose of seeking out and bringing the enemy to fight'.[16] In fact, the RFC policy of attrition sought to wear down the enemy simply by maintaining a high level of contact with him, ignoring in the process the principle of concentration of force. The German air forces, in keeping with the overall strategic posture of their parent army, were generally content to remain on the defensive and deal with a proportion of the British offensive patrols on terms of their own choosing, while leaving the remainder alone.

British calculations as to their offensive's effectiveness were unbalanced by two factors. The first was the failure to realize that the undoubted success of the offensive policy in the opening stages of the Somme campaign was due in large measure to German deficiencies in organization and equipment. With the strengthening of its command structure and the re-equipment of its fighter squadrons with more modern aircraft in the autumn and winter of 1916, the *Luftstreitkräfte* entered the new year as a considerably more effective fighting force. Offensive action against the *Jagdstaffeln* of VI *Armee* around Arras in April 1917 cost British fighter squadrons dearly. The ordeal of the two Nieuport Scout equipped units stationed at Izel le Hameau with 13th (Army) Wing, opposite the German fighter concentration around Douai, was fairly representative. During April, No. 29 Squadron lost eleven pilots killed or taken prisoner and two more wounded. No. 60 Squadron fared even worse with personnel casualties totalling sixteen missing, two wounded and two injured in crashes – more than 100 per cent of the unit's flying strength.[17]

The second factor clouding the British perception of the offensive policy's impact was the failure of air intelligence to provide a realistic assessment of the enemy's losses. While Trenchard did tend to view air superiority very much in moral terms, he and many of his senior subordinates remained convinced that the battle forced on the enemy far behind his lines was costing more German lives than British. At its worst this confidence manifested itself in a desire that British casualties themselves remain high: as Brancker wrote to Trenchard when casualties began to mount in September 1916, 'I rather enjoy hearing of our heavy casualties as I am perfectly certain in my own mind that the Germans lose at least half as much again as we do'.[18]

The reports of returning pilots were generally accepted as sure evidence of the damage being done to the enemy's fighting strength.[19] In fact, pilot's reports were a notoriously inaccurate guide to the extent of the enemy's losses. In the air battles behind German lines only a fraction of the enemy aircraft listed as crashed or sent down out of control were actually destroyed. As most of the fighting took place over their territory, many of the German airmen who were actually brought down survived to fight another day.

The *Jagdstaffeln* opposing the British were gradually worn down, and in the last eighteen months of the war, the German air service, like its parent army, suffered a slow loss of fighting efficiency in the face of a relentless battering. For much of the period, however, the *Luftstreitkträfte* remained a potent adversary, giving far better than it received in its contest with British fighter aviation. In the VI *Armee* area in early 1917, for example, German flying casualties in the five weeks between 31 March and 3 May totalled only 21 killed, 15 wounded and 14 missing. Over the same period, German air units in the sector accounted for 176 British aircraft.[20]

The limitations of British air doctrine were ultimately to blame for the extreme length of the RFC's casualty list. Although the dependence on a strategy of attrition meant an inevitable acceptance of heavy loss, the rigidity of tactical practice made the cost far higher than it might have been. In a sense, military air policy on the Western Front was a microcosm of the strategy employed by Haig against Germany's commanding position in northeast France. The clumsy application of force to an imperfectly perceived object resulted in an unnecessarily high cost in lives. The combination of the pursuit of a strategic offensive, a course dictated to the RFC by the stance of the army it was supporting, and the casualty rate produced by the clumsy handling of this offensive, placed the army air service in the same position relative to the air effort as that occupied by the BEF in the wider context of the overall war effort. The intensive air support offered to the BEF placed a strain on Britain's air resources which could only be relieved by the subordination of all other forms of air activity.

The increasing cost of the air support of the BEF was apparent as early as the first months of 1916. The early strain of providing an air contingent for an army which was itself undergoing a tremendous burst of growth was too much for either a field force which had expanded only very slowly through 1915 or its support organization at home, which was still suffering from its prewar immaturity. The actual level of attrition remained relatively low. Nonetheless, the expanded programme of growth which Trenchard requested, 32 squadrons with 18 or 20 pilots each instead of 27 with 12, was quite beyond the RFC in Britain. Brancker told him in mid-March that he would be lucky to get them by the end of

Plate 1   Sir Sefton Brancker, second in command of military air organization in Britain, August 1914–October 1917.

Plate 2   Major Frederick Sykes (front row, 3rd from right) with military and naval personnel of the pre-war Flying Corps.

Plate 3   Sir David Henderson (right) escorting William Joynson-Hicks, MP, one of the first parliamentary critics of the flying service, around installations on Salisbury Plain.

Plate 4   Winston Churchill while serving as First Lord of the Admiralty.

Plate 5   Captain Murray Sueter, Director of Air Department, Admiralty, August 1912–September 1915.

Plate 6   The German Fokker EI, the prototype of the modern fighter.

Plate 7   The B.E.2c, the mainstay of the RFC for the first half of the war.

Plate 8   Naval Zeppelin L48 in flight.

Plate 9   The French ambassador inspecting the wreck of naval Zeppelin L33, brought
down in Essex in September 1916.

Plate 10 Lord Derby, Chairman of the Joint War Air Committee, February–April 1916.

Plate 11 Lord Curzon, President of the Air Board, May–December 1916.

Plate 12 Lord Northcliffe, Lloyd George's first choice as political head of the RAF.

Plate 13 Lord Rothermere, Secretary of State for the Royal Air Force, January–April 1918.

Plate 14   Sir Hugh Trenchard, GOC, RFC in the Field, September 1915–December 1917 and Chief of the Air Staff, January–April 1918.

Plate 15   Sir David Henderson, Director-General of Military Aeronautics, April 1912–October 1917.

Plate 16 A. J. Balfour, First Lord of the Admiralty, May 1915–December 1916 (right) and Sir Edward Carson, First Lord of the Admiralty, December 1916–June 1917.

Plate 17 Jan Christian Smuts, South African soldier-statesman and author of the report leading to the formation of the Royal Air Force.

Plate 18 Albatros DII fighter aircraft of *Jagdstaffel* 9.

Plate 19 F.E.2d of No. 20 Squadron, RFC.

Plate 20   Sopwith 1½ Strutters of No. 3 Wing, RNAS at Luxeuil.

Plate 21   Aircraft under construction at the Austin works.

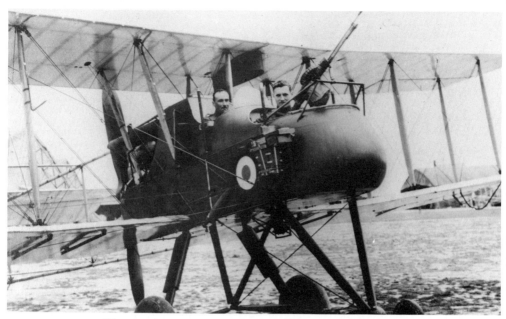

Plate 22   Camera-equipped F.E.2 of No. 18 Squadron, RFC.

Plate 23   S.E.5a of No. 56 Squadron, RFC.

Plate 24   Sopwith Camels of No. 9 Squadron, RNAS on Bray Dunes aerodrome. This photograph gives some impression of the conditions under which aircraft on the Western Front frequently had to operate.

Plate 25   S.E.5a fighters of No. 29 Squadron, RAF lined up on Oudezeele aerodrome in August 1918.

Plate 26   Gotha GIV of *Kampfgeschwader* III.

Plate 27   Bomb damage near King's Cross in London, caused by the German raid of 7 July 1917.

Plate 28 Handley-Page bombers on an airfield on the Western Front.

Plate 29 D.H.9 of the Independent Force, captured by the Germans.

Plate 30   Lord and Lady Cowdray after the war. Cowdray served as President of the Air Board, January–November 1917.

Plate 31   Lord Weir, Secretary of State for the Royal Air Force, April 1918–January 1919.

September. This prediction was to prove quite accurate: in September the RFC was still one squadron short of requirements established half a year earlier.[21]

The official estimates of requirements for the new year proceeded more from an appreciation of what had taken place in 1915, than of what might happen in 1916. While the RFC did manage a substantial quantitative improvement in pilot and aircraft output, it did so without altering to any great extent the methods and equipment of the earlier period. The failure to reach targets should not be allowed to overshadow the considerable expansion which was achieved. Two new squadrons left Britain for the Western Front in December 1915, two more in January, and three each in February and March. This result, however, was only achieved by completely outrunning the resources of the support organizations. Only three more squadrons reached France before the Somme offensive began on 1 July. In mid-April, Trenchard was still 70 pilots short of establishment.[22]

By the time the Somme offensive began it seemed as if the RFC had emerged from the worst phase of its crisis of growth. While Trenchard did not command a force appreciably larger than the one he had originally expected to have at his disposal at the beginning of the year, there were signs that expansion was once again about to accelerate.[23] The air war itself was also going very well. The daily reports from RFC Headquarters reveal a rapidly developing optimism about the results of the new offensive policy.[24] The Fokker was no longer an opponent to be feared, and although British penetrations of German air space did occasionally meet considerable resistance, the D.H.2 and F.E.2 aircraft making up the bulk of the service's fighting strength were more than capable of holding their own. British army co-operation machines were now enjoying almost complete protection from fighter patrols, only two being lost to enemy action in June.[25]

On 1 July 1916 the RFC in France mustered 27 squadrons and 421 front-line aircraft. Cautious optimism about the state of aircraft and pilot supply, unfortunately, was largely based on calculations derived from the casualty rate of the preceding months. In the first quarter of 1916 the average percentage of B.E.2s struck off the strength per month was established to be 14·4. It was therefore calculated that the average number of B.E.2s required to supply one squadron of twelve aircraft each month was between one and two. The figures for F.E.2 two-seater fighters were only slightly higher. According to the Directorate of Air Equipment, this data appeared 'to confirm the estimate made at home that a monthly supply of one-sixth of the establishment of B.E.2c and F.E.2b aeroplanes was required to maintain units in the Field up to strength'.

Figures for the second quarter of the year did not significantly change the picture, although they do make it clear that the major problem confronting the Corps remained the large number of take-off and landing accidents (due largely to the poor state of grass airfields and the chronic unreliability of most aero engines). In all 198 aircraft were struck off – 134 of them through accidents, 33 through deterioration and 31 through hostile action. The average wastage rates remained low; 17 per cent per squadron per month for B.E.2cs, 22 per cent for F.E.2bs and 30 per cent for D.H.2s. In view of later developments, the most significant statistic was the low overall percentage of losses due to enemy action. When the offensive policy got under way at full stretch in July, this figure changed dramatically.[26]

RFC casualties in the early days of the Somme offensive reached hitherto unparalleled heights. The rate of slightly more than ten flying personnel killed, wounded or missing for every hundred aircraft available in the first week of July was not equalled until the following April.[27] Trenchard's appreciation of the opening day's losses did not show undue concern: 'Considering it is practically a bare two percent of the whole lot engaged and it is not as if they only went over the lines once as most of them did two or three trips, I think it is a very small percentage for pilots.' Nor did Brancker, at the other end of the supply network, seem any more worried: 'The casualties are certainly not very large considering. I do not suppose that you will keep up such a high average after the first day or two, and if not, they should work out to just about what I expected ...'[28]

Losses did drop, but the level remained high enough to call into doubt Brancker's belief that they might be covered by fresh replacements from Britain. Personnel casualties for the four weeks ending on 28 July totalled 111.[29] A comparison of aircraft losses in July with those suffered in the previous month demonstrates the impact of intensified operational activity. In June, 11 aircraft had been struck off due to enemy action, and 22 as a result of accidents or deterioration; a further 14 had been seriously damaged in action and 51 due to other causes. In July, overall losses more than doubled to 210 aircraft lost or seriously damaged. Significantly, the increase in casualties attributable to the enemy had actually approached a factor of four, the number of machines put out of action in this fashion growing from 25 to 97.[30]

The effort required to keep abreast of this level of attrition was prodigious. A huge drive by the Directorate of Air Equipment managed to produce 200 of the 219 aircraft required by the RFC in France in July. The next month, however, MacInnes supplied only 196 of the 257 machines that Trenchard requested.[31] Before July was over, Brancker was sounding the alarm over the supply of pilots as well: 'We are doing our best to meet your heavy demands, but I must try and keep things going at home, as if we let training drop too low, you will suffer severely for it in a month's time'.[32]

There had been difficulties with the quality as well as the quantity of new pilots earlier in 1916. The pressure on the training organization was such that a substantial number of trainees went overseas so inadequately schooled as to need remedial tuition in France. Trenchard had complained to some effect, and by the summer a minimum standard of proficiency had been established, although only at the cost of watering down the original expansion scheme.[33] The need to produce pilots at a much greater rate from July onwards swept these reforms aside. By September the RFC was caught in a tighening spiral of increasing losses and decreasing training standards from which it did not escape until the following summer. As a complaint from Brancker makes clear, these personnel problems were inextricably connected with the continuing shortage of aircraft:

> I am not quite happy about the output of pilots: your demands of late have been big, and we have not quite come up to them. The main reason is that so many machines were sent out to you in the first week of September that training was absolutely starved in war machines. MacInnes arranged this with you apparently without telling me, and I heard nothing of it until Salmond [GOC Training Brigade] complained.[34]

The military air service had not yet completely rid itself of the prewar misconception that it could hold all the strings of aircraft procurement in its own hands. With the average interval between initial design and production in bulk running at approximately half a year for aircraft and a year for aero engines, the Directorate of Air Equipment found it next to impossible to keep abreast of the demands of the air war.[35] Brigadier-General D. S. MacInnes, the head of this department until the end of 1916, was the frequent target of Trenchard's attacks on the air organization in Britain. There is little evidence to suggest that MacInnes was the 'blithering idiot' Trenchard made him out to be. Rather he was the conscientious and overworked victim of a procurement system which simply could not respond to the demands made upon it.[36] After the Somme offensive raised the tempo of air operations, aircraft supply was simply too big a problem, impinging too heavily on the overall war production priorities of the nation, to be handled by a compartmentalized section of one small War Office directorate.

Apart from the undoubted strain placed on the procurement apparatus by the increasing rate of attrition, the supply situation suffered as a result of the growing size of the military air effort relative to the total productive capacity of the industry behind it. Over the first six months of 1916, engine procurement, including deliveries from foreign suppliers, had totalled 3,114, giving an average monthly output of 519 powerplants. In the second half of the year, total engine procurement reached 3,969, an average monthly output of 662. The increase in average monthly engine production from the first half of the year to the second was therefore approximately 28 per cent.[37] In July 1916, at the beginning of the Somme offensive, the average strength of the RFC contingent on the Western Front was 390 serviceable aircraft. In December the figure had risen to 566, an increase of approximately 45 per cent.[38] The BEF's air needs were clearly growing more rapidly than the procurement system's ability to support them.

During the actual course of the Somme campaign, between the beginning of July and the middle of November, the RFC in the Field was reinforced by seven new army squadrons and one naval squadron. Expansion over this period, and on into the spring of 1917, was dominated by the build-up of fighter strength. On 1 July 1916, Trenchard had mustered 15 Corps squadrons, used almost entirely for close co-operation work with the ground forces, and 12 Army squadrons, used for offensive duties behind the enemy's lines. On 9 April 1917, the first day of the Arras offensive, he commanded 21 Corps squadrons and 29 Army squadrons. No fewer than 17 of the 22 additional squadrons were thus allocated to offensive operations. Four of the new fighting squadrons came from the RNAS, the products of the Admiralty's surrender to army demands for priority within the air effort.

It would be simplistic to portray the growing dominance of fighting machines in the RFC's expansion plans as the result only of Trenchard's adoption of the offensive policy. In the summer of 1916, the single-seater fighter in particular was still a relative newcomer to the air war, most machines, such as the German Fokker *Eindecker* and the British D.H.2, representing little more than transitional stages in design and armament.[39] Over the following six to nine months all the combatants concentrated on introducing a new and more effective generation of aircraft (of which the German Albatros, the French Spad, and the British Sopwith Pup and S.E.5 were the most important examples) and developing the specialized organization, training and doctrine for large-scale employment. German total front-line air strength on 30 June 1916 comprised only 199 single-seater fighters out of a total of 1,465 aircraft. On 30 April 1917, the Germans deployed 688 fighters out of a total of 2,341, the proportion of such aircraft having thereby increased from 14 per cent to 29 per cent.[40]

Nonetheless, the British pursuit of offensive air warfare did depend on a higher proportion of fighters to army co-operation aircraft than the defensive stance of their opponents. Army co-operation forces, along with their parent armies, had effectively reached their maximum strengths by the spring of 1917. Indeed, the RFC deployed exactly the same number of Corps squadrons at Arras in April 1917 as its successor, the Royal Air Force, was to do during the Amiens offensive of August 1918. By the latter date, however, the number of Army squadrons had more than doubled to 72.[41] It was this concentration on fighting aviation which was to make the army's air needs so large and to require the concentration of manufacturing resources to the detriment of other forms of air operations.

In the period between the Somme offensive of 1916 and the Arras offensive of 1917, before the British aircraft industry had reached full maturity, the army's air programme could only be kept in approximate touch with its objectives by making sacrifices elsewhere. The RNAS's long-range bombing force was one victim, the army's own home establishment was another. The latter's inadequate resources were partially to blame for the generally low level of training received by new pilots until the summer of 1917.[42] Indeed, the RFC squadrons which received such a mauling over Arras as to earn the fourth month of 1917 the sobriquet 'Bloody April' were arguably at their lowest state of operational effectiveness of the last two years of the war.

Throughout the winter of 1916–17, Trenchard's correspondence with his colleagues in London was heavily punctuated with complaints about the Directorate of Military Aeronautics's failure to sustain the growth of his command in anticipation of the spring air offensive.[43] While his efforts did not prevent the RFC from suffering heavy losses in the spring, they did contribute to the establishment of the military domination of air procurement. The army did not succeed in its efforts to block the intervention of the Ministry of Munitions into the supply process. Nonetheless, the new procurement system, in which a rejuvenated Air Board served as a tenuous link between the services and the responsible munitions officials, was overwhelmingly concerned with the support of the Trenchardian vision of the air war.

In 1917–18 the British air effort was devoted first and foremost to the battle for air superiority on the Western Front, a battle which was conducted to the harsh tune of attrition dictated by the offensive policy, leaving little in the way of a surplus for other activities. 1916 has been seen as the year of the army's greatest influence over strategic decisions.[44] While Lloyd George was able to reduce military strength during the remainder of the war, he was never to destroy it, leaving Haig in the end to win his war exactly the way he had always said he would. Aviation followed closely in the course of these greater developments. The advantage gained in 1916 survived the creation of an independent air service and left the air contingent attached to Haig's command fighting the war defined for it by Trenchard right up to the armistice. The cost of this offensive remained high enough to doom a fresh experiment in the strategic use of airpower to a failure only marginally less total than that of the earlier victim of the army's air plans, the RNAS bombing force of 1916.

Notes

1   RFC HQ memorandum, Offence and defence, 22 September 1916, PRO, AIR 1/522/16/12/5.
2   ibid.
3   L. E. O. Charlton, *War from the Air. Past, Present, Future* (London: Nelson, 1935), p. 56; P. R. C. Groves, *Behind the Smoke Screen* (London: Faber, 1934), pp. 126–7; Sykes, *From Many Angles*, pp. 219–21.
4   *WIA*, Vol. 6, pp. 552–7.
5   M. Smith, *British Air Strategy between the Wars* (Oxford: Clarendon Press, 1984), pp. 13–43. For Baring's own account of his service with Trenchard see M. Baring, *R.F.C. HQ* (London: Bell, 1920), *passim*.
6   Trenchard's autobiographical notes and his biography, which depends heavily on his own testimony, are particularly revealing as to his attitude towards the man he generally referred to simply as 'the chief'. See Trenchard Papers, MFC 76/1/61; Boyle, *Trenchard, passim*.
7   Boyle, *Trenchard*, pp. 165–71.
8   Trenchard to Brancker, 23 November 1916; Brancker to Curzon, n.d., Trenchard Papers, MFC 76/1/8.
9   RFC HQ memorandum, Offence and defence, 22 September 1916, PRO, AIR 1/522/16/12/5.
10 See for example CGS to BEF armies, 5 August 1917, PRO, AIR 1/522/16/12/5.
11 Trenchard to Brancker, 19 August 1916, Trenchard Papers, MFC 76/1/7.
12 Trenchard to RFC brigades, 10 June 1917, PRO, AIR 1/971/204/5/1111.
13 Compiled from casualty returns in PRO, AIR 1/847–52.
14 As an example, the Bavarian fighter unit *Jagdstaffel* 23b lost 4 pilots killed and 2 wounded during its stay on the French sector (17 November 1916 to 4 February 1918) and 9 pilots killed, 9 wounded and 2 taken prisoner on the British sector (4 February 1918 to 11 November 1918).
15 A. G. Lee, *No Parachute. A Fighter Pilot in World War I* (London: Jarrolds, 1968), pp. 217–18.
16 Trenchard to GHQ, 13 June 1917, PRO, AIR 1/971/204/5/1111.
17 PRO, AIR 1/847/204/5/381–2.
18 Brancker to Trenchard, 22 September 1916, Trenchard Papers, MFC 76/1/7.
19 Trenchard to Henderson, 9 April 1917, Trenchard Papers, MFC 76/1/76; Papers relating to policy on amalgamation of the RFC and the RNAS, Henderson Papers, RAF, AC 71/4/4.
20 Kofl, 6 Wochenberichte, General d. Pionere 6, Nr. 58, Bayerisches Hauptstaatsarchiv-Kriegsarchiv.
21 Brancker to Trenchard, 18 March 1916, Trenchard Papers, MFC 76/1/5.
22 Trenchard to Brancker, 17 April 1916, Trenchard Papers, MFC 76/1/5.
23 Army Council to Haig, 30 May 1916, PRO, AIR 1/521/16/12/2.
24 Summaries of RFC operations for GHQ, PRO, WO 158/34.
25 PRO, AIR 1/844/204/5/371.
26 Brooke-Popham to Brancker, 2 April 1916, Brancker to Trenchard, 6 April 1916, Brooke-Popham to MacInnes, 30 June 1916, PRO, AIR 1/878/204/5/586.
27 PRO, AIR 1/509/16/3/54.
28 Trenchard to Brancker, 2 July 1916, Brancker to Trenchard, 4 July 1916, Trenchard Papers, MFC 76/1/7.
29 PRO, AIR 1/509/16/3/54.
30 Compiled from casualty returns in PRO, AIR 1/844/204/5/372.

31 PRO, AIR 1/878/204/5/586; AIR 1/2302/215/12.
32 Brancker to Trenchard, July 1916, Trenchard Papers, MFC 76/1/7.
33 PRO, AIR 1/141/15/40/218.
34 Brancker to Trenchard, 10 September 1916, Trenchard Papers, MFC 76/1/7.
35 *History of the Ministry of Munitions*, Vol. 7, pt 1, p. 62.
36 Macmillan (ed.), *Sefton Brancker*, p. 65; Trenchard to Brancker, 7 July 1916, Trenchard Papers, MFC 76/1/7.
37 PRO, AIR 1/2302/215/12.
38 PRO, AIR 1/509/16/3/54.
39 The *Eindecker* was little more than a prewar airframe wedded to a synchronized machine-gun; the D.H.2 was of a pusher configuration, with the engine mounted behind the cockpit and the tail attached to the rest of the airframe by a clumsy system of struts and booms.
40 Frontbestand an Flugzeugen vom 31 August 1914 bis 31 August 1918, Grosz Collection.
41 *WIA*, Vol. 3, pp. 412–13; Appendices, p. xxiv.
42 Lee, *No Parachute*, pp. 4–7.
43 M. Cooper, 'A house divided. Policy, rivalry and administration in Britain's military air command, 1914–1918', *The Journal of Strategic Studies*, vol. 3, no. 2 (1980), pp. 187–9.
44 P. Guinn, *British Strategy and Politics, 1914 to 1918* (Oxford: Clarendon Press, 1965), pp. 130–1.

[7]

The Aircraft Industry –
Reorganization and Expansion

Throughout 1916 the growth of the British air effort had been hampered by the uncertain progress of the industry behind it. In the first half of 1917, this situation underwent a dramatic transformation. The production of airframes and aero engines under the authority of the War Office and Admiralty had become increasingly difficult as industrial potential had been absorbed by the remainder of the munitions industry. Controlled by small service procurement agencies, aircraft manufacture had suffered as a result of its position outside the national organization constructed around the Ministry of Munitions. Following the transfer of responsibility for air procurement from the army and navy to the Ministry of Munitions, the output of aircraft doubled in a matter of months. The possibility of a surplus of modern machines appeared to open the way to just that sort of strategic experimentation which the RNAS had found so difficult in the straitened circumstances of the previous year. The conjuncture of this development and the reappearance of the German aerial threat to London proved of crucial significance to the debate over the creation of an independent air service in the summer of 1917.

Unfortunately, the new air procurement apparatus created in the winter of 1916–17 experienced severe difficulties in sustaining its momentum. Ministry of Munitions and Air Board officials overestimated the rate of productive expansion, and by the end of 1917 their programmes were falling foul of labour and material shortages and a host of technological problems. The industry failed to produce all the aircraft expected of it, leaving the long-range bombing force, on which the air service's claim to independence was based, almost completely starved of the means of operation. Before considering either the decision to form a united air force or the fate of that service after its creation, it is therefore necessary to study the incomplete revolution in aircraft production which attended the transformation of British air organization in the last two years of the war.

84

Lloyd George's handling of the impasse over the report of Curzon's Air Board, inherited from his predecessor, brought out some of the better characteristics of his war administration. He undoubtedly benefited from the presence of more pliant ministers. Sir Edward Carson, the new First Lord of the Admiralty, accepted the separation of aircraft supply from naval control. He was also prepared to appoint a new Fifth Sea Lord with specific responsibility for aviation, and to remove Vaughan-Lee from his post as Director of the Air Department because of his close association with the disputes of the Curzon era.[1] Derby at the War Office did not prove any more obstructive, and Brancker, who attempted to revive the military case against the Ministry of Munitions, soon found himself effectively isolated.[2] Indeed service opponents of the proposed reorganization of supply discovered that the new government was not to be treated as lightly as the old. When the new First Sea Lord Jellicoe objected to the War Cabinet's approach to aircraft supply, he too received short shrift.[3]

On 22 December, the War Cabinet gave executive substance to the tentative arrangements agreed by the War Committee almost a month before. The Air Board, invested with true authority as a result of the New Ministries and Secretaries Act, was to concern itself first and foremost with 'allocating the aerial resources of the country between the Admiralty and War Office wherever there is conflict or competition between them'. The two services were expected to co-ordinate their air policies in consultation with the Board, which in turn would adapt their programmes to available resources and place orders with the Ministry of Munitions.[4] Effective control of aircraft supply thus lay with the newly appointed Controller of Aeronautical Supplies, William Weir.

Weir was an influential voice in Britain's air councils right up to the Second World War. A successful industrialist in his own right, he had served as Scottish Director of Munitions before he came south to participate in the experiment of 'a mixed department of khaki and blue'. In view of the over-optimistic projections of aircraft output which originated in his office, it is important to stress his self-proclaimed ignorance 'as regards running a Central Supply Department in London'.[5] Weir and his colleague Percy Martin, a former Daimler executive who served alongside him as Controller of Petrol Engine Supply, were responsible for that rationalization and expansion of the British aircraft industry which finally allowed it to realize its potential. Unfortunately, their relative inexperience in the complicated business of aircraft procurement led them to underestimate the difficulties attending their task. This inexperience, and the attenuated communications network connecting their offices with the actual air commands abroad, conspired to allow policy and supply to drift dangerously far apart.[6]

The man charged with the vital role of providing a link between the services and the Ministry of Munitions was the new President of the Air

Board, Lord Cowdray. The most prominent public works contractor of his age, Cowdray has been well served by recent historiography, having generally been portrayed as the architect of service co-operation and air expansion.[7] There is considerable justice in this judgement: as the arbiter of aircraft procurement, Cowdray possessed a blend of administrative experience, leadership and tact sufficient to convince one senior airman that 'he was almost Napoleonic in his outlook on the position of aviation'.[8] This notwithstanding, Cowdray was very much in the hands of his munitions experts as regards the co-ordination of production and never really challenged the military control of available resources or the Trenchardian air policy behind it. His support of the formation of a separate strategic air command was conditioned by the belief that sufficient resources existed to create this force without in any way interfering with the existing requirements of the army. Lloyd George's cavalier treatment of him in the aftermath of the decision to form an Air Ministry was ultimately the product of Cowdray's weak position within the government. His tenure as President of the Air Board had no aura of permanence. Cowdray himself was prepared to leave the post in June over the issue of his business connections with the Admiralty,[9] while Hugh Cecil's cruel jibe that he was 'in truth, a superannuated man of business' is apt comment on his position as an essentially transitional figure.[10]

The management of the air effort in 1917 was dominated by the Ministry of Munitions. While this arrangement was quickly to show signs of weakness, it did result in an immediate improvement in aircraft supply. The inflated estimates of air capability which so affected the policy decisions taken in the summer of 1917 grew out of a justified sense of achievement with regard to airframe and engine production.

At the Air Board's second meeting under Cowdray's chairmanship on 4 January, an attempt was made to gauge the country's air needs over the following six months. It was estimated that 300 engines must be manufactured each month to maintain the 3,300 up-to-date engines currently in the RFC's possession (wastage was estimated at approximately 100 per cent per annum). If the RFC was to expand to a strength of 106 service squadrons, as then required by the army, a total strength of 8,000 engines would be necessary, occasioning the manufacture of another 800 engines per month. The maintenance of these additional engines would require a further expansion of monthly output by 400. Naval requirements (300 engines per month) and the need for a reserve capacity to meet any new demands which might arise (200 engines per month) pushed the total monthly requirement up to 2,000. It was therefore necessary to produce approximately 500 engines each week. Existing weekly output, however, had only just reached 150, while domestic procurement for the previous year had been 5,363 (an average of 103 per week), having been increased to 7,227 (an average of 139 per week) by purchases from foreign (almost exclusively French) suppliers.[11]

The Air Board clearly had a monumental task before it. British engine procurement had increased by 275 per cent from 1915 to 1916, but still had not matched German output, which had reached 7,823 in the same year.[12] The French engine industry which had contributed 24 per cent of the British total in 1916, remained in a class of its own, producing more powerplants (16,149) than Britain and Germany combined.[13] Even if the total of 2,000 engines a month required over the first six months of 1917 was duplicated without further increment in the second half of the year, the increase in output between 1916 and 1917 would have to be in the order of another 330 per cent.

This requirement was made all the more difficult by the fact that expansion could not be based on the engines already in production. The aircraft of 1917–18 would have to be powered by a new generation of engines, mostly stationary, water-cooled designs of between 200 and 400 horsepower. Such designs as the Sunbeam Arab and the B.H.P., earmarked for mass production in January 1917, were still at that stage largely experimental. If the Air Board was to produce them in time, then orders would have to be placed before they had been properly refined and tested. There were further outstanding problems with the supply of both raw materials and manufactured components, and with the overall division of the country's engine production capacity. The new Controller of Petrol Engine Supply told his colleagues in January that facilities for the production of high-grade steel, essential for such components as crankshafts, 'did not at present exist in Great Britain'.[14] Ball-bearings were likely to prove another problem: even if the existing domestic output was handed over entirely to the aircraft programme it would not have proved sufficient to meet freshly extended needs.[15] As far as the general supply of engines was concerned, the aircraft procurement campaign was now in direct competition with the army's tank programme which, despite the tank's uncertain operational debut on the Somme, was in the process of expansion.[16]

The British aircraft industry at the beginning of 1917 showed all the signs of two and a half years of unplanned growth under competing Admiralty and War Office procurement authorities. The services continued to depend upon a bewildering array of different aircraft and engine types, produced in small quantities by a large number of relatively underdeveloped firms. In January 1917 the RFC was using 48 different aircraft designs and the RNAS 43, of which 15 were shared between the two. The engine situation was only marginally less complicated, the services employing 30 and 39 types respectively, only 12 of which were in common usage.[17] The total domestic output of 583 aero engines in the same month was divided between 15 manufacturers, only five of which produced more than 50. No fewer than 19 engine designs were involved, none of which alone accounted for more than 20 per cent of the total.[18]

In their efforts to expand production, the Air Board and Ministry of Munitions concentrated on reducing the number of designs in service, standardizing fighter, bomber and reconnaissance machines, and placing fewer orders of much greater size than had hitherto been the case. Established firms were brought under tighter control than had been possible in the days of divided military and naval responsibility. Rolls Royce, for example, was instructed to lower its obsessively high quality controls to avoid the persistent defaulting on deadlines for which it had always been notorious.[19] Relative newcomers to the field were given the incentive of large orders to expand their capacity as rapidly as possible. One firm, the Siddeley-Deasy Motor Company of Coventry, was encouraged to spend £100,000 in order to increase potential output from 400 to 600 engines per month. As a guarantee, the company asked for and received a promise of contracts for 3,000 engines, instead of the 2,000 originally intended – all this in spite of the fact that Siddeley-Deasy had built only 509 engines of a relatively simple design up to the end of 1916.[20]

By the beginning of March there were almost 20,000 aero engines on order, but problems of design and construction were already emerging. Technological advances in the field of internal combustion engines lagged behind the operational requirements of the air war, and as early as 19 March Weir felt obliged to warn the Board of the possibility of one or more of the models upon which the expansion programme depended failing before full production efficiency was attained. At the same meeting, Weir had to admit that 62 per cent of the crank-cases in the new designs were currently failing to meet qualitative standards.[21]

The most immediate problem affecting expansion, however, was the need for urgent remedial action with regard to the RFC in the Field, which, in the spring of 1917, was reaping the full results of earlier procurement difficulties. Cowdray and his colleagues came on the scene at a time when the services were struggling to hurry a new generation of aircraft to the front in time to avoid being caught at a technological disadvantage in the Arras campaign. In December, before the reorganization of the supply apparatus had been completed, the Board had asked the Ministry of Munitions to accelerate the production of more powerful engines for fighter aircraft.[22] Such measures had generally been left too late, and the effect, as far as the Air Board was concerned, was that the overall aircraft programme was projected into such a state of disarray that expansion was doubly difficult.

With no apparent improvement in the state of his command, Trenchard was soon pressing the Cowdray Board as hard as he had its predecessor the year before. In early February he persuaded Haig to send home a general statement regarding RFC deficiencies, emphasizing the need for immediate action.[23] In mid-April, with the situation at the front having if anything worsened, a further statement was issued, stressing that 'the difficulties to be overcome were increased by the number of out-of-date machines and new-type machines which came too late for pilots to become accustomed to them.'[24] The Air Board reply to the second letter, reviewing the overall state of the supply situation, is worthy of detailed consideration.

The Board began by emphasizing that 'the real difficulty' to be overcome before the supply of aircraft could be improved was the development and production of new high-power engines. Earlier administrators had to a certain extent jeopardized the future by depending on French designs for the previous generation of large engines, with the result that 'it is only to-day that we are reaching the stage of production in substantial quantities of an engine suitable for fighter and fighter/reconnaissance aeroplanes of British design and manufacture'. The Board went on to explain the other shortcomings of the aircraft and engine procurement system as it had found it, stressing that present failures were due to mistakes in 'the development of aircraft during last summer and autumn'.

It was in every way reflective of the growing feeling of confidence among Cowdray, Weir and their associates that the Board should have gone on to offer its critics a glowing vision of the future. With regard to the crucial problem of engine deliveries, the Board reported an immediate and dramatic increase, with even more to follow in the course of the year:

If the average monthly deliveries of engines for 1916 be taken as a standard figure of   8
then the average actual deliveries for January and February 1917 would be represented by   16
the guaranteed deliveries for the period 1st March to 30 June by   19
and the guaranteed deliveries for the period 1st July to 31st October by the figure   29

The report's conclusion afforded a pleasing contrast to the constant stream of postponements and excuses of the preceding year:

There can thus be no question but that the supply of aircraft to the Expeditionary Force will steadily and materially improve during the remaining months of the year. There have already been sent to the Front since the 1st January machines of new types amounting to an addition of some 80 engines and, further, 3½ squadrons already at the Front have been equipped with new aeroplanes and engines. This process will be continued as rapidly as the manufacturing and transport conditions permit.[25]

It rapidly became apparent that the goal of 2,000 engine deliveries per month by the middle of the year, effectively representing a threefold increase in output over a six-month period, was unrealistic. The Air Board's first projection of future output, presented in a report to the cabinet on 24 March, predicted only an average figure of 973 deliveries per month between March and June.[26] While even this target was not quite reached, monthly engine output did exceed the 1,000 level for the first time in May, and, after a small drop in June, remained above that figure for the remainder of the year.[27] In May the Air Board provided the cabinet with the first evidence of a possible acceleration in engine production which seemed to open the way to a host of fresh options in air policy.

According to the Air Board report of 12 May, engine deliveries could be expected to reach the 1,500 per month level by August, increase by a further 500 by October, and reach the almost fantastic figure of 2,500 at the end of the year.[28] Weir had, in fact, revised his figures slightly downwards by the time he presented a fresh summary to the War Cabinet in July in the wake of the first Gotha attacks. He had, however, projected his figures forward into the summer of 1918, and was predicting a monthly output by that time in the vicinity of 4,000 engines.[29]

It is easy enough to explain the general air of optimism that pervaded the Air Board's outlook on engine production in the summer of 1917. The preceding six months had witnessed a steady and substantial increase in output. In fact, the average monthly production figures for engines in the first six months of 1917 (including deliveries from foreign sources) was 1,045, an increase of 74 per cent over the same figure in the last six months of 1916.[30] The campaign for standardization was by this time promising a considerably simpler future, and by September the Board would be working to a programme involving only 13 engine and 14 aircraft types.[31] Finally, the modernization of the actual fighting equipment of the forces in the field was also well under way. In a letter sent by Haig to the Army Council on 18 May, the 51 squadrons then under Trenchard's command were divided under three headings: 22 equipped with 'new type machines', 14 with 'types which will become obsolete during this summer and early autumn', and 15 with 'types which are already obsolete'. If this system of classification is adapted to the RFC order of battle at the end of July, modifying the assignation of categories to individual types of aircraft to take account of the changing operational conditions, a considerable upgrading in equipment becomes apparent: of the 51 squadrons then available, 37 fell into the first category, 3 into the second and 11 into the third.[32]

None the less, a retrospective study of the air production situation in the summer of 1917 demonstrates that real problems had already surfaced which ought to have given the Air Board cause to be more cautious about the future. At the beginning of May, Weir warned the Air Board that the average time between the inception and mass production of new designs was likely to increase 'as the standard of performance required rises, and as the manufacturing difficulties increase'.[33] A week later, in the very same report in which the Board first revealed to the cabinet the prospect of a substantial surplus in aero engines, it also expressed 'a good deal of anxiety' as to the development of the new high-power engines on which the future so heavily depended. Both the 200 horsepower Sunbeam and the 200 horsepower Wolseley-built Hispano-Suiza were found to be displaying design faults and, in the latter case at least, these were held to be sufficiently serious to warrant the placement of a supplementary order for 400 of the proven 150/180 horsepower Hispano-Suiza 'as a measure of insurance'.[34]

Domestic engine output had reached the 1,000 per month level by the middle of 1917. Average monthly output over the last six months of the year only reached 1,145. Total monthly procurement, after the injection of 3,423 foreign-built engines, stood at an average of 1,715 for the same period – a profound improvement, but still far short of the original projection. The major problems rested with precisely those modern engines which comprised the most significant part of the expansion programme.

The production history of the 200/230 horsepower B.H.P. engine provides the best example of the perils of heavy dependence on an untried design. The small Galloway works in Dumfries produced only 43 of these engines between April and December 1917. The other producer, Siddeley-Deasy, began to supply the B.H.P. to the RFC in July, but of the 11,500 eventually ordered from their Coventry works only 274 had appeared by the end of the year. Similar shortfalls were experienced with the 200 h.p. Sunbeam Arab, the 190/200 h.p. Rolls Royce Falcon, the 250/360 h.p. Rolls Royce Eagle and the 200 h.p. Hispano Suiza. Overall, these five engines on which so much depended made up only 21 per cent (2,417 of 11,763) of British domestic engine production in 1917.[35]

There is little doubt but that Weir and his technical advisors failed adequately to anticipate the problems associated with the development of much larger and more powerful engines than those which had proved themselves in service up to the end of 1916. This was a problem common to the aircraft industries of all the combatant powers. The Germans, for example, were never successfully to break the 200 horsepower barrier in fighter engine design, and several of the promising aircraft they introduced into service in 1918 were to have their careers ruined by unsatisfactory powerplants.[36] Similarly, the American Liberty engine experienced a prolonged and difficult development which delayed its frontline use until the closing months of the war.[37] Nonetheless, the technological difficulties associated with the production of more powerful engines were exacerbated in Britain by particular problems of organization and supply. In explaining the British aircraft industry's failure to clear the qualitative and quantitative hurdles confronting it in the middle of 1917, it is necessary to consider three factors of this sort: the inexperience of the new arbiters of aircraft supply, the structural weakness of the procurement system within which they operated, and the unbalanced relationship between that system and the remainder of British war industry.

The official history of the Ministry of Munitions quite correctly pointed out that there was little solid basis for the calculation of a large programme of supply when that department first assumed responsibility for aircraft production.[38] It might almost have gone further and commented upon the lack of real aeronautical expertise among those who eventually undertook this task. Cowdray, Weir and Martin certainly possessed a varied wealth of industrial experience, but none of them could bring more than general administrative skill to bear on the highly specialized task of producing a complicated and still relatively novel piece of war machinery. In this regard it is worthy of note that one of the senior officers whose services were dispensed with during the general reorganization of the air command in the winter of 1916–17 was the army's Director of Air Equipment, Brig.-Gen. D. S. MacInnes. This much maligned officer returned to the Royal Engineers, eventually to die on active service in 1918. Given his long experience of the problems of meeting constantly rising quantitative and qualitative standards in aircraft production, it is difficult to avoid the conclusion that better use might have been made of his talents within the new Air Board.

The departures of MacInnes and his naval opposite number Sueter were symbolic of the widening of the administrative gap between the air services at the front and their supply organizations caused by the formation of the Cowdray Air Board. The relationship had never been an easy one, as Trenchard's complaints about the Directorate of Air Equipment in 1916 made clear. Despite its campaign to retain control of procurement in the final months of the Curzon Board, the army in particular seems almost to have washed its hands of aircraft supply when the Ministry of Munitions entered the field at the beginning of 1917.[39] The New Board was very much dominated by civilians and established only erratic consultative links with the operational components of the air services. The result was a progressive loss of touch between the aircraft industry and the air command, a development which led the latter to plan its future campaigns without real knowledge of the problems which would affect both the performance of the new machines on which their plans depended, and the rate at which they would appear at the front.

The official history of the Ministry of Munitions once again provides a valuable insight into the Air Board's problems:

Aeronautical supply was the last large service to impose its claims on industry during the war. It had therefore to be content with a comparatively small ratio of skilled labour, though it actually required an exceptionally large one . . . [40]

Britain's war industry had already expanded to a point where fresh calls on manufacturing potential could only be met at the expense of other industries. The aircraft industry itself had little reserve capacity, and any increase in output would have to be underwritten by new facilities created in an environment in which expansion of any kind was no longer easy. In the first two months of 1917 alone, 65 firms, making up the bulk of those then engaged on aircraft work, took on approximately 7,000 new hands, an increase of almost 10 per cent in their total workforce.[41] Such growth could only be achieved at the cost of ongoing dilution of skilled labour. The level of dilution (the replacement of skilled by unskilled workers) in the aircraft industry had already reached 31 per cent by August 1916. It was to increase steadily throughout the remainder of the war, finally reaching a level of 46 per cent.[42]

Struggling to increase their plant with an increasingly inexpert work-force, individual manufacturers found it very difficult to accelerate production. Siddeley-Deasy, which had built 509 engines up to the end of 1916, produced 974 in 1917, 700 of these as part of an outstanding contract for the low-powered RAF 4a engine. Indeed only two manufac-turers averaged more than 100 deliveries per month in 1917. Significantly, both of these concerns, Daimler and Rolls Royce, were well-established firms producing engines which had already entered production the year before.[43] Skilled labour, raw materials, machined components and factory space were all in short supply by the time Britain launched an expanded air programme. The new central air procurement apparatus operated at some disadvantage in competing with established military and naval organizations for control of the residuum, and in arguing for a reallocation of resources otherwise intended for other sectors of the war effort. Some victories would be won, such as the assignation of priority in engine supply of aircraft over tanks, but Weir and his colleagues had also to be on guard against the transfer of portions of their hard-earned industrial resources to well entrenched parts of the British war machine such as the Admiralty's shipyards or the War Office's shell factories.[44]

British aircraft and aero engine procurement in 1918 did experience continued growth. The total output of aircraft more than doubled (from 14,832 in 1917 to 30,782 in 1918), while the total output of engines only just fell short of following suit (16,665 in 1917 and 31,269 in 1918).[45] In fact, only the rapid cut-back in production immediately after the armistice prevented the figures for growth assuming even more impressive propor-tions. The existing squadrons of what in April 1918 became the Royal Air

Force were able to sustain far heavier casualties during the last seven and a half months of the war, while actually enjoying a steady if slow increment in their strength. Not only on the Western Front, but in the secondary theatres of Italy, Salonika and the Middle East, and in the home defence command as well, British flying units generally utilized equipment which was at least as modern and as efficient as that of their allies and enemies.

On the other hand, the British aircraft industry did fall a long way short of the targets projected for it in the previous year. In July 1918, for example, it produced only 2,616 of the 4,000 engines Weir had promised twelve months earlier. The failure of certain of the advanced engine designs to achieve either expected levels of performance or easy transition to mass production also undermined the re-equipment of certain crucial components of the air force. The B.H.P. engined D.H.9, expected to become the mainstay of the day bombing force, proved inferior in many ways to the machine it was intended to replace. Although its shortcomings were already obvious before it entered service in the winter of 1917–18, the D.H.9 still made up the bulk of the RAF's bombing strength at the armistice, largely because the appearance of its successor, the D.H.9a, was delayed by design and production difficulties with its Liberty engine.[46] Similarly, plans to replace the R.E.8 army co-operation aircraft with the higher performance Bristol F.2b, remained unfulfilled twelve months after their inception. Once again the culprit was the engine, in this case the Sunbeam Arab, of which only 1,195 out of a total order of 5,160 had been produced by the end of 1918.[47]

The most obvious victim of the shortfall in production was the independent strategic bombing force, which never achieved more than a fraction of its intended strength. Thus, the failure of the aircraft procurement programme to attain the expected level of growth effectively undermined the redirection of air effort attempted through the creation of the Royal Air Force. As late as March 1918, Churchill, then Minister of Munitions, was expressing concern 'that production would soon outstrip the man-power requisite for utilizing its results'.[48] Far from this proving to be the case, aircraft and engine output never completely outran the demands of the air war on the Western Front. In the autumn of 1918, Britain's factories were still primarily concerned with supporting this campaign and could provide little material sustenance to efforts at bombing Germany.

The basic error of those charged with the mobilization of Britain's aerial resources in 1917–18 was to equate the allocation of resources with the resulting level of production. Money and orders poured into an immature industry did not elicit an immediate return in completed aircraft or aero engines. In a sense, Weir and his colleagues repeated the mistake of the munitions experts charged with the manufacture of guns and shells earlier in the war. To produce a heavier flow of the instruments of war it was necessary to do more than simply open wide the tap of the nation's industrial potential. Mobilization of resources was a slow business compared to mobilization of existing facilities. Only when plant had been constructed, a labour force trained and a series of complicated design problems resolved, would the finished products begin to flow from the production lines. Far from achieving full capacity in the winter of 1917–18, the British aircraft industry was only just approaching it when the war ended a year later.

The airframe and aero engine industry at the end of 1916 was still a small and unhealthy organism, untuned to the necessities of mass production as a result of divided control and limited military and naval objectives. Like Britain's overall industrial base at the time when efforts were first made to set it on a war footing, the air industry had been starved of resources too long to permit a rapid expansion. There were to be no surplus air fleets in Britain during the First World War, just as there was to be no surplus of guns, shells, ships or fighting men. Further strategic innovations such as an independent bombing force could only be underwritten by reallocating existing material resources.

Notes

1 Carson to Bonar Law, 20 December 1916, BL Papers, 81/1/63; Carson to Curzon, January 1917, Curzon Papers, Eur.F.112/170.
2 Private diary, 6 January 1917, Addison Papers, Bodleian Library, 98; Brancker to Trenchard, 6 January 1917, Trenchard Papers, MFC 76/1/9.
3 War Cabinet 15, min. 19, 22 December 1916, PRO, CAB 23/1.
4 ibid.
5 Weir to Addison, 3 January 1917, Addison Papers, Bodleian Library, 66.
6 Weir's biography tends to be uncritical of his achievements both during and after the war. See W. J. Reader, *Architect of Air Power. The Life of the First Viscount Weir of Eastwood, 1877–1959* (London: Collins, 1968), *passim*.
7 Dean, *The Royal Air Force*, pp. 23–4; Boyle, *Trenchard*, p. 245.
8 Macmillan (ed.), *Sefton Brancker*, p. 141.
9 Cowdray to Lloyd George, 3 and 9 June 1917, LG Papers, F/11/2/2–3.
10 H. Cecil to Milner, 11 October 1917, Milner Papers, Dep.357/97–101. For Cowdray's life generally see J. A. Spender, *Weetman Pearson, First Viscount Cowdray, 1856–1927* (London: Cassell, 1930), *passim*; D. Young, *Member for Mexico. a Biography of Weetman Pearson, First Viscount Cowdray* (London: Cassell, 1966), *passim*.
11 Air Board minutes, 4 January 1917, PRO, AIR 6/4.
12 Morrow, *German Air Power in World War I*, p. 210.
13 Laux, 'Gnôme et Rhône', p. 20.
14 Air Board minutes, 10 January 1917, PRO, AIR 6/4.
15 Weir and Martin to Addison, 16 June 1917, PRO, MUN 4/3235.
16 Air Board minutes, 2 and 5 February 1917, PRO, AIR 6/5.
17 Weir to Addison, 31 January 1917, PRO, MUN 4/3231.
18 PRO, AIR 1/2302/215/12.
19 Air Board minutes, 12 February 1917, PRO, AIR 6/5.

20 PRO, AIR 1/2302/215/12.
21 Air Board minutes, 19 March 1917, PRO, AIR 6/6.
22 Secretary, Air Board to Secretary, Ministry of Munitions, 18 December 1916, PRO, MUN 4/3231.
23 Haig to Robertson, 13 February 1917, PRO, AIR 1/503/16/3/17.
24 Haig to Robertson, 14 April 1917, PRO, AIR 1/522/16/12/5.
25 Air Board to War Cabinet, 17 April 1917, PRO, AIR 8/2, pt 2.
26 G.T. 306, Air Board report to Cabinet, 24 March 1917, PRO, CAB 24/9.
27 PRO, AIR 1/2302/215/12.
28 G.T. 718, Air Board report to Cabinet, 12 May 1917, PRO, CAB 24/13.
29 War Cabinet 179, min. 6, 9 July 1917, PRO, CAB 23/3.
30 PRO, AIR 1/2302/215/12.
31 *History of the Ministry of Munitions*, Vol. 7, pt 1, pp. 157–8.
32 Haig to Army Council, 18 May 1917; Army Council to Haig, 7 July 1917, PRO, AIR 1/2267/209/70/34; *WIA*, Vol. 4, pp. 414–18, 426–30.
33 G.T. 662, Air Board report to Cabinet, 5 May 1917, PRO CAB 24/12.
34 G.T. 718, Air Board report to Cabinet, 12 May 1917, PRO, CAB 24/13.
35 PRO, AIR 1/2302/215/12.
36 Morrow, *German Air Power in World War I*, pp. 121–41.
37 I. B. Holley, *Ideas and Weapons. Exploitation of the Aerial Weapon by the United States during World War I; a Study in the Relationship of Technological Advance, Military Doctrine and the Development of Weapons* (New Haven, Conn.: Yale University Press, 1953) pp. 119–33.
38 *History of the Ministry of Munitions*, Vol. 12, pt 1, p. 68.
39 Brancker to Trenchard, 6 January 1917, Trenchard Papers, MFC 76/1/9.
40 *History of the Ministry of Munitions*, Vol. 12, pt 1, pp. 60–1.
41 G.T. 398, Air Board report to Cabinet, 7 April 1917, PRO, CAB 24/9.
42 *WIA*, Vol. 6, p. 95.
43 PRO, AIR 1/2302/215/12.
44 See for example G.T. 5829, Man power and air power, 25 September 1918, PRO, CAB 24/64.
45 *History of the Ministry of Munitions*, Vol. 12, pt 1, pp. 173–4.
46 L. A. Pattinson, *History of 99 Squadron, Independent Force, Royal Air Force, March 1918–November 1918* (Cambridge: Heffer, 1920) pp. 6–18; War Cabinet 361, mins. 13–14, 7 March 1918, PRO CAB 23/5; PRO AIR 1/2302/215/12.
47 PRO, AIR 1/2302/215/12.
48 War Cabinet 361, min. 17, 7 March 1918, PRO, CAB 23/5.

[8]

The Smuts Report

By the summer of 1917, Britain had not been seriously threatened from the air for nine months. Four Zeppelins had been destroyed over southeast England between 3 September and 2 October 1916, and two more off the east coast on the same day in late November. In the face of improving night flying and fighting techniques, and the new incendiary bullet, the airship had become more of a threat to its own crew than to its enemies. Those which did still pay occasional visits to the British mainland were forced to operate at such a height as to be almost entirely ineffectual. As a result of this freedom from attack, home air defence and its frequent partner, retaliatory bombing action against Germany, had fallen from the public attention. The appearance of German bomber aircraft over Folkestone on 25 May and Sheerness on 5 June did inject a note of uncertainty into the situation, causing the War Cabinet to consider both defensive and offensive countermeasures.[1] When, however, the raiders appeared over London on 13 June, they found the capital unprepared and almost undefended.

The Gotha raids on London of 13 June and 7 July probably contributed more to the future development of air warfare than any other event during the entire war. Not only did they lead to the formation of the first independent air service in the world; they also cast a shadow over British perceptions of war which, distorted by the passage of time and darkened by the rebirth of German airpower under Hitler, profoundly affected the preparations made for war in 1939.[2] The first three decades of the air age were, however, characterized by a persistent overestimation of the effectiveness of the bomber. It is therefore advisable to preface any discussion of the British response to the first concerted aircraft campaign against the island with a consideration of the true nature of the German threat.

At the distance of more than half a century, the Gotha raids of 1917–18 appear only marginally more impressive than the Zeppelin attacks during the first half of the war. The *Luftstreitkräfte* utilized only about one quarter of its heavy bomber strength – at the very most 40 aircraft – on sorties against southeast England. Based around Ghent in Belgium, the aircraft of *Kampfgeschwader* III (the unit was reclassified as *Bombengeschwader* III in early 1918) were often diverted to operations on the Western Front. Between May and August 1917 formations of approximately 20 aircraft carried out eight day raids, only two of which reached London. In the face of intensifying fighter opposition, the Germans then switched to night operations. A further 19 attacks were launched from September 1917 to May 1918, 15 of which reached the capital, although seldom at full strength. Just under 120 tons of bombs were dropped. The total damage caused was valued at approximately one-and-half million pounds sterling; total casualties were under 3,000, almost a quarter of them military.[3]

The raids were conceived only as a sideline to operations in France, and were given up after one last full-strength effort on the night of 19/20 May 1918, as much because the bombers were needed elsewhere as because of the high casualty rate (15 per cent, due more to accidents than British action).[4] The Gotha campaign in no way represented a major attempt to alter the course of the war through an attack on either the physical or moral fabric of British society. The important thing about it, however, was that this was how it was perceived by the British.

The British reaction to the Gotha raids was conditioned by three factors. The general nervousness of attacks on the home island has already been mentioned. This fear was exacerbated in the summer of 1917 by a real concern at the course the war was taking. The Russian collapse, the mutinies in the French army and the heavy toll taken by U-boats all hinted at disaster for the allies. Finally it must be remembered that attack from the air was all the more frightening for its sheer novelty. The sight of a formation of aircraft, dropping bombs with apparently studied precision, undisturbed by either British aircraft or heavy fire from the ground, was a far more menacing prospect than the hit-and-run visitations of nocturnal Zeppelins. It is little wonder that the War Cabinet should have acted, in one senior soldier's estimation at least, as if the world was coming to an end.[5] The appearance of the Gothas certainly did seem to indicate that the nature of warfare had changed in a manner which could only spell danger to Britain's long-enjoyed insular fastness.

One other extraneous factor ought also to be taken into account. During his first six months in office, Lloyd George had clearly demonstrated his resolve to break the strategic stranglehold of the military command. He had also shown himself willing, if not even overwilling, to seek advice and administrative talent outside the normal channels of politico-military decision-making.[6] The prime minister's distrust of his own military servants had manifested itself most clearly in his naive acceptance of French promises of success on the Western Front in the spring. In the wake of the daylight Gotha raids, he found another potential saviour in the South African soldier–statesman, Jan Christian Smuts.

Smuts, a lawyer turned politician who had played a central role in his country's diplomacy during and after the Boer War, had arrived in London in March 1917 to represent South Africa at an imperial conference. Although he had successfully overseen the conquest of German Southwest Africa and inflicted a major defeat on von Lettow-Vorbeck's guerrilla army in Tanganyika, his military experience was scarcely broad enough to merit the respect it was granted by Britain's war leadership. Smuts's charisma and enthusiasm for the imperial cause hypnotized the War Cabinet, which looked to him to point a way through Britain's tangled problems of command and strategic direction.[7]

As a result of the early raids on the southeast coast, the War Cabinet had already begun to show interest in retaliatory strikes against Germany. After the first raid on London, these discussions took on greater urgency, the perceived need for action contributing not only to the decision to bring Haig and Trenchard home to discuss reprisals and their possible effects on operations on the Western Front, but also to that of 2 July to approve the expansion of the RFC from 108 to 200 service squadrons.[8] It was the second daylight raid on the capital, however, which convinced the War Cabinet that a prolonged campaign against the seat of government had become a likely possibility. Agreeing with *The Times*'s assertion that 'all our arrangements in connexion with air campaigning, both offensive and defensive, require fresh investigation', it nominated a two-man committee, comprising Smuts and the prime minister himself, to examine both 'the defence arrangements for Home Defence against air raids' and 'the air organization generally and the direction of aerial operations'.[9]

Lloyd George took little real part in the committee's deliberations, but Smuts, working on his own, produced two reports in little more than a month. The first, dealing entirely with home defence measures, recommended a unified command for the various fighter squadrons, searchlight and gun batteries, and observation posts. As such it simply gave form to the existing consensus of opinion and consolidated the general strengthening of these services undertaken in a piecemeal fashion since May. In fact, only five days before the appearance of Smuts's first report, Henderson had suggested precisely the same sort of consolidation in a letter to the CIGS, Robertson.[10]

The most significant aspect of the reformation of the British home defence system was its cost in terms of the far from adequate supply of modern fighter aircraft. Early engagements with Gotha formations had proved conclusively that dependence could no longer be placed on the obsolescent machines that had defeated the Zeppelin.[11] By the winter of 1917–18, Major-General E. B. Ashmore, the commander of the newly created London defence area, was to have eight full squadrons of fighter aircraft at his disposal – a total of approximately 150 aircraft, many of them modern Sopwith Camel and Bristol F2b machines.[12] Trenchard's predictable reaction to the temporary transfer homewards of several of his fighting squadrons in the aftermath of the summer raids had been that, if the bombing of London was to be stopped, 'the only way to do it is to completely knock the German aviation out here'.[13] When it became obvious that opinion in London was demanding not only improved home air defence, but the bombing of Germany as well, Trenchard began to worry that the provision of the necessary aircraft would interfere with the expansion of his forces up to the level considered necessary to win the air war on the Western Front.[14] Both the growth of the home defence force and the ambitious programme for a long-range bombing force were to prove his fears justified.

Nonetheless, it was Smuts's second report, produced on 17 August, which offered the more serious threat to the military control of air policy. In some senses at least, its recommendations were less revolutionary than might at first seem to be the case. In the atmosphere of urgency prevailing in London after the second Gotha raid, Smuts, who had little if any technical knowledge of his subject, was expected to move rapidly. Many of his political colleagues were already half-convinced that some form of separate air organization was necessary. The memory of inter-service rivalry in the days of Derby and Curzon, the fact that the army had obstructed and finally destroyed an earlier naval effort at bombing Germany, and the evidence that the two existing air services seemed incapable of interfering effectively with recent German attacks, all seemed to point in the same direction. As Leo Amery told Smuts two days after the second German raid:

> the real crux of the air situation is the refusal to treat the air seriously as a separate department of warfare which, for the purposes of offensive and defensive strategy, requires its own separate Air Staff and Air Force over and above the General Staffs of Armies at home or in the field or of the Naval detachments at Dunkirk, etc.[15]

The available specialist advice underlined this judgement. In a memorandum to Smuts dated 19 July, Henderson placed great emphasis on the deleterious effects of inter-service competition. He stressed that the Air Board exercised only partial control over the air effort, and that 'on the adoption of any policy, the responsibility of carrying it out is completely divided at present'. His conclusions appeared to make the military message clear:

> It is difficult to indicate any method of overcoming the present illogical situation of divided responsibility in aeronautics, except by the formation of a complete united service dealing with all operations

in the air, and with all the accessory services which that expression implies. A department would have to be formed on the general lines of the Admiralty and War Office, with a full staff, and with full responsibility for war in the air.[16]

Henderson spoke with the authority of the nominal head of the RFC, but from a position which had over the previous year become progressively more isolated from that held by the majority of his senior colleagues. Smuts was probably not aware that Henderson's views were unlikely to command the support of air officers in the field. Furthermore, Cowdray, Smuts's other major source of information, was himself dependent on Henderson, the senior military representative on his Board, for details of RFC policy. Thus, from the beginning, there was little chance of Smuts's findings reflecting the views of much of Britain's larger air command.

Naval opinion was divided, but while the First Sea Lord Jellicoe was opposed to the creation of a new air service, his recently appointed civilian master Sir Eric Geddes eventually came to support the move. Geddes was undoubtedly impressed by the views of Beatty, Jellicoe's successor as commander of the Grand Fleet. Following the collapse of the strategic bombing campaign, naval air policy seemed to have lost its way. Beatty had become frustrated by the RNAS's failure to provide adequate resources for fleet reconnaissance, anti-submarine patrols and offensive maritime air operations. Although his most recent biographer has criticized Beatty's acceptance of the Smuts Report as naive, there was considerable truth in that officer's claim that the existing organization of naval aviation 'kills progress'.[17]

Indeed, the RNAS command itself contributed little to the debate on unification. Naval air administration was dominated not by officers of the like of Trenchard, Brancker or Henderson, but rather by non-aviators, generally selected more for their soundness than for any independence of thought.[18] A body of opinion did remain within the naval air service which would only applaud the creation of a separate air force. During the hiatus between the acceptance of the Smuts Report and the implication of its recommendations, at least one senior officer, Rear-Admiral Mark Kerr, echoed Sueter in pressing the case for the rapid formation of such a service. For much of the critical period of transition, however, the RNAS acted only as a passive spectator to its own demise.

Henderson's memorandum had alluded to 'a considerable force of bombing machines' which would become available for offensive operations early in 1918.[19] It was left to the Air Board to provide Smuts with details of this potential strategic reserve. On 28 July, Cowdray wrote to Smuts about the certainty of a 'surplus aircraft fleet' of 400 to 500 machines being ready for use within the following six months. He further claimed that production, now standing at roughly 1,000 aircraft per month, could be expected to double by the end of 1917, treble by 31 March 1918, and quadruple three months after that.[20] Cowdray, of course, was not himself responsible for these figures, which depended entirely on the calculations already laid before the cabinet by his munitions expert Weir.[21] In view of the inaccuracy of Weir's projections, it is perhaps significant to note that their author shortly emerged as one of the most committed adherents to the strategic vision at which they seemed to hint. Once again, Smuts could only take the evidence presented to him at face value, and draw the inevitable conclusion.

Cowdray's biographer has quite correctly pointed out that his subject did not at this stage support the wartime creation of a separate air service, an undertaking which he believed would cause administrative difficulties unacceptable as long as hostilities continued.[22] What Cowdray did recommend was that the powers of the Air Board be extended to embrace the co-ordination of air policy beyond the reaches of simple procurement, for which purpose the Board 'should now be turned into a permanent Ministry, presumably by Act of Parliament, so as to place it in a position to secure a War Staff of recognized experts'. As regards the new strategic force, Cowdray felt that it should fall only notionally under military control.[23]

It is not necessary to place too much stress on Smuts's own turn of mind in explaining the document he produced. He does not seem to have been exposed at any time before he wrote his report to the military version of air organization as practised by Trenchard in France. Taken together, the memoranda of Henderson and Cowdray represented an authoritative statement of administrative needs and material possibilities. The resulting recipe was further seasoned by the demands for protection and retaliation pressed not only in the newspapers, but also in public petitions to the government.[24] Smuts did not single-handedly bring Britain into the air age; he simply gave coherent form to widely held desires and expectations.

Smuts began his second report by stressing the urgency of the questions involved, and endorsing the general view that the German raids represented the first step in a campaign which might win the war unless rapidly countered. He defined his brief in such a way as to demonstrate that the changes under consideration were far more sweeping than the bombing itself might seem to require. The questions he posed clearly reflected the sort of advice he had received:

1 Shall there be instituted a real Air Ministry responsible for all Air Organization and operations?
2 Shall there be constituted a unified Air Service embracing both the present R.N.A.S. and R.F.C.? And if this second question is answered in the affirmative, the third question arises:
3 How shall the relations of the new Air Service to the Navy and the

Army be determined so that the functions at present discharged for them by the R.N.A.S. and R.F.C. respectively shall continue to be efficiently performed by the new Air Service?

Smuts proceeded with his consideration of these points by reviewing the unhappy history of inter-service co-operation. He went on to discuss the limitations of the Air Board, dismissing it as 'not really a Board, but merely a Conference'. Citing the Board's total dependence on service representatives, Smuts claimed that the lack of a professional staff rendered its authority to discuss questions of policy merely nominal. Under such a restraint, he argued, 'it is useless for the Air Board to embark on a policy of its own, which it could neither originate nor execute under present conditions'.

Having thus illustrated the limitations of the existing system, Smuts claimed that recent events proved that the air service could be used as an 'independent means of war operations'. In what might easily be considered the most important statement of aviation's utility for war issued in Britain to date, Smuts presented a vivid picture of the prospect unveiled by the Gotha raid of 7 July and argued for the immediate creation of a unified and independent air service:

> Unlike artillery, an air fleet can conduct extensive operations far from, and independently of, both army and navy. As far as can at present be foreseen, there is absolutely no limit to the scale of its future independent war use, and the day may not be far off when aerial operations with their devastation of enemy lands and destruction of industrial and populous centres on a vast scale may become the principal operations of war, to which the older forms of military and naval operations may become secondary and subordinate. The subjection of the Air Board and Service could only be justified on the score of their infancy. But that is a disability which time can remove, and in this respect the march of events has been very rapid during the war. In our opinion there is no reason why the Air Board should any longer continue in its present form as practically no more than a Conference room between the older Services, and there is every reason why it should be raised to the status of an independent Ministry in control of its own War Services.

Smuts proceeded to explain that aircraft production was increasing at such a rate that the requirements of naval and military co-operation would soon be met, and a substantial strategic reserve become available which only an independent air authority would be able to use to proper effect. Regarding the effects of this strategic reserve upon the conduct of the war, Smuts drew a picture which must have held a special attraction to the prime minister and many of his colleagues, opposed as they were to

Haig's war of attrition on the Western Front. In the following summer, he argued, the 'air battle front' would be far behind the Rhine, bringing intense and perhaps war-winning pressure to bear on enemy industry, at a time when the army in France was still only moving forward at 'a snail's pace'. The Germans were 'no doubt making vast plans to deal with us in London', and unless the British were quick to make up the ground which had already been lost, their chances of winning the war might well end under a hail of bombs. Smuts rounded off his case by pointing out that manpower resources were short, and that the aircraft, like other mechanized means of war, could bring victory without heavy casualties – once again an argument likely to appeal to political opponents of the war in the trenches of Flanders.[25]

The War Cabinet discussed the Smuts Report on 24 August, and despite some opposition from the military and naval representatives, accepted all of Smuts's recommendations in principle. Smuts himself was made chairman of a new cabinet committee charged with investigating the arrangements necessary to implement the planned unification of the RFC and RNAS.[26] There was nothing surprising about the political acceptance of the Smuts Report: the air situation had become very embarrassing and indeed potentially dangerous, the government was committed to quick action, and Smuts seemed to have produced the necessary solution. While many of Smuts's crucial assumptions were later to prove fallacious, his report appeared at the time to constitute something of a panacea for Britain's air ills, and as such it was accepted.

It has recently been suggested that the Smuts Report was little more than political window dressing, produced to protect the government from the popular backlash set loose by the Gotha raids, but not intended as the first stage in a systematic restructuring of air objectives.[27] While there is little doubt that Smuts's remedy did appeal to the prime minister in particular as a package which might be expected both to defuse the mini-crisis in air policy and to remove control of one part of the nation's war machinery from the grip of the army, it would be a mistake entirely to ignore political awareness of airpower as a factor leading to the decision. The air raids on London placed the government, however briefly, in the frontline, and many of its members were sufficiently nervous of attack from the air seriously to consider drastic organizational remedies.

This is not to say that there were convinced adherents of the barely formed doctrine of strategic airpower within the ranks of the Lloyd George government. A few ministers, most notably Milner, Curzon and Churchill, were certainly air-minded to a limited extent; but the lack of consistent interest in bombing Germany, particularly when the immediate stimulus of German raids on London faded away in 1918, is sufficient proof that the shadow of the bomber was not as yet sufficiently menacing to occupy the political mind to the extent it was to do in the 1930s.[28]

Advocates of all-out bombing operations against German cities tended to occupy peripheral positions on the political stage, and some of them certainly adopted the role of the prophet of airpower for motives that had at least as much to do with personal ambition as with deeply held strategic belief.

While, however, the cabinet was not by any means convinced that aerial armageddon was as likely or as imminent as Smuts had suggested, the Gothas left in their wake a residual fear that they might indeed just prove to be the harbingers of something altogether more menacing. British air intelligence remained relatively poor throughout the war, persistently producing inflated estimates of German strength and distorted interpretations of German intentions.[29] Nowhere was this more apparent than with reference to the enemy's bombing potential, which was not only exaggerated in size, but granted a strategic mission far beyond the imagination of most of its commanders. Even in the last months of the war, British home defence forces stood ready to repel an all-out assault on London of which the German *Bombengeschwadern*, understrength and committed on an almost nightly basis to attacks on military targets in France, could hardly have attempted.[30] In this sense at least, the Smuts plan did not represent a real commitment to the doctrine of strategic air warfare, but rather an effort to provide for the possibility of such a doctrine becoming necessary. Even with the arrival in 1918 of an air administration committed to such a policy, there remained no real impulse to bring the contingency plan into operation as long as the Germans stayed away.

Ironically, the very fact that the momentum towards a concerted strategic effort was never sufficiently strong to threaten existing military or naval operations limited opposition from the quarter where it would have proved most inimical to the smooth process of unification. Even at the time of the first discussions of the Smuts Report, service resistance was slight. Such criticism as was put forward was calculated largely to ensure that the special interests of the army and navy were protected within the new arrangement. Neither the Admiralty nor the War Office could put forward a case for maintaining the status quo which was likely to impress the War Cabinet; neither had ever been very keen to hold responsibility for home air defence, and neither was ready to undertake a bombing campaign for vague strategic reasons. As long as they were guaranteed their own air support requirements, the two services were not disposed to protest too hard at their airmen changing uniforms. Beatty, the commander of the Grand Fleet, considered the unification of air forces to be 'a move in the right direction'.[31] The Army Council was not as enthusiastic, but Brancker at least was convinced it would agree to Smuts's plan from the moment it appeared.[32]

The Smut's Report was based on four main premises: first, that aircraft had come of age as weapons of strategic importance; secondly, that the

Germans appreciated this fact and had begun a campaign designed to bomb Britain into submission; thirdly, that the British aircraft industry had progressed to the point where it was capable of supporting a new bombing campaign as well as extensive army and navy co-operation services; and finally, that the existing air organization would no longer serve to direct the air effort. Each of these premises was to a certain extent mistaken. The truth regarding the first three was at least partially obscured at the time of the report's preparation. The real nature of the German bombing campaign and the shortcomings of the British air production programme have already been discussed, while a final judgement of the strategic efficacy of airpower is best postponed until Britain's own attempt at long-range operations in 1918 has been analyzed. The dismissal of the existing organizational arrangements, however, was based on a faulty evaluation of facts and opinions readily available to Smuts.

Cowdray had argued against the unification of the air services during the war, recommending instead that the Air Board's supervisory powers be extended and consolidated by reforming it as a ministry of state. Such an expedient was more in line with the expectations of the services themselves, and would have represented a continuation of Cowdray's existing policy of expanding his Board's authority to cover those areas of air policy not previously connected with the ancillary needs of the army and navy. There seems little justice in either Smuts's deprecation of the Board's usefulness as a co-ordinating agency, or the official historian's prediction that action along the lines suggested by Cowdray would have resulted only in 'three policies instead of one'.[33] Following the decline of naval interest in strategic bombing in the winter of 1916–17, there was little conflict between naval and military air policy save in the field of aircraft procurement. The first six months of Cowdray's presidency seemed to indicate that the latter could be solved within the framework of the Air Board. That being the case, the two air services could presumably have been left to pursue their air plans in separate theatres without superimposing a new air organization above them.

Such an arrangement would have left open the question of responsibility for strategic bombing. The army, however, had long argued that it was quite willing to undertake the bombing of Germany as soon as the requirements of the ground co-operation war at the front had been met. As the satisfaction of these requirements was a precondition for the strategic bombing plans put forward in the Smuts Report, it seems possible that the RFC could have been left to the task, with general policy decisions particularly as regards targeting being made by a War Cabinet committee, or by the Air Board in its new form as a ministry. The precedent for establishing new departments to deal specifically with matters on the boundaries of existing service responsibilities had already been set: Lloyd George himself had created ministries of labour and shipping control, while the patently successful Ministry of Munitions dated from the middle of the previous war administration.

Quite simply, the questions posed by the Gotha raids might well have been solved within the existing framework of two separate air services, co-ordinated by the Air Board. Smuts's decision to dismantle this organization and create an entirely new one seems an over-reaction based on an inadequate appreciation of the progress made towards a comprehensive air policy during the preceding six to nine months. Until the Gotha raids delivered a shock to the government, the future of British air policy lay with Cowdray's Air Board. The new arrangements which followed represented a break with developments to date, a break which both the experience of British aviation during the rest of the war and the departmental struggles of the inter-war years were to call seriously into question.

Smuts's creation did not seek to dismantle the system in which the army and navy effectively decided and controlled their own air policies and resources. Rather, it imposed a new independent strategic force upon the existing arrangement. This organization depended not on the resources of the army and navy air services, but on a potential material surplus, for its aircraft. When this surplus failed to materialize, the portentously named Independent Force could not call on the army or navy for a share of their resources, even though the personnel of these contingents had been placed in different uniforms. Thus the Royal Air Force represented little more than old wine in new bottles, an organizational innovation which did little to alter the existing priorities of the British air effort. As the following chapter will begin to make clear, even this limited transformation caused a degree of dislocation which might well have destroyed the new force at birth.

Notes

1 War Cabinet 150, min. 9, 30 May 1917; War Cabinet 154, mins 2 and 3, 2 June 1917, PRO, CAB 23/2–3.
2 U. Bialer, *The Shadow of the Bomber. The Fear of Air Attack and British Politics* (London: Royal Historical Society, 1980), *passim*.
3 Cole and Cheesman, *The Air Defence of Britain*, pp. 207–436.
4 Several raids were planned in the summer of 1918 but cancelled at the last moment. See ibid., p. 416.
5 Sir W. Robertson, *Soldiers and Statesmen, 1914–1918*, Vol. 2 (London: Cassell, 1926), p. 17.
6 The most recent study of Lloyd Geroge as a war leader suffers from a narrow approach. See D. R. Woodward, *Lloyd George and the Generals* (Newark, Del.: University of Delaware Press, 1983). The best balanced account remains Guinn, *British Strategy and Politics*.
7 J. Sweetman, 'The Smuts report of 1917: Merely political window-dressing?', *The Journal of Strategic Studies*, vol. 4, no. 2 (1981), pp. 152–74; W. K.

Hancock, *Smuts. The Sanguine Years, 1870–1919* (Cambridge: Cambridge University Press, 1962), *passim*.

8 War Cabinet 150, min. 9, 30 May 1917; War Cabinet 154, mins 2 and 3, 2 June 1917; War Cabinet 163, min. 7, 14 June 1917; War Cabinet 173, min. 25, 2 July 1917, PRO, CAB 23/2–3.

9 *The Times*, 8 July 1917.

10 Henderson to Robertson, 14 July 1917, PRO, AIR 1/512/16/3/61.

11 PRO, AIR 1/2267/209/70/41; Cole and Cheesman, *The Air Defence of Britain*, pp. 209–19.

12 PRO, AIR 9/69.

13 Trenchard to Henderson, 9 July 1917, Trenchard Papers, MFC 76/1/76.

14 Trenchard to GHQ, 15 July 1917, PRO, AIR 1/522/16/12/5.

15 Amery to Smuts, 9 July 1917, Smuts Papers, Cambridge University Library, 680.

16 Air defence, aerial operations and organization of the air services, 19 July 1917, PRO, CAB 21/27.

17 Beatty to Geddes, 22 August 1917, PRO, ADM 116/1606; S. Roskill, *Admiral of the Fleet Earl Beatty. The Last Naval Hero. An Intimate Biography* (New York: Atheneum, 1981), pp. 239–40.

18 Roskill, *Documents Relating to the Naval Air Service*, p. xi.

19 Cowdray to Smuts, 28 July 1917, Pearson Papers, Science Museum, A.9.

20 ibid.

21 War Cabinet 179, min. 6, 9 July 1917, PRO, CAB 23/3.

22 Young, *Member for Mexico*, p. 207.

23 Cowdray to Smuts, 28 July 1917, Pearson Papers, Science Museum, A.9.

24 See for example G.T. 1437, Demand for reprisals from Cardiff, 12 July 1917; G.T. 1514, Demand for reprisals from the League of Londoners, 23 July 1917, PRO, CAB 24/20–21.

25 G.T. 1658, Second report of the committee on air organization and home defence against air raids, 17 August 1917, PRO, CAB 24/22.

26 War Cabinet 223, min. 12, 24 August 1917, PRO, CAB 23/3.

27 Sweetman, 'The Smuts report of 1917', pp. 152–74.

28 Bialer, *The Shadow of the Bomber, passim*.

29 See for example, Bombing strength of Germany on the Western Front, 31 August 1918, PRO, AIR 1/1578/204/80/109.

30 Only after the German withdrawal from Flanders in October 1918 were the British prepared to reallocate home defence fighters to the Western Front: G.T. 5999, correspondence on the posting of home defence aircraft to France, 9–15 October 1918, PRO, CAB 24/66.

31 Beatty to Geddes, 15 August 1917, PRO, ADM 116/1606.

32 Brancker to Trenchard, August 1917, Trenchard Papers, MFC 76/1/16.

33 *WIA*, Vol. 6, p. 19.

[9]

Unification and Dislocation

The War Cabinet's approval of the Smuts Report on 24 August 1917 did not produce an immediate revolution in air policy. There was a lull in the air war over Britain following the final German day raid on the southeast coast on 22 August, and although Smuts's new committee began to investigate unification measures, there seemed a real chance that Lloyd George and his colleagues might not push their initial decision to its logical conclusion. It was only the renewal of the German bombing campaign under cover of night, and in particular an intensive period of raiding in late September, which reactivated the government and set the process of unification permanently under way. In the meantime, however, the Smuts Report had already set tremors running through the air command which unbalanced its organization to such an extent as ultimately to prevent the new Royal Air Force from enjoying strong central direction for the remainder of the war.

It is important to realize that the administrations of both the RFC and the RNAS had begun to show signs of instability and lack of direction before the Gotha raids placed any additional strain upon them. In each service's case, the real damage was done by the emergence of the army in the field as the effective arbiter of air priorities in the winter of 1916–17. By the following summer, neither the Directorate of Military Aeronautics nor the Naval Air Department was making a significant contribution to the control of the air effort, a factor of some significance in evaluating the relative enthusiasm each manifested for the creation of a new service.

Sir David Henderson, Director General of Military Aeronautics and titular head of the RFC, had become progressively more isolated from the remainder of the military air command since early 1916. Although his stand on the reorganization of aircraft supply proved in many ways far-sighted, it had met with little approval from his colleagues, who generally took the narrow view of army air organization. This situation, combined with an obvious decline in Henderson's health, rendered an attempt at his removal inevitable, and there is some evidence to suggest that such a move was considered as early as September 1916.[1]

Derby, Secretary of State for War after the change of government in the winter, considered Henderson 'a good man at his job' but at the same time 'slow'.[2] On 21 April 1917 he wrote confidentially to Haig explaining that he was 'not at all happy about the management of the R.F.C. on this side of the channel'. Claiming that a director of greater vigour than the tired Henderson was required, he asked if Trenchard could be spared for the post. Haig was not willing to part with his air commander and would only consider an arrangement whereby Trenchard would hold his post as GOC, RFC in the Field concurrently with that of DGMA. Derby quite correctly did not believe that this compromise was practicable, but returned to the issue at the end of May. A further rebuff from Haig put a temporary end to the matter, but it was clear that Henderson's days at the War Office were numbered.[3]

If the army air command was suffering by the spring of 1917 from a divergence of opinion as to the future of the air effort, its naval counterpart could almost be said to have lost its way altogether. The relative failures of both the Churchill–Fisher and Balfour–Jackson administrations to find a secure niche for the RNAS in the naval establishment had prevented the emergence of a coherent air policy. While the purely maritime possibilities of aviation had been inadequately explored, the creation of a land-based force, oriented towards offensive action against land targets, had led only to a wasteful and ultimately unsuccessful competition with the army. By the first half of 1917, the RNAS was devoting a great deal of energy to supporting its erstwhile rival, the RFC in the Field .

As a result of the Admiralty's surrender to combined army–Air Board pressure, five naval fighter squadrons were serving under Trenchard's command by the summer of 1917. In terms of the quality of pilots and equipment, these units were as good, if not better, than the best RFC fighting squadrons. Like their army counterparts, however, they suffered steady attrition as a result of their commitment to intensive offensive patrol work. Unfortunately, the RNAS replacement programme was less able to absorb such losses than its far larger military counterpart. As early as 20 May, Trenchard noted that his naval squadrons were falling below strength, and by mid-June the Admiralty was forced to admit that it had 'become impossible to keep the squadrons up to their maximum strength at present without impeding the Naval work of the Royal Naval Air Service'.[4]

The Ypres campaign came close to ending naval assistance altogether. On 21 August, Trenchard reported that naval units under his command were 27 pilots and 15 aircraft under strength, and asked if the position was likely to improve. The day before, however, the First Sea Lord had informed the War Office: 'There is absolutely no place from which I can draw pilots and machines for bringing the RNAS Squadrons up to establishment, except by taking them from Dunkerque.'[5] The Dunkirk command was at this time undertaking its own offensive against German naval establishments on the Belgian coast and could certainly not be depended upon as a reserve for the field contingent without further prejudicing the navy's own air effort. Under the strain of recurrent casualties and associated shortages of men and machines, naval morale began to decline. At the end of September there was an ugly incident when an RNAS unit, which had compiled an enviable record in the fighting earlier in the year, first failed to press home an attack on a German aerodrome, and then refused to undertake the mission afresh.[6] In the end, the Admiralty took the only course left open to it and withdrew some units from Trenchard's command in order to maintain the remainder on a more adequate footing. When 1917 drew to a close, only two RNAS squadrons remained attached to the RFC in the Field.[7]

With the Grand Fleet pressing for the expansion of its ship-borne air contingent, the Mediterranean commands for aircraft for convoy duty, and the Vice-Admiral, Dover Patrol for the means both to combat the strengthened German air presence over the Channel and to attack the naval bases at Zeebrugge and Ostend, it is not surprising that the opposition mounted to the formation of a new air force was not backed up by Beatty and his fellow active service commanders.[8] While senior officers both inside and outside the naval air command laid plans for a more intensive use of airpower at sea throughout the second half of 1917, the period of uncertainty following the acceptance of the Smuts Report saw little change in the RNAS hierarchy. The independence of the naval air service had been curtailed in the Balfour-Jackson era, and the successors of Sueter and Vaughan-Lee were left to await the arrival of the Royal Air Force by an Admiralty confident that the existing command could be depended upon to foster naval interests even after it had been placed in new uniforms. The Army Council was not so sanguine about the future. Despite the fact that RFC officers were always likely to dominate the new service, the army undertook a series of desperate expedients to ensure that the interests of the BEF would remain supreme, whatever organizational changes 1918 brought in its train.

The first consequence of the approval of the Smuts Report was Henderson's departure from the Directorate of Military Aeronautics. As the major military participant in the discussions leading up to the publication of the report, the DGMA was the obvious choice to assist Smuts in overseeing its implementation. The replacement of Henderson brought a new feature of internal army politics clearly to the surface. Feeling in the Army Council had been running high against military airmen for some months. Having generally supported the RFC command in its squabbles with the navy during 1916, the Council had woken up to the possibility of the developing independence of some airmen moving the air service dangerously far away from the rest of the army.[9] There is no doubt that Henderson's support of the removal of aviation from military control contributed to the Council's acquiescence to his transfer away from the War Office. Brancker was probably correct in assuming that he, with considerably less justification, had been tarred with the same brush.[10] The Army Council seemed determined to rescue something from a situation which threatened to undermine its *de facto* control over air policy. To this end it attempted to insert Major-General Sir John Capper as Henderson's successor and Brancker's new superior. Capper, lately a divisional commander in France, had no experience of aviation since his days as prewar commander of the Royal Engineers' balloon detachment. Like the reigning chiefs of the RNAS, he had evidently been appointed because he could be expected to follow the wishes of his parent service.

Brancker was understandably incensed by the appointment. On the day he heard the news he wrote to Trenchard:

> Evidently I am considered perfectly useless and I propose to get out of this job as soon as I can. It is a little too hot to be expected to educate a D.G.M.A. whose knowledge of aviation is limited to balloons of five years ago!
>
> I really think I'd better try to get back to soldiering, for the only job in front of me now is bottlewasher to David [Henderson] again when the Air Ministry is formed.

The next day Brancker wrote again, demanding to know if the army in France had anything to do with the appointment, reasserting his desire to leave the Directorate, and complaining: 'It really is a little trying to be discredited and disgraced in the eyes of the whole army and my friends because I haven't got a sufficiently bald head or pot-belly for the Army Council.' Always inclined to express his views forcefully, Brancker also wrote to Derby in a similar vein.[11]

Brancker's resistance put the army in a difficult position. With Capper a relative novice in the ways of military aviation, it would obviously have been unwise to dispense with Brancker's services as well as those of his former chief. Nor was Brancker without supporters outside the War Office. Curzon, for one, opposed Capper's appointment from inside the War Cabinet.[12] The Capper affair demonstrated that political interest in aviation had developed to such an extent that the army could no longer expect to arrange appointments simply to serve departmental interests. Lord Hugh Cecil, serving as a staff officer in the RFC in Britain, wrote to Smuts pointing out that the War Office's decision 'transgresses the main principle on which the creation of our air service depends – that aviation is a thing *sui generis* which cannot be efficiently controlled by soldiers or sailors'.[13] Cecil, along with Sir John Simon, who joined Trenchard's Headquarters in France in the autumn of 1917, was to be heard from again in the course of the reorganization of the air command. Aviation, for so long subject only to service control, was now to be ordered with increasing reference to the opinions of a wider audience.

Within a week of the issue emerging the proposed appointment of Capper was a dead letter, notwithstanding an attempted compromise by Derby which would have kept Henderson, Brancker and Capper all nominally within the air command without any clear delineation of authority.[14] Brancker, whose position had been reinforced by letters of support from the army in France, had a private interview with Derby, and while the former was given a gentle reprimand, he was allowed to stay on as Deputy Director.[15] Brancker underlined his victory in another letter to Derby pointing out that the commander of the flying corps must himself be an aviator and that a number of senior officers were currently to be found who might be considered eminently qualified for high administrative authority.[16]

A second attempt at overhauling the RFC command structure in London followed a little over a month after the first had failed. On this occasion the military chiefs had prepared their ground more carefully, and there was no chance of successful resistance. In early October, Henderson's departure from the Directorate of Military Aeronautics was confirmed. His successor was Major-General J. M. Salmond, most recently GOC of the RFC's training division. The office of Deputy Director was temporarily abolished (it was later filled by Brigadier-General E. L. Ellington, like Salmond a future Chief of the Air Staff) and Brancker was dispatched to take command of aviation in Egypt and Palestine. As this organization comprised little more than one under-sized brigade, which had its own commander (by coincidence the new DGMA's elder brother), there can be little doubt that Brancker, who had all but run the central office of military aviation in Britain for most of the war, had simply been got rid of.[17] His last bitter letter to Trenchard is apt comment on the atmosphere of doubt and recrimination prevalent in the military air command in the aftermath of the Smuts Report:

They have got me alright at last ...
    It is very clever, and I don't know how far you have helped them indirectly – Wully [Sir William Robertson, the CIGS] (backed by you) is up against the Air Ministry – he *thinks* I am an ardent supporter of it (I am not very much really) – His first effort was to try to push Capper in – I frustrated that and got myself disliked in consequence.
    This is a brilliant stroke. He has never seen Salmond and knows nothing about him; but he gets rid of D. H. and sidetracks me with one blow – and I have no case against the move this time – except that

I was definitely told the reason I could not go on to the Army Council was that I was too junior! [Salmond was more junior still.] It makes me smile – Of course your everlasting criticism of everything at home has given them a good lever – and as I already told you, everybody's sins have eventually fallen on my head.[18]

Salmond, who had started the war as a major commanding one of the RFC's original squadrons, was a highly competent officer who would eventually rise to the top of the Royal Air Force, succeeding Trenchard as Chief of the Air staff in 1929–30.[19] In 1917 he was only 36 and like so many of his colleagues in the air service had little general administrative experience. Salmond did not like his new position and, even when Ellington, a trained staff officer, was brought in as his deputy, tended to rely on his former commander Trenchard for support. Indeed, it was indicative of the latter officer's all but ubiquitous influence that almost all of the young brigadier-generals and major-generals holding important posts in the air administration looked back to their apprenticeships under Trenchard for inspiration in the execution of their duties. This being the case, the future of the new air service would depend very heavily on Trenchard's far-from-assured support.

While Salmond proved as resolute a defender of the interests of the army as any, he was certainly no pliable instrument. When Lord Rothermere was appointed designate Air Minister later in the year, he complained that Salmond was 'small', 'no good' and 'impertinent'.[20] In reality, the latter was simply manifesting the disenchantment felt by most of the established army air command at the prospect of serving in the new air force. It was obvious that Salmond had been introduced as a stopgap and would not stay in command when the Royal Air Force was eventually formed. He did not show himself disposed to wait for the end and talked to Trenchard of resigning. On 18 December this evoked the Olympian response, 'You cannot resign in war'.[21] Three months and a day later the unsatisfactory state of the reformed air command was to drive Trenchard to attempt precisely that.

The whole military air organization was seriously disturbed by the changes and rumoured changes attendant on the unification of the air services. Salmond's complaint to Trenchard in early December that he was being kept in the dark over proposed appointments and as a result felt as if he was 'standing on water' was indicative of a loss of momentum and purpose regarding aviation right through the civil–military edifice.[22] More than a month after Smut's recommendations had first been accepted, one of the more strident advocates of unification could still complain with considerable justification at 'the real mischief of having at the crisis of the war our air administration without a head and under a divided and mutually jealous control'.[23] At the root of all this uncertainty stood the vexed problem of the selection of the civil and military heads of the new service. In order then to develop a deeper appreciation of the crisis of reorganization, it is necessary to return to the War Cabinet's efforts to see the Smuts Report through to fruition.

Following the War Cabinet's acceptance of his recommendations, Smuts had been appointed to chair a new committee to inquire into the precise measures necessary to implement unification.[24] Henderson was seconded to act as his assistant and undertook most of the basic administrative and organizational work. On 21 September the War Cabinet decided as a result of complaints from the army regarding the uncertainty of future aerial operations to appoint the seemingly omniscient Smuts chairman of a newly constituted Aerial Operations Committee. This body, composed of Smuts, Derby, Geddes, Churchill and Cowdray, was charged with settling the matter of priority in the allocation of air resources to the existing military and naval campaigns and to the planned bombing of Germany.[25]

By early September, however, the campaign to form a united air service was in danger of losing momentum. The daylight Gotha raids, which had provided the initial impetus for change, had ended after a costly and ineffectual attack on coastal targets on 22 August. Between that date and 24 September, *Kampfgeschwader* III returned only twice by night, reaching the capital on the second occasion, but causing only slight damage. With aircraft production already showing signs of falling short of expectations, the War Cabinet seemed likely to give up plans to create an independent strategic bombing force in the face of continued army concern for its tactical air contingent, even though these plans represented the major justification for undertaking reorganization in the first place.[26] The administrative difficulties of amalgamation, not least the selection of a responsible minister, also seemed to promise a long period of readjustment, and convinced Smuts at least of the need for a full-blown interim controlling body.[27] As late as the beginning of October, the appearance of the Royal Air Force while the war lasted remained far from certain.

It has been argued that a strongly-worded memorandum, produced on 11 October by Rear-Admiral Mark Kerr, finally brought the War Cabinet's interest back to strategic bombing and the organizational reforms necessary to undertake it. Kerr, a recent appointee to the Air Board, was undoubtedly a more dynamic officer than most of his contemporaries in the senior echelons of the RNAS. In language reminiscent of Smuts's report, he reiterated the view that Britain had been forced into a race to build a bombing force, and argued that this race and the war itself would be lost if immediate action was not taken. Kerr's memorandum, however, can hardly have done anything but confirm the War Cabinet in an opinion which it had already formed. By the time it appeared, a renewal of the

German bombing offensive had injected fresh urgency into a situation which in any case was beginning to attract the attention of far more influential supporters of a unified air service.[28]

Between 24 September and 2 October, the Germans launched six raids on Britain. Only one failed to reach London, and although casualties and damage were relatively light, the simple frequency of the attacks was sufficient to convince many that they were about to become almost a routine feature of the war. As a result, October saw the heaviest concentration of government attention on air policy of the entire war. At the beginning of the month the War Cabinet discussed aviation at no fewer than six consecutive meetings, producing a flurry of quick decisions which set aviation irrevocably on the road to independence and a renewed long-range bombing commitment.[29] One of the prime motivators of the push for immediate action was Milner, who, encouraged by Weir, Baird and Cecil, told his colleagues: 'The whole question is so important, future developments in the Air are surrounded by so many unknown possibilities, that I feel that we cannot accept with a light heart the responsibility of continuing with the ill-defined organization, which is all we at present appear to possess.'[30] A similar message came from Geddes, the First Lord of the Admiralty, who argued that if a fully-fledged air ministry could not rapidly be created it was necessary that 'an interim arrangement ...should be come to and should be given executive functions as early as possible'.[31]

By 15 October the War Cabinet had decided that 'immediate arrangements should be made for the conduct of long-range offensive operations against German towns where factories existed for the production of munitions of all kinds', and had set up a new Air Policy Committee composed of Smuts, Derby, Geddes and Cowdray 'to advise the War Cabinet on all questions relating to air policy'.[32] In early October, in response to the War Cabinet's orders, three bombing squadrons, two army and one navy, were moved south to Ochey (near Nancy at the southern end of the Western Front) to form the nucleus of a strategic strike force. On 17 October, 11 aircraft attacked industrial targets in Saarbrucken to get the campaign under way.[33]

The British long-range bombing campaign did not achieve real momentum until the following year, but in London the preparatory work for the formation of the new air service finally began to accelerate. At one time in October, no fewer than four different committees, all under Smuts's chairmanship and composed of very much the same collection of ministers and aviation experts, were in existence at the same time. The Air Raids Committee was responsible for passive and active defence measures against German attacks; the Air Reorganization Committee dealt with the constitution of the new air ministry; the War Priorities Committee (the successor to the Aerial Operations Committee) was charged with all questions of priority regarding the production of munitions, particularly aircraft; and the Air Policy Committee held the general brief of advising the War Cabinet on all matters relating to air policy.[34]

The Air Policy Committee, the most important of these bodies as regards the evolution of air strategy, met six times between 16 October and 30 January. Its discussions were concerned almost entirely with the long-range bombing campaign against German cities. These discussions made it clear that no simple recipe for a strike force either existed or was likely to exist without a drastic reordering of aerial priorities. Difficulties were already emerging regarding the provision of an adequate number of bombers of sufficient performance to make intrusions into German air space a worthwhile experiment. Problems also arose with the control of the new force which, in its existing guise, was an army formation, commanded by the former chief of Trenchard's Headquarters Wing with the RFC in the Field, and still very much under the sway of the last-named organization.

Both Trenchard's evidence before the committee and a memorandum prepared by Henderson entitled 'Progress of Aerial Offensive' indicated that the bombing campaign could not begin in earnest until the summer of 1918.[35] While hopes for a large reserve of modern bombing aircraft had not yet been totally deflated, the committee became increasingly preoccupied with obtaining a drastic reallocation of resources to help with the expansion of the bombing effort. It was indicative of the Air Policy Committee's concentration on such material concerns that little real progress was made with the formulation of a strategic policy to guide the new bombing force in its operations. Milner's October memorandum had expressed well-founded concern at the lack of a clearly defined set of objectives and questioned the efficacy of unthinking retaliatory action. The Air Policy Committee did nothing to provide answers to the questions he had raised, leaving the RAF to embark upon its career without established strategic direction. In the absence of any sense of purpose beyond that of simply dropping bombs on German soil, the Ochey Wing, and its successor the Independent Force, were easily diverted to objectives other than those for which they had first been created. Both bodies remained under the influence of the army command in France, a command which was no more interested in establishing an aerial presence across the Rhine in 1918 than it had been in 1916.

As the old air administration at home gradually atrophied, the new united organization evolved from a host of committees to take its place. The conduct of the air war at the front went on largely unaffected by this process, except for the removal of three squadrons to form the nucleus of the long-range bombing force. As the time for the actual formation of the new air command approached, however, the vexed question of who was actually to direct the air arm along its poorly defined course threatened to bring the whole edifice down in ruins.

Unfortunately, neither Smuts nor Cowdray, at first glance the obvious candidates, were considered eligible to undertake cabinet responsibility for a new air ministry. Smuts, in any case, would not allow himself to be considered for the post.[36] Cowdray's newspaper the *Westminster Gazette* had published an account of the prime minister's alleged fear of air attacks in September.[37] While this incident can hardly have endeared him to his political master, it is important to realize that his appointment as president of the Air Board had never been seen as an apprenticeship for a ministry.[38] Churchill, once considered as a candidate, was now established at the Ministry of Munitions, and although Milner inclined towards Weir, Lloyd George was thinking less in terms of established aeronautical expertise than of overall political expedience in his own search for an air minister.[39]

In early November the press magnate Lord Northcliffe returned to London from a mission to the United States. Northcliffe, perhaps the most powerful and least stable of Britain's newspaper owners, had taken a periodic interest in aviation since the days of the Wright brothers, and had generally lent the support of his publications to any inquiry into the state of the air effort.[40] With the Passchendaele campaign a running sore in the government's side, he seemed on the point of launching a campaign against Lloyd George's conduct of the war.[41] Northcliffe had always tended to support the services against their political masters; the availability of a new cabinet post appeared to present Lloyd George with a unique opportunity to get him into the government, thus silencing a potentially dangerous critic by pandering to one of his special interests.

Northcliffe quickly gave Lloyd George opportunity to regret his decision. On 15 November the prime minister approached Northcliffe privately to sound him out on the prospect of his becoming Britain's first Secretary of State for Air. Northcliffe apparently gave a favourable response, but the following day published an incredible letter of refusal in *The Times*, claiming that he could best serve the nation by maintianing his position as an independent critic of the government.[42] Cowdray, who had not been consulted prior to Lloyd George's overture to Northcliffe, was naturally offended and resigned as President of the Air Board on the same day. The prime minister had no real answer to Cowdray's charge that 'it ought not to have been left to me to receive from Lord Northcliffe's letter to *The Times* the first intimation that you desire a change at the Air Ministry', although it might be noted that Cowdray himself had not at the time been given ministerial rank. The explanation Lloyd George eventually proffered, that he wanted to exploit Northcliffe's recently acquired knowledge of aerial developments in the United States, hardly rings true.[43] The ultimate proof of his real objective lies in the appointment of Northcliffe's younger brother Lord Rothermere, a newspaper owner in his own right, to the post Northcliffe had spurned. As Ernest Lane, secretary to Smuts, explained to the latter's wife:

> The reason why he [Rothermere] was appointed was that Lloyd George found that it was highly necessary to gather round him in these ministerial appointments a certain number of men who had a large circle of influence and carried also some Press influence, so that when he had any project in mind and wanted to carry out some particular line of policy he would have the Press at his disposal to put his views before the public. You see that Mr. Asquith still is regarded by the Liberals as their particular man, and therefore he has the Liberal Press, and the Tories look on Bonar Law as their man, and while they support Lloyd George they would always be prepared if Bonar Law were to start in and try to be Premier to support him, and thus you can see that Lloyd George's Press is a very weak one. For these reasons he has had to gather round him in his appointments men like Rothermere, and one or two others, who can supply his requirements.[44]

Although Rothermere was to serve his master loyally enough, he was to prove a disastrous choice. His failings were not to be revealed in full until early 1918, but even before he took up his full responsibilities, he showed himself to be a difficult colleague. He was almost immediately on bad terms with the caretaker DGMA Salmond. Furthermore, his contribution to the selection of his service partner, the Chief of the Air Staff, was to go a long way towards making that appointment as unsatisfactory as his own.

The choice of candidates for the senior professional appointment lay between Henderson and Tenchard. Of these two, Henderson was on the surface the more likely candidate. As Smuts's main service adviser, he was the major military architect of the new service, a qualification to which he could add a wealth of experience in both administration and civil–military relations which his competitor could not match. Even Trenchard later admitted that he was easily the more qualified of the two.[45] Henderson, however, had aroused the suspicions of the army hierarchy through his close connection with an organizational reform which seemed to threaten military air interests. He was also isolated from most of his colleagues, did not command any real reputation within the RFC, and seems almost to have been considered by those who did not know him as a spent force unlikely to inject vigour into a new service.

Trenchard, on the other hand, commanded almost unequalled respect both inside and ouside the Flying Corps, having moulded Britain's most important air command, the RFC in the Field, into one of the most frequently acclaimed military institutions. Most of the officers who would hold posts of responsibility within the new air organization were in one way or another his protégés. In political terms alone, the administration could hardly afford not to make Trenchard Chief of the Air Staff. Unfortunately, both Trenchard's and Haig's dislike of the planned appointment, and the clumsy manner in which the change was ultimately forced upon them, turned Trenchard's presence in London from a potential asset to a disadvantage which threatened the future of the RAF before its formation was complete.

Whatever Trenchard's qualifications as long-time senior operational commander, there were disturbing portents in his single-minded domination of the RFC in France which might have suggested that his energy and determination would not easily be harnessed within the entirely different environment of Whitehall. The manner of his appointment would, in any event, have infuriated even a man of less well developed views on the subject of political perfidy. Trenchard did not want to leave the field command he had done so much to make what it was; Haig was only willing to let him go home if he could simultaneously retain his post at GHQ.[46] If politicians were at the bottom of Trenchard's moral hierarchy, Haig was at the top. Nonetheless, Rothermere, with the co-operation of his brother Northcliffe, tried to use Trenchard's devotion to Haig to blackmail him into becoming Chief of the Air Staff, threatening to launch a press campaign against Haig if Trenchard would not return to London.[47]

Trenchard left France in December to take up a post he did not want, already prepared, one suspects, to find that the new arrangement would not work. His place as GOC, RFC in the Field was taken by Salmond whose old post as DGMA had become redundant. Thus British aviation faced a new year in which more was to be expected of it than ever before with an operational commander who had not served at the front since early 1916, a chief of staff who had never been enthusiastic about either his post or the organizational change that had created it, and a political head who rapidly showed himself to be endowed with neither the tact nor the experience to handle such a difficult situation.

Although the war had less than eleven months to run, the dawn of 1918 did not find the soon-to-be victorious allies in a happy position. The prospects for British aviation were as uncertain as those of the allied cause. The air services had weathered the storms of the preceding year with a fair degree of success, but it remained to be seen whether the new air organization and the policies associated with it would stand the test of operational application. The Air Force (Constitution) Bill was passed in November 1917, but the Royal Air Force itself did not come formally into being until 1 April 1918. With many senior airmen opposed to the new arrangement, and with civil–military bickering already disrupting the workings of the Air Council, the future of the new air service remained in doubt.

The Air Council, charged with implementing the changes embodied in the government legislation and then overseeing the administration of the RAF, formally took over the remnants of the Air Board and the army and navy air commands at the beginning of 1918. Under Rothermere's presidency, the council began to work its way through an extensive programme of organizational arrangements in a series of twice-weekly meetings. The schedule was an onerous one, not least because of the difficulties encountered in meeting such requirements as discipline and seniority, hitherto subject to separate service practices.[48] Even office space was hard to find in war-stretched London, a proposal to house the Air Ministry in the British Museum provoking a predictable storm of resistance.[49]

The difficulties of carving a niche for the Air Ministry were compounded by the low priority generally accorded the air effort in governmental deliberations. With German air raids no longer concentrating ministerial attention as forcibly as in the previous autumn (three raids in December, two in January, two in February and one in March), and all the major decisions apparently made, the air service was generally crowded off the War Cabinet agenda by more pressing matters. This trend was probably accelerated by Rothermere's lack of political prestige and isolation within the cabinet. The Secretary of State for the Royal Air Force was an infrequent participant at War Cabinet meetings – indeed, even when air policy did appear on the agenda, he was frequently not invited to attend. Aviation was discussed at sixteen of the seventy War Cabinet meetings held in the first three months of 1918, but Rothermere was only present at six of these.[50]

Eventually, most of the problems attendant on the establishment of the new ministry were solved. On 8 January it was finally decided to call the new service the Royal Air Force, and on 5 March the date for the RAF's formation was set as the first day in April (the Order in Council transferring the personnel of the old services to the new was passed on 27 March).[51] In the meantime a 20 per cent increase in establishment had been approved, and a formal division of responsibility within the new air command agreed upon within the Council.[52]

Had either the top civilian post or its military equivalent been filled by a different man, the first Air Council should have survived. Both Rothermere and Trenchard were able men blessed with just those qualities of energy and initiative the air command in Britain had so often lacked in the past. Neither, however, worked well as part of a team and, as early as February, it was clear that the two together comprised a disastrous combination. Rothermere was at least as difficult a man as his more famous elder brother. His rise to power in the frenetic world of the great London newspaper proprietors fitted him more for rule by decree than administration by committee. Under the severe pressure of his first months in office, his brittle temperament, already suffering as a result of the fatal wounding of a favourite son in France, began to show signs of giving way altogether.[53]

Trenchard was no more inclined to work in a dual harness. His two-year tenure as GOC, RFC in the Field, during which he had ruled his command as if it was his private fief, had served to rigidify Trenchard's single-minded ideas on the exercise of authority. His letters home had often featured explicit references to the need for him to become sole arbiter of air policy, and he was not long in seeking such a mandate as Chief of the Air Staff.[54] Trenchard's unsuitability as Rothermere's service partner had been rendered more acute by the clumsy manner of his appointment. Even in January, Trenchard was telling Haig that Rothermere was 'quite ignorant of the needs of workings of the Air Services' and expressing his conviction that the force 'cannot last as an independent ministry, and that air units must again return to army and navy'.[55]

Trenchard expected to be Rothermere's premier adviser on all matters of policy. The latter, poorly versed in the intricacies of departmental administration, seemed more inclined to treat his senior air officer as he might a more pliable newspaper editor. By the middle of March, Rothermere's habit of dealing directly with some of Trenchard's fractious junior colleagues without reference to him had drained the latter's shallow reserve of patience to the bottom. On 18 March Trenchard wrote Rothermere questioning whether he retained his confidence:

> I would now point out that the failures and shortcomings and delays of the past were supposed to be due to these very methods, and there is no doubt that this is the case. I would further point out that I was appointed Chief of the Air Staff, and as I am responsible to you, I am your adviser on these matters and I am able and willing to obtain for you all the information you desire. I am far from denying that you have a perfect right to see whom you like, but at the same time if you have not sufficient confidence in me even to tell me what is happening in the branches of my own department I consider, and I feel sure that you will agree with me, that the situation created is an impossible one.[56]

Rothermere did not agree, and, having dismissed Trenchard's complaints as 'unnecessary', proceeded to lecture him on the right of political heads of department 'to confer at any time they like with whomsoever they please without consultation with their Chief of Staff or anyone else'. With regard to Trenchard's own advice, Rothermere cautioned, 'I cannot regard the advice of any of the members of the Air Council as pontifical', and that 'it is impossible in the early days of a new service, for a Secretary of State to accept the advice of any professional adviser entirely without demur'.[57]

On 19 March, the same day in which he received Rothermere's rebuff,

Trenchard tendered his resignation.[58] According to Trenchard's own account, he had a private interview with his chief after the letter arrived. Rothermere told him that he himself would be resigning in a few weeks and asked him if he would be willing to withdraw his own resignation in the light of this knowledge. Trenchard did not believe him and refused to go back on his decision, but when the Germans broke through on the Somme two days later he was persuaded to let the matter rest until the crisis had been surmounted.[59] On 13 April, however, with the situation in France still far from promising, Trenchard's resignation was suddenly accepted. Rothermere's extraordinary letter revealed the failings of its author at least as clearly as those of its recipient:

I now accept your resignation tendered to me on the 19th March.

I cannot say I do so with any particular reluctance. Every man is the best judge of what he does but I believe your act in resigning your post of Chief of Staff twelve days before myself and the large staff here were going into action to accomplish the gigantic task of the fusion of the Royal Naval Air Service and the Royal Flying Corps is an unparalleled incident in the public life of this country.

Two days ago you reproached me for not accepting your resignation when proffered and suggested I had temporized. It is true. I could do nothing else. I was filled with profound anxiety lest your resignation might become public and rumour with its thousand tongues might allege you had resigned in protest against some policy of mine which would be disastrous to the interests of the 25,000 officers and 140,000 men who were just going to become the Royal Air Force.

Under such circumstances your resignation might have jeopardized the whole scheme of amalgamation on which I and many others had been working night and day for some months. I can only attribute it to instability of purpose, which I have observed in you on several occasions recently, and which, in my opinion, is due to the overstrain and work of the last three years.

For anything you have done since I have been here I wish most cordially to thank you.[60]

As Beaverbrook later pointed out, the delays and secrecy attending the acceptance of Trenchard's resignation had been occasioned by fears that the early revelation of the antagonism within the Air Ministry might be used by the pro-military opposition against the Lloyd George administration.[61] When the crisis did break, the anti-government press took just such a line, connecting Trenchard's departure with the earlier losses of Jellicoe and Robertson, and observing: 'The list is steadily growing of acknowledged masters of their craft for whose services in the crisis of our fate the Government has no serious use'.[62] The inevitable casualty of the resulting inquest was Rothermere, already isolated and unpopular, who found himself exposed to attack in the Commons by members whose position as RAF staff officers left them in little doubt as to where their loyalties lay.

The parliamentary campaign against Rothermere centred around two men, Sir John Simon and Lord Hugh Cecil. Simon, a member of Trenchard's staff since the preceding autumn, seems to have fallen under the latter's spell. Although not unaware of Trenchard's failings, he took the view that 'Lord Rothermere, without real knowledge and with a low standard of both manners and truthfulness, vexed him beyond endurance'.[63] Cecil, who had already shown himself a supporter of a strong, unified air force, clearly felt that Rothermere was not up to his job, and made his removal his first object.[64]

Rothermere, who had retired ill to the country, was particularly offended to have junior officers of his own service attack him in the House, and did not accept Simon's explanation of his freedom of action as a member of parliament.[65] The attacks made on him were sufficient to confirm Rothermere in his desire to resign. Fortunately for the government, he was persuaded to withdraw the first draft of his resignation, which contained ill-considered attacks on several of his political antagonists, and to substitute another referring only to his bereavement and the decline in his health.[66] Rothermere was promised a viscountcy, as much to keep him from reopening the matter at a later date as for any service rendered to the nation. In private letters to Bonar Law and Sykes (Trenchard's successor as Chief of the Air Staff), Rothermere penned a typically unhappy postscript to his time in office. To the former he wrote that Trenchard's 'dull, unimaginative mind ... would within twelve months have brought death and damnation to the Air Force'.[67] To the latter, no friend of Trenchard in any case, he sounded a similar note of discord:

> In getting rid of the late C.A.S. I flatter myself I did a great public service. The mere thought of the Air Service being in the hands of anyone without precision, elasticity of outlook and receptivity of mind caused me grave anxiety. Starting on such a basis there was no possible hope of the great Air Force being what I am now assured it will be in your hands.[68]

Within a month of its formation, the Royal Air Force had lost both its political and its professional head. The major cause of this rupture was an irredeemable clash of personalities, but beneath this antagonism there did exist a significant divergence over policy. While Rothermere did not display any deep understanding of the material and strategical aspects of the situation, he was wedded to the concept of a long-range bombing offensive against Germany.[69] Trenchard, on the other hand, had not been converted to this vision of the aerial future, and still saw his task primarily in terms of providing as much tactical support as possible to his old service. If the Royal Air Force was to become that strategic instrument which Smuts had envisioned, then the government was faced not only with the problem of finding a civil–military partnership which could function harmoniously, but with that of finding men who actually believed in the future of the bomber as an independent vehicle of victory.

The resignations of Trenchard and Rothermere ultimately proved that the transformation of British air policy was not to be achieved through a simple reorganization of the air forces into a united service. The navy, and more particularly the army, remained in possession of the bulk of available air strength and could continue to depend on the loyalty of the bulk of the air command. While some airmen certainly were to show themselves converts to the doctrine of strategic airpower, most of their collegues remained at heart the soldiers or sailors they had been before their change of uniform. At the time of its creation, the Royal Air Force became an independent service only in name. If Britain was indeed to effect a transformation in the practice of war, it remained for the government to find the leaders to preside over the last rites of the RFC and RNAS.

Notes

1 Brancker to Trenchard, 8 September 1916, Trenchard Papers, MFC 76/1/7.
2 Derby to Lloyd George, 5 April 1917, Derby Papers, Liverpool Record Office, 920 DER (17) 27/1.
3 Derby to Haig, 21 April and 30 May 1917; Haig to Derby, 22 April and 4 June 1917, PRO, AIR 1/522/16/12/5.
4 Trenchard to GHQ, 20 May 1917; Admiralty to War Office, 14 June 1917, PRO, AIR 1/913/204/5/851.
5 Trenchard to RNAS Dunkirk, 21 August 1917; Jellicoe to War Office, 20 August 1917, PRO, AIR 1/913/204/5/851.
6 PRO, AIR 1/770/204/4/258. For a full account of the incident see S. F. Wise, *Canadian Airmen and the First World War* (Toronto: University of Toronto Press, 1980), pp. 432–4.
7 PRO, AIR 1/2267/209/70/41.
8 Beatty to Admiralty, 25 August 1917, PRO, ADM 1/8486; C. in C. Mediterranean to Admiralty, 10 August 1917; SNO RNAS Dunkirk to Admiralty, 10 June 1917, PRO, AIR 1/641–2.
9 J. Barnes and D. Nicholson (eds.), *The Leo Amery Diaries*, Vol. 1 (London: Hutchinson, 1980), p. 174.
10 Derby, however, thought that Brancker was 'too erratic' and too junior to succeed Henderson. See Derby to Sassoon, 3 April 1917, Derby Papers, Liverpool Record Office, 920 DER (17) 27/3.
11 Brancker to Trenchard, 29 and 30 August 1917, Trenchard Papers, MFC 76/1/16; Macmillan (ed.), *Sefton Brancker*, pp. 159–61.
12 H. Cecil to Curzon, 31 August 1917, Curzon Papers, Eur.F.112/118A.
13 H. Cecil to Smuts, 31 August 1917, Smuts Papers, Cambridge University Library, 681.

14 Derby to Bonar Law, 1 September 1917, BL Papers, 82/4/1.
15 Sassoon to Derby, 2 September 1917, Derby Papers, Liverpool Record Office, 920 DER (17) 27/3; Brancker to Trenchard, 1 September 1917; Trenchard to Brancker, 4 September 1917, Trenchard Papers, MFC 76/1/17; Macmillan (ed.), *Sefton Brancker*, p. 159.
16 Brancker to Derby, 2 September 1917, Trenchard Papers, MFC 76/1/17.
17 Macmillan (ed.), *Sefton Brancker*, pp. 163–70.
18 Brancker to Trenchard, 12 October 1917, Trenchard Papers, MFC 76/1/17.
19 Salmond's biography reveals little beyond the bare details of his career and is closely based on his unpublished autobiography. See J. Laffin, *Swifter than Eagles. The Biography of Marshal of the Royal Air Force Sir John Maitland Salmond* (Edinburgh: Blackwood, 1964); Salmond Papers, RAF, AC 71/14.
20 Notes on resignation, Trenchard Papers, MFC 76/1/19.
21 Trenchard to Salmond, 18 December 1917, Trenchard Papers, MFC 76/1/91.
22 Salmond to Trenchard, n.d., Trenchard Papers, MFC 76/1/91.
23 H. Cecil to Milner, 11 October 1917, Milner Papers, Dep. 357/97–101.
24 War Cabinet 223, min. 12, 24 August 1917, PRO, CAB 23/4.
25 War Cabinet 237, min. 8, 21 September 1917, PRO, CAB 23/4.
26 G.T. 2058A, Formation of a separate air ministry, 23 October 1917, PRO, CAB 21/21; G.T. 2234, Air raids and the bombing of Germany, 6 October 1917, PRO, CAB 24/28.
27 War Cabinet 249, min. 11, 15 October 1917, PRO, CAB 23/4.
28 Jones, *The Origins of Strategic Bombing*, pp. 152–3; Roskill (ed.), *Documents Relating to the Naval Air Service*, p. 563; G.T. 2284, Air policy, 11 October 1917, PRO, CAB 24/28.
29 War Cabinet 242A, min. 2; War Cabinet 243, min. 13; War Cabinet 244, min. 2; War Cabinet 245, min. 12; War Cabinet 246, min. 4; War Cabinet 247, min. 9, PRO, CAB 23/4.
30 G.T. 2409, Air organization, 24 October 1917, PRO, CAB 24/30.
31 Geddes to Smuts, 17 October 1917, PRO, ADM 116/1602.
32 Minutes of War Cabinet committee on air policy, 16 October 1917, PRO, AIR 1/678/21/13/2102; War Cabinet 249, min. 15, 15 October 1917, PRO, CAB 23/4.
33 War Diary, 8th Brigade, RFC, Newall Papers, RAF, B.392.
34 War Cabinet committees on aerial questions, 22 October 1917, PRO, AIR 1/678/21/13/2102.
35 G.T. 2422, Progress of aerial offensive, 28 October 1917, PRO, CAB 24/30.
36 Milner to Smuts, 16 October 1917, Smuts Papers, Cambridge University Library, 682.
37 P. Rowland, *Lloyd George* (London: Barrie & Jenkins, 1975), p. 419.
38 Cowdray, however, clearly did expect the appointment. See Young, *Member for Mexico*, p. 209.
39 Milner to Lloyd George, 20 November 1917, LG Papers, F/38/2/22.
40 See for example Northcliffe to Bonar Law, 30 January 1916, BL Papers, 52/2/52.
41 P. Ferris, *The House of Northcliffe. The Harmsworths of Fleet Street* (London: Weidenfeld & Nicolson, 1971), p. 211.
42 *The Times*, 15 November 1917.
43 Cowdray to Lloyd George, 15 November 1917; Lloyd George to Cowdray, 16 November 1917, Pearson Papers, Science Museum, A.9.
44 Lane to Mrs Smuts, 18 December 1917, Smuts Papers, Cambridge University Library, 682.
45 Autobiographical notes, Trenchard Papers, MFC 76/1/61.

46 Derby to Haig, 12 January 1918, Derby Papers, Liverpool Record Office, 920 DER (17) 27/2; autobiographical notes, Trenchard Papers, MFC 76/1/61.
47 Autobiographical notes, Trenchard Papers, MFC 76/1/61.
48 Air Council minutes, January 1918, PRO, AIR 6/12.
49 G.T. 3252, Curzon memorandum on the use of the British Museum for Air Ministry, 7 January 1918, PRO, CAB 24/38; War Cabinet 318, min. 1, 8 January 1918, PRO, CAB 23/5.
50 War Cabinet minutes, PRO, CAB 23/5.
51 PRO, AIR 6/12, nos 2 and 21; AIR 6/16, no. 84.
52 PRO, AIR 6/12, no. 13; AIR 6/16, no. 44; War Cabinet 361, min. 7, 7 March 1918, PRO, CAB 23/5.
53 Ferris, *The House of Northcliffe*, pp. 212–15.
54 Trenchard Papers, various, MFC 76/1/8 and 92.
55 Blake (ed.), *The Private Papers of Douglas Haig*, p. 280.
56 Trenchard to Rothermere, 18 March 1918, Trenchard Papers, MFC 76/1/19. This letter, and the others cited below with reference to Trenchard's resignation, were all reprinted in G.T. 4321, PRO, CAB 24/49.
57 Rothermere to Trenchard, 19 March 1918, Trenchard Papers, MFC 76/1/19.
58 Trenchard to Rothermere, 19 March 1918, Trenchard Papers, MFC 76/1/19.
59 Autobiographical notes, Trenchard Papers, MFC 76/1/61.
60 Rothermere to Trenchard, 13 April 1918, Trenchard Papers, MFC 76/1/19.
61 Lord Beaverbrook, *Men and Power, 1917–1918* (London: Hutchinson, 1956), pp. 222–3
62 *Daily Mail*, 15 April 1918.
63 Memorandum on Trenchard's resignation, Simon Papers, Bodleian Library, 55/77–82.
64 H. Cecil to Simon, 26 April 1918, Simon Papers, Bodleian Library, 55/100–1; *Hansard*, vol. 105, HC Deb., 5s., 22 April 1918, col. 670; 24 April 1918, cols 971–2; 29 April 1918, cols 1305–72.
65 Simon to Rothermere, 23 April 1918, Simon Papers, Bodleian Library, 55/84–5. Rothermere also found himself at odds with his parliamentary under secretary. See Baird to Rothermere and Baird to Lloyd George, 22 April 1918, LG Papers, F/44/5/5.
66 Rothermere to Lloyd George, 23 and 25 April 1918, LG Papers, F/44/5/6–7.
67 Rothermere to Bonar Law, 3 May 1918, BL Papers, 83/3/9.
68 Rothermere to Sykes, 26 April 1918, Sykes Papers, RAF, MFC 77/13/52.
69 G.T. 3727, PRO, CAB 24/42; G. T. 3833, CAB 24/44.

[10]

The Independent Force

The almost simultaneous departure of Rothermere and Trenchard presented an obvious problem to the government. Trenchard's resignation in particular cast a shadow of illegitimacy over the newly formed Royal Air Force, while the administrative hiatus attendant on unification was prolonged into the late spring by constant changes of senior personnel. If a long-range air offensive was to become an important part of the British war effort in the summer months of 1918, it was vitally important that the new air service be provided with leaders who could work harmoniously towards a new strategic policy. The need to act swiftly in order to take advantage of the good summer flying weather was only one factor pointing towards the need for rapid action. The bulk of British air strength was still committed to the support of the BEF in France, and neither the change of service affiliation nor the change of commanders had in any way impaired the tight interdependence between the field air detachment and the army. The German spring offensives beginning on 21 March 1918 had led to a dramatic increase in the level of air activity, with a contingent rise in personnel and equipment losses. With the aircraft industry already falling short of its production objectives, and the potential strategic reserve shrinking continuously, only a reallocation of resources was likely to produce a bombing force of any size before the end of the year. Such a reallocation could only be achieved by an administration strong enough both to dominate the rump of the army air command and to galvanize the lukewarm supporters of the bombing offensive within the government.

A new partnership was found for the Air Ministry which did seem to fulfil the necessary conditions. Rothermere's replacement as Secretary of State was Sir William Weir, who was elevated almost immediately to the House of Lords. As one of the men most responsible for the organizational changes of the previous year, he could be expected to lend full support to an active bombing policy. Weir was indeed to prove a dedicated proponent of the doctrine of strategic airpower.[1] Like many of the other professional experts introduced into Lloyd George's government, however, his effectiveness was limited by lack of political experience and influence. Weir did begin his tenure of office by dealing firmly with the recalcitrant Trenchard, who sulked in London, demanding to be sent back to the army, until forced by Weir to assume command of the newly constituted Independent Force.[2] Thereafter, he made little impact on either the government or the air force. Despite frequent espousals of the merits of the strategic offensive from Weir's pen, the army's air contingent continued to command the lion's share of air resources. The government showed little inclination to wrest any portion of that share away from Salmond's command to make good the failure of the air industry to provide the Independent Force with the tools of its intended trade.

Weir's impact on air policy was limited from the start by his insistence that his appointment should only last for the duration of the war. His Chief of the Air Staff, Frederick Sykes, also failed to make any real impression on the aerial future of his country and was destined to be removed from his post soon after Weir's retirement. During his year in office, Sykes remained at a considerable disadvantage in dealing with his senior subordinates because of his position outside the mainstream of air thought. He had been removed from the RFC early in the war as the result of a suspected intrigue against his chief, Henderson, and after a short spell attached to the RNAS in the Mediterranean, had left aviation altogether, Henderson's unremitting hostility blocking all attempts at his reinstatement. His return to the senior professional post in the new air force from the relative obscurity of the British Military Mission at Versailles marked an attempt to find a Chief of the Air Staff more in sympathy with the objectives of the RAF than the departed Trenchard. Sykes had been an exponent of the widest possible application of airpower since before the war.[3] His outlook on strategic operations might best be described as visionary, in that he anticipated the weapons and doctrines of the next war. He was to pursue his ideal of a long-range aerial armada with all of his energy, even after the war, when his ambitious plans were a major cause of his dismissal. While the war lasted, Sykes remained an isolated figure, unable to find any consistent support among his colleagues for his unconventional policies.

The decision to replace Trenchard with Sykes was not arrived at easily. It was only after prolonged discussion and consultation with the War Office that the appointment was finally made.[4] The reaction from within the air command immediately underlined the causes of this hesitation. Henderson, the Vice-President of the Air Council, could hardly have been expected to serve under the man whom he had banished from the Flying Corps in 1915. On 12 April, before the new posting had become public knowledge, he decided to resign, telling his son (himself an air force officer), 'I expect many more will refuse to transfer to the Air Force'. Two weeks later Henderson explained to Bonar Law that his relations with

Sykes were a matter of record, and that in any case, he 'earnestly desired to escape from the atmosphere of intrigue and falsehood which had enveloped the Air Ministry for the last few months'.[5]

The departure of Henderson, the major service architect of the RAF, gave some credence to the feeling that the entire edifice was about to collapse. Other resignations did little to allay these fears, although at least one important would-be departure, the Master-General of Personnel Major-General Godfrey Paine, was eventually persuaded to change his mind. In the end, the Air Council and its subordinate organizations were only stabilized by a wholesale shuffle of responsibilities and a purge of those identified as dissidents.[6]

The Air Staff was composed more of the ex-army and navy officers available in London at the time of its formation than of convinced adherents of the concept of a separate air force. While Trenchard's brief and stormy period in charge had certainly not provided an atmosphere conducive to the emergence of a united command, the introduction of Sykes did nothing to make such a development a more likely prospect. A more politically adroit man than his predecessor, Sykes was certainly at home in the complicated world of wartime administration. His political contacts, some of whom had laboured in his interests during his period of exile, gave him advantages which Trenchard had never enjoyed. Indeed, his appointment can be seen as part of the government's campaign to replace men identified with the entrenched military opposition to Lloyd George with those less under the influence of Haig or his vision of civil–military relations. This very factor could only contribute to Sykes's isolation from his colleagues in the service. While his advocacy of strategic bombing did receive the support of some officers within the Air Ministry, particularly those of Brigadier-General P. R. C. Groves's Directorate of Flying Operations, the majority remained true to the interests of their former masters.[7] Typical of these officers was Major-General E. L. Ellington, Controller-General of Equipment, whose response to the suggestion that independent air action might win the war was that 'the decision must be by offensive action on the part of the army, and the detachment of Air Force from the army to the Independent Air Force required to be very carefully watched, lest the result should be a weakening of the offensive power of the Army'.[8]

The suspicion surrounding Sykes in the early days of his career followed him throughout the war, weakening his authority as CAS in the eyes of men who had no personal reason to distrust him. Salmond, his senior operational commander and, as GOC, RAF in the Field, the defender of the army's tactical air policy, had apparently inherited the suspicions of his predecessors to the extent that he did everything in his power to avoid dealing directly with his chief.[9] Sykes's isolation was sufficiently marked to cause one of his closest political admirers, the Unionist leader Bonar

Law, to write to the king's secretary Lord Stamfordham asking him to put private pressure on Weir to improve the position of his professional adviser. This Stamfordham duly did, but Weir's attempt to promote Sykes to Lieutenant-General was blocked on procedural grounds by his opponents within the Air Council.[10]

The correspondence concerning Sykes's position within the Air Ministry is heavily larded with references to the antagonistic factions operating inside the air command. This fragmentation was not simply the product of personality clashes, but also reflected the lack of consensus regarding the role of the air service. A minority of officers did, as has already been suggested, support the concept of a truly independent force with a strategic function of its own. Others, however, remained true to the service traditions in which they had first risen to prominence, and defined their doctrinal horizons in terms of the aerial needs of the army or navy. As Bonar Law himself mentioned in his letter to Stamfordham, the Air Ministry lacked the 'solid foundations' of the War Office and Admiralty. In the brief period of its wartime existence, it tended to perpetuate rather than resolve the divisions and contradictions inherent in the dualistic organization it was intended to replace. This had the effect of leaving the established dominance of the military element in the air command relatively untouched, despite the best efforts of Weir and Sykes to overturn it. The most important victim of this residual army influence was the independent bombing force.

When the War Cabinet first approved the formation of this bombing contingent (known initially as 41st Wing, RFC) in the autumn of 1917, it was in the belief that it would soon be reinforced by new squadrons formed from the surplus of aircraft predicted by its air experts. Taking account of the fact 'that the feeling of the public generally was in favour of immediate counter-attacks', the War Cabinet impressed on Trenchard in early October 'the importance of making a success of the forthcoming air offensive, having regard to the effect that such a success would have on the morale of the people at home'.[11] By the time the Germans launched their attempt to break the stalemate on the Western Front in March 1918, 41st Wing had been operating for five months. Although it was upgraded to a brigade command (VIII Brigade) in anticipation of the arrival of reinforcements, its original complement of three squadrons had not in fact been expanded. The weather through much of the winter was bad, and the existing units were hampered by their inability to bomb targets more than 100 miles behind enemy lines. Up to the end of March, only 56 tons of bombs had been dropped on objectives scattered through Alsace–Lorraine and the Saar basin. Major German cities such as Stuttgart and Mainz had received isolated visits, and Cologne, at the very edge of even the long-range Handley-Page two-engined bomber's radius of action, had only been raided by a single aircraft.[12]

Brigadier-General Cyril Newall, the commander of VIII Brigade, was generally left to form his own bombing policy. The government's original instructions had referred only to the bombing of German towns in which munitions factories were situated, while the efforts of Smuts's Air Policy Committee to provide more effective guidelines had been hamstrung by the temporary nature of its brief.[13] Strategic bombing policy fared no better in the early days of the Air Ministry. The supreme organ of the new administration was the Air Council, but throughout the first half of 1918 its attention was largely occupied with the formalization of its relations with other departments and the settlement of the internal disputes which threatened its very existence. The first real step towards the formulation of a coherent bombing policy was not taken until 18 April when a Strategic Committee was created within the ministry.[14]

In the meantime, Newall had been getting used to being his own master. As a former commander of one of Trenchard's high echelon formations in the field, he was hardly fitted by experience to forging an independent bombing strategy. With the influence of the parent service still strong, VIII Brigade favoured targets more in line with army bombing policy, such as railways and aerodromes near the front, than the more distant munitions and population centres originally intended as its objectives. When the crisis on the British sector in the north broke on 21 March, the brigade was drawn away to full-time employment against the enemy's supply network behind the lines in France. Between 25 March and 15 May only a single Handley-Page, on a sortie to Cologne, dropped any bombs on a German city. Thus, even near its launching, Smuts's plan for 'continuous and intense pressure against the chief industrial centres of the enemy',[15] displayed its vulnerability to the recurrent demands of the main theatre of operations.

The advent of intense aerial activity on the British sector of the Western Front also made serious inroads into the supply of aircraft for the bombing campaign. By the winter of 1917–18, shortfalls in aircraft and engine production were already threatening the existence of the 'Surplus Air Fleet' on which bombing operations depended. Nonetheless, air staff planners remained sanguine about the prospects. In mid-November the Air Policy Committee had received figures which projected the formation of nine Handley-Page night bombing and fifteen D.H.9 day bombing squadrons by the end of July 1918.[16] A memorandum prepared for the Supreme War Council in January lowered this estimate, but still talked in terms of two night and thirteen day squadrons by July, with the numbers increasing to eight and twenty respectively by the end of September.[17] By the spring, a combination of heavy losses on the Western Front and production problems at home had made a mockery of these figures.

British aircraft losses at the front had risen dramatically after 21 March 1918. The traditional policy of the army had always emphasized the need to meet the demands of the front before any operations of a strategic nature were undertaken. In the absence of any initiative from a divided ministry, the RAF in the Field was able to press its claims for new equipment in the same fashion as the RFC before it. Salmond was able to demonstrate that the struggle for superiority over the Western front demanded continuous large-scale infusions of men and machines, and to ensure that resources which would otherwise have been used to build up a bombing force went instead to him as replacements and reinforcements.[18] In this he received support from the command of the bombing force itself. Still true to the beliefs of his old service, Newall argued as late as 23 June that the time when a significant proportion of air strength could 'be diverted from the Battle front to the work of bombing the industrial centres of Germany' would only come 'when the aviation of each of the Allies is strong enough to hold and beat the German aviation'.[19]

The history of the RAF's strategic bombing campaign was to be marred by heavy losses, ill-defined objectives and inadequate resources. Trenchard arrived to take command of the newly renamed Independent Force in late May. By that time Newall had renewed the interrupted offensive against German cities with several raids on Saarbrucken and Mannheim. The first of what was still expected to be a large number of new squadrons had by then arrived but, significantly, was already experiencing severe serviceability problems with its B.H.P.-powered D.H.9 bombers.[20]

Trenchard's early experience of his unwanted command was prophetic of the difficulties the Independent Force would encounter. By the end of May he was already complaining to Weir that the Air Ministry was paying insufficient attention to his requirements.[21] He was also receiving requests from Salmond to bomb tactical objectives on the Western Front which he quite correctly saw as indicative of the difficulties he would encounter in maintaining his command's independent posture.[22] At the same time, strategic bombing advocates inside the Directorate of Flying Operations at the Air Ministry were beginning to worry about the lack of direction coming from the Air Council and the strategic planning committee it had formed more than a month before. As one staff officer complained, such a situation would hinder efforts to persuade the allies to co-operate in the bombing campaign:

On the 22nd April the Strategic Council held its first meeting and it was then decided that a paper should be drawn up on the policy of bombing Germany, and submitted to the War Cabinet. Although many papers have been put forward, nothing has been decided since that date and the Council has not met since the 30th April. Of the papers put forward, only one on the 3rd May put forward any definite plan for this year, and the plan therein set forth was so general in its nature that it clearly would not induce the French to help.[23]

Despite much discussion of the 'obliteration' of selected German industries, and the advancement of theoretical calculations as to the number of bombs required to visit this fate upon various kinds of factories, little of substance had been achieved by the summer except the rough allocation of chemical works, steel and iron works, and railways – in that order – as priority targets.[24] A report from Newall on 27 May demonstrated that the field command was taking little notice of the deliberations in London. Not only did the GOC, VIII Brigade put the bombing of aerodromes and rolling stock at the top of his target list, but he showed no awareness of available intelligence on the state of the German chemical industry, the target his masters at the Air Ministry most wanted him to bomb.[25]

However confused his own objectives might have been, Trenchard maintained the bombing campaign as intensely as possible during the summer. Until August, he received only two D.H.9 squadrons to augment the three squadrons originally assigned to the force in the previous autumn. Fighter opposition to day raids was frequently very fierce: seven of nine D.H.9s of No. 99 Squadron were lost attacking Saarbrucken on 31 July, and seven of twelve from No. 104 Squadron did not return from a raid on Mannheim on 22 August.[26] The intensity of German fighter activity was sufficient to cause Trenchard to divert many of his bombers against the source of the trouble, enemy aerodromes close to the front in the area of operations of the German army.

A statistical breakdown of the attacks carried out in June, July and August gave the air staff in London adequate proof that its bombing plans were chaff in Trenchard's hands. The chemical industry had only received 14 per cent of the raids launched in June, 9·5 per cent in July and 8 per cent in August. The other prime industrial target, steel and iron works, got off just as lightly with 13·3 per cent, 9 per cent and 7 per cent of the attacks respectively in the three months concerned. Aerodromes had come in for an increased amount of attention – 13·3 per cent, 28 per cent and 49 per cent – while railways, a target which the field command persistently favoured against the wishes of the Air Ministry, received most of the rest – 55 per cent in June, and 46 per cent and 31 per cent in the following months. Seriously concerned, the Director of Flying Operations wrote to his chief, Sykes, 'that this policy is a violation of the policy of the Independent Force'.[27]

Whatever the policy, and whatever the theoretical base from which it should have been developed, targetting decisions remained firmly the prerogative of Trenchard at Independent Force Headquarters. Reinforced during August by three new night bomber squadrons and one day bomber squadron equipped with the improved, Liberty-engined D.H.9a, he launched his heaviest attacks yet. During September, 179 tons of bombs were dropped – more than a quarter of the total for the entire campaign.

Aerodromes and railways together received no less than 83·3 per cent of the attacks – many of them as a result of Trenchard's agreement to a request from Generalissimo Foch for support for the St Mihiel offensive.[28]

The air fighting in the Independent Force's area of operations remained heavy until the end of the war, although deteriorating weather in October and November limited the amount of bombing that could be done. An increasing part of this activity took place at night. The Handley-Page, with its greatly superior bomb load, achieved some fine results, but also began to suffer as a result of improving German defence techniques. By far the worst night was that of 16/17 September, when seven of a raiding force of 21 aircraft, drawn from all five squadrons, failed to return.

By day as well, German opposition showed no signs of slackening. Losses were increased by the Independent Force's diversion to supply and communications targets in the rear of the St Mihiel salient. These sorties took the unescorted day bombers into the midst of one of the largest concentrations of German fighter aircraft on the Western Front. On 26 September, for example, five of ten D.H.9s sent to bomb the railways at Metz-Sablon were lost to a formation of between thirty and forty enemy fighters.[29]

The statistics presented by the official historian give an inflated impression of the Independent Force's effectiveness. Jones pointed out that only 3·9 per cent of the bombers which set out did not return, although he did admit that a further 24 per cent turned back without dropping their bombs and 20·5 per cent bombed a target other than the allotted objective.[30] In fact, a substantial portion of the raids carried out successfully without loss were mounted against aerodromes and railways less than thirty miles behind the lines. Many of the supposedly successful attacks on German industrial centres were actually interfered with by gunfire and fighters to the extent that most bombs fell harmlessly wide of the objective.[31] In addition, losses among the four day bombing squadrons were heavy enough to force each out of action for periods as long as three to four weeks.[32]

The achievements of the Independent Force, as measured by a postwar commission working in Germany, give the best measure of the early bomber's limited destructive capacity. The intensive raids against railways had produced delays but little permanent damage. Steel and iron works had proved too solidly constructed to sustain anything but superficial injury from the relatively small bombs dropped on them. The one factory which attracted almost all of the attacks directed against the chemical industry, the *Badische Anilin und Soda Fabrik* at Mannheim, was 'never forced to stop work owing to damage done by air raids'.[33] Doubt must be cast on the committee's conclusion that the raids had at least made real inroads into the morale of Germany's industrial population. Certainly the German government did make desultory diplomatic efforts to stop air raids on civilian targets.[34] Similarly, the attacks did cause some panic and unrest in southwest Germany. Visits to major cities, however, were rare: the Independent Force raided Bonn only once, Cologne three times, and Frankfurt, Coblenz and Karlsruhe six, seven and eight times respectively.[35] With the exception of one or two isolated instances when early warning precautions broke down, casualties were light. Total German casualties to air raids (including those launched by the French) were just in excess of 2,500, approximately one third of which were deaths.[36] There is no evidence to suggest that these brought the end of the war one day nearer, or forced the German government into any major changes of policy.

Trenchard's own assessment of the performance of his command provides an apt postscript to Britain's abortive adoption of a strategic bombing policy:

> I am certain the damage done both to buildings and personnel is very small compared to any other form of war and the energy expended. The moral effect is great – very great – but it gets less as the little material effect is seen. The chief moral effect is apparently to give the newspapers copy to say how wonderful we are, though it does not affect the enemy as much as it affects our own people.[37]

Weir and Sykes in London continued to advocate a massive strategic effort until the end of the war.[38] In the face of the supremacy of the army's air policy, they could achieve little. With Salmond's command success-fully demanding all but a fraction of Britain's operational air resources, Weir's claim that he had established with the War Cabinet 'the principle that just as long as we can maintain our same relative superiority to German aviation, on the purely naval and military fronts, then the balance of our resources must be concentrated on the long-range work', was meaningless.[39]

During 1918, the Independent Force received only 427 of the 1,817 bombing aircraft sent to the various front-line air commands in France.[40] At the armistice, only 10 of the 99 squadrons and 140 of the 1,799 aircraft of the Royal Air Force on the Western Front were under Trenchard's direction. The latter officer, who had just been made commander of the Inter-Allied Bombing Force which Sykes had finally pushed into existence on paper, was unequivocal in his verdict on the past campaign: 'Thus the Independent Force comes to an end. A more gigantic waste of effort and personnel there has never been in any war.'[41]

During the last six months of the war, the Weir–Sykes administration had devoted itself to the creation of a combined allied strategic bombing force. The obstructions they encountered within the Surpeme War Council at Versailles amply demonstrated that the ideas of Britain's small circle of air visionaries were out of step not only with those of the bulk of the British military command, but also with those held by their allies. The British objective, as laid before the Inter-Allied Aviation Committee by Sykes in his capacity as British representative, was simply that an allied air striking force should be created under united command and made responsible directly to the Supreme War Council, thus by-passing the newly appointed Commander-in-Chief of the Allied Armies.[42] The creation of this force around the nucleus of the Independent Force had the theoretical support of the Lloyd George government, although in this, as in so many other aspects of air policy in the final year of the war, it is difficult to detect signs of anything more than lukewarm official interest. The prime minister did generally respond to Weir's proddings by reiterating his government's commitment to the concept of a combined force to his French, American and Italian colleagues. This notwithstanding, Lloyd George clearly felt that he had more pressing matters to discuss than a prospect of aerial action which even the Air Ministry had been forced to admit had receded until 1919 at the earliest.[43]

The Inter-Allied Aviation Committee, which had grown out of an earlier body formed to co-ordinate aircraft supply, rapidly proved to be a dead letter. In three meetings held in May and July, Sykes failed to convince his French counterpart of either the availability of sufficient surplus resources or the feasibility of separate command for an air striking force. The French remained particularly nervous of any interference with the authority of Foch, and preferred to keep the entire air force at his disposal for the decisive battle on the Western Front. Although the American and Italian representatives proved more amenable to Sykes's plans, they could make little immediate contribution to any strategic striking force, and were thus not likely to object too strenuously to French arguments in favour of postponement until the German military stronghold in northeast France had been destroyed.[44]

In one sense, the French outlook on strategic bombing was similar to that held by the British military since the days of the RNAS bombing offensive of 1916. The French insistence on regarding the bombing of Germany as a luxury to be indulged in after the battle at the front had been won was given added force by their understandable fixation with clearing German troops from their soil. It is also important to realize that earlier French flirtations with a long-distance air offensive were not proof of their conversion to the doctrine of strategic bombing. French attacks on German cities, undertaken as early as 1915, were conceived of as acts of retaliation for specific enemy 'outrages'. Even in the mounting of such retaliatory strikes, the French proved themselves circumspect, particularly with regard to attacks launched by their allies from French soil. Air attacks undertaken on targets close to the lines at the behest of the BEF excited French apprehension on the grounds that they, and not their British comrades, were likely to be the main victims of any German adoption of tit-for-tat bombing.[45]

Following the failure of the Inter-Allied Aviation Committee to come to a decision on a co-operative bombing venture, the question was referred to the Military Representatives on the Supreme War Council. True to its own interests, this body recommended the formation of a bombing force under the command of the Allied Commander-in-Chief of Armies.[46] Weir complained to the War Cabinet that this decision was 'in complete disaccord with the policy previously put forward by the Chief of the Air Staff and concurred in by the War Cabinet'.[47] Under pressure from Weir, Lloyd George finally managed to gain grudging acceptance of the principle of an independent allied force from the French.[48] By the time Trenchard finally assumed command of this organization, the end of the war was only a few days away. No non-British units came under his direction, and the allied force, like the ambitous British plan to bomb Berlin from Czech territory opened up by the collapse of the Austro-Hungarian empire, died with the armistice.[49]

Proponents of strategic bombing have criticized Britain's air commanders for devoting insufficient attention to such operations.[50] While it is certainly true that the bomber did not receive a fair trial during the First World War, it remains doubtful whether any possible reallocation of resources could have produced a weapon of consequence. Aviation's strategic potential remained just as limited as its capability for direct decisive intervention on the battlefield, and analyses of the former have tended to proceed more in terms of the air weapon of the Second World War than that of the First World War. The last British raid on a German city in November 1918, carried out against Saarbrucken five days before the armistice, delivered a bombload appreciably smaller than that dropped by just one of the four-engined bombers which raided the Third Reich in their hundreds during the later years of Hitler's war. Had the Independent Force received the full complement of squadrons originally intended for it, it is very doubtful whether any one part of the German war machine could have been dislocated, let alone destroyed. Even if air operations on the Western Front had been cut down, or British aircraft factories provided more bombing machines, the vision of air warfare encapsulated in the Smuts Report and subscribed to by Sykes and Weir, must have remained an elusive goal.

Notes

1 See for example Air Council minutes, 15 July 1918, PRO, AIR 6/13; G.T. 5076, Aerial policy, 10 July 1918, CAB 24/57; Weir to Lloyd George, 27 August 1918, LG Papers, F/47/3/8.
2 Weir to Lloyd George, 27 April 1918, Weir Papers, Churchill College, Cambridge, 1/6; Reader, *Architect of Air Power*, pp. 73–4.
3 Smith, *British Air Strategy between the Wars*, p. 51.

4   Smuts to Lloyd George, 13 April 1918, LG Papers, F/45/9/12; private diary, 8–13 April 1918, Milner Papers, Dep. 89.
5   D. Henderson to I. Henderson, 12 April 1918, Henderson Papers, RAF, AC 71/12; Henderson to Bonar Law, 26 April 1918, BL Papers, 83/2/30.
6   For the composition of the new Air Council see *WIA*, Vol. 6, pp. 26–7.
7   Bombing industrial objectives in Germany, November 1917 – November 1918, PRO, AIR 1/460/15/312/101.
8   Air Council minutes, 15 July 1918, PRO, AIR 6/13; Ellington to Air Council, 14 July 1918, AIR 6/17.
9   Laffin, *Swifter than Eagles*, p. 134.
10 Bonar Law to Stamfordham, 27 August 1918; Stamfordham to Davidson, 31 August 1918, BL Papers, 84/7/73 and 83/6/46; Weir to Brancker, 14 October 1918; Brancker to Weir, 15 October 1918, Sykes Papers, RAF, MFC 77/13/53.
11 War Cabinet 242A, min. 2, 1 October 1917; War Cabinet 244, min. 2, 2 October 1917, PRO, CAB 23/4.
12 PRO, AIR 1/451/15/312/20; War diary, 8th Brigade, RFC, Newall Papers, RAF, B.392.
13 PRO, AIR 1/678/21/13/2102.
14 Air Council minutes, 18 April and 2 May 1918, PRO, AIR 6/12.
15 G.T. 1658, Second report of the committee on air organization and home defence against air raids. 17 August 1917, PRO, CAB 24/22.
16 PRO, AIR 1/678/21/13/2102.
17 PRO, AIR 1/463/15/312/137.
18 Private diary, Trenchard Papers, MFC 76/1/32; draft autobiography, Salmond Papers, RAF, AC 71/14.
19 The bombing of Germany, 23 June 1918, PRO, AIR 1/2422/305/18/11.
20 Pattinson, *History of 99 Squadron*, pp. 6–18.
21 Trenchard to Weir, 26 May 1918, PRO, AIR 1/2422/305/18/11.
22 Private diary, 27 May 1918, Trenchard Papers, MFC 76/1/32.
23 Tiverton to DFO, 22 May 1918, PRO, AIR 1/460/15/312/101.
24 PRO, AIR 1/450/15/312/4 and AIR 1/460/15/312/97 and 101.
25 The scientific and methodical attack of vital industries, 27 May 1918 and Directorate of Flying Operations notes thereon, PRO, AIR 1/460/15/312/101.
26 War diary, 8th Brigade, RAF, Newall Papers, RAF, B.392.
27 DFO to Sykes, n.d., PRO, AIR 1/460/15/312/101.
28 PRO, AIR 1/451/15/312/19 and 20.
29 War diary, 8th Brigade, RAF, Newall Papers, RAF, B.392; Tätigkeitsbericht der Fliegerverbände der Armee-Abteilung C dur die Zeit vom 20.9 mit 26.9.1918, Williams collection.
30 *WIA*, Vol. 6, p. 163.
31 Newspaper accounts of raids on southwest Germany, Nebel Papers, Deutsches Museum, Munich.
32 War Diary, 8th Brigade, RAF, Newall Papers, RAF, B.392.
33 D.A.1, no. 5, Results of air raids on Germany carried out by the 8th Brigade and the Independent Force, RAF, January 1st – November 11th, 1918, 1 January 1919, PRO, AIR 1/2104/207/36.
34 War Cabinet 353, min. 7, 25 February 1918; War Cabinet 358, min. 9, 4 March 1918, PRO, CAB 23/5
35 PRO, AIR 1/460/15/312/101.
36 PRO, AIR 1/711/27/13/2214.
37 Private diary, 18 August 1918, Trenchard Papers, MFC 76/1/32.

38 G.T. 6218, Establishment of a base in Bohemia for aerial operations against Germany, 6 November 1918, PRO, CAB 24/69; Weir to Lloyd George, 29 October 1918, LG Papers, F/47/3/12; Notes by the Chief of the Air Staff on the Independent Force, Royal Air Force, and the proposed Inter-Allied Strategic Bombing Force, 7 August 1918, Sykes Papers, RAF, MFC 77/13/53; J. Kuropka, 'Die britische Luftkriegskonzeption gegen Deutschland im Ersten Weltkrieg', *Militär-geschichtliche Mitteilungen*, no. 1 (1980), pp. 7–24.
39 Wier to Trenchard, 29 June 1918, PRO, AIR 1/2422/305/18/11.
40 PRO, AIR 1/162/15/124/11.
41 Private diary, 11 November 1918, Trenchard Papers, MFC 76/1/32.
42 Proces-verbal of the 1st, 2nd and 3rd sessions, Versailles Inter-Allied Aviation Committee, 9 and 31 May and 21 July 1918, PRO, CAB 25/121.
43 Weir to Lloyd George, 12 and 27 August, 17 and 28 September and 29 October 1918; Derby to Weir, 6 September 1918, LG Papers, F/47/3/7–12.
44 Proces-verbal of the 1st, 2nd and 3rd sessions, Versailles Inter-Allied Aviation Committee, 9 and 31 May and 21 July 1918, PRO, CAB 25/121.
45 Petain to Haig, 20 September and 21 October 1917; Haig to Petain, 15 and 24 October 1917, PRO, AIR 1/2266/209/70/24.
46 Military representatives, Supreme War Council, memorandum no. 35, Bombing air service, 3 August 1918, LG Papers, F/47/3/11.
47 G.T. 5536, Weir to Hankey, 28 August 1918, PRO, CAB 24/62.
48 Clemenceau note, 17 October 1918, Sykes Papers, RAF, MFC 77/13/53.
49 Private diary, 30 October 1918, Trenchard Papers, MFC 76/1/32; G.T. 6218, Establishment of a base in Bohemia for aerial operations against Germany, 6 November 1918, PRO, CAB 24/69; private diary, October–November 1918, Read Papers, IWM, 72/76/2.
50 See particularly Jones, *The Origins of Strategic Bombing, passim.*

[11]

Airpower and Victory

The history of the Royal Air Force between the wars has been dominated by the image of the omnipotent aerial armadas of the Second World War. The *Luftwaffe*'s contribution to the blitzkrieg victories of 1939–41, the ordeal of the Mediterranean Fleet off Crete, the destruction of the Imperial Japanese Navy around the Philippines and, most importantly, the devastation of the cities of both Germany and Japan by fleets of multi-engined bombers, have lent heroic overtones to the RAF's struggle for survival in the 1920s and the race to rearm in the 1930s. While modern scholarship has now begun to reveal the confusion of interwar strategic air thought, it remains to place Britain's first experience of aerial warfare in the context of its own time. Any overview of the British air effort between 1914 and 1918 must begin with an appreciation of the central position occupied throughout the war by the air contingent attached to the BEF in France and Belgium. Home defence, long-range bombing, maritime operations and the support of military campaigns in Italy, Palestine, Mesopotamia and Salonika, all made demands on air resources, but the burgeoning training and manufacturing facilities in Britain remained devoted first and foremost to the air war on the Western Front.

It was largely in terms of its contribution to Haig's victory on the Western Front that the air command measured its performance during the war. Strategic bombing was considered by all but a minority to be of almost incidental importance to the air effort. The Independent Force received less than 6 per cent of the aircraft sent to France in 1918; 5 Group, the semi-autonomous formation charged with attacks on German naval installations on the Channel coast, received less than 4 per cent.[1] Postwar inquiry gave the lie to Sykes's claim that 'the effect, both morally and materially, of the raids on German territory carried out during the summer of 1918 can hardly be over-estimated'.[2] In the immediate aftermath of the liberation of the Channel ports, Weir had made similarly inflated claims for the raids carried out against these targets.[3] Once again, however, an investigation undertaken after the armistice had demon-

141

strated that neither the damage nor the consequent interruption of the enemy's operations had been in any way severe.[4]

Aerial operations in the Mediterranean and Middle Eastern theatres had never assumed major importance. In the wake of the disaster at Caporetto, the RFC in France had been seriously weakened by the withdrawal of front-line squadrons to support the Italians. In 1918, the air contingent in northeast Italy had been itself reduced and some of the units returned to France, and while the remaining squadrons played their part in the victorious battles on the Piave, the main burden of aerial operations was undoubtedly carried by the Italians.[5] In Salonika, Palestine and Mesopotamia, the small British air contingents generally had to make do with obsolete equipment until the last year of the war. Thereafter they had little difficulty in establishing dominance over very weak opposition, but although they achieved some of the most dramatic results of the war against ground targets, in particular the retreating Bulgarians in Salonika and the Turkish Eighth Army in Palestine, the enemy was to all intents beaten before attacked from the air.[6]

It was in France and Belgium that the bulk of British air strength was deployed, and it was there that the ability of the aircraft to intervene decisively in the war was most thoroughly tested. The Western Front was in a state of almost continuous flux from the beginning of the first German offensive on 21 March 1918 until the armistice in November, and air operations attained a level of intensity hitherto without parallel. The resulting attrition in aircraft would have been insupportable, a year before. Indeed, over the ten full months of combat in 1918, monthly losses almost equalled the full strength of the RFC at the beginning of 1917. On 1 January 1917, Trenchard had commanded 691 serviceable aircraft; in 1918 his successor Salmond lost an average of 670, either to the enemy or in accidents, each month.[7] Even in the expanded RAF of 1918, these losses represented a high percentage of available resources. On 21 March 1918, the front-line strength of the air units under Salmond's command was 1,232; between then and 29 April, a total of 1,302 aircraft were struck off his strength.[8]

British aircraft production continued to keep up with these heavy losses. In May, June and July, no fewer than 2,139 new aircraft were sent over the Channel to the RAF in the Field.[9] While this flow represented a considerable achievement on the part of the British air industry, sacrifices had to be made elsewhere to meet Salmond's requirements. New units did not appear on schedule, and the Air Ministry had to resort to the old expedient of breaking up fresh cadres to supply men and machines to existing units. The most prominent victim of this policy was the Independent Force which by the end of August, had received only seven of the 23 squadrons planned for January 1918. While Britain was able to sustain the high rate of attrition on the Western Front, the effort stretched its aerial resources to a point where a new strategic bombing effort was all but impossible to support.

The air war on the Western Front had been prosecuted only half-heartedly between the end of November 1917 and early March 1918. The weather, of course, was largely to blame – even in 1918 military aircraft were unable to operate in moderately poor conditions. The dramatic drop in the level of air activity following the Battle of Cambrai was also the result of deliberate attempts to harbour strength for the coming spring. The Germans began to form the first of 40 new fighter squadrons in November 1917. Between the end of October and the end of February, the pursuit of the *Amerika* programme (so named because it was intended to counter the expected arrival of large numbers of American aircraft at the front) resulted in a 28 per cent increase in front-line German fighter strength, from 1,251 to 1,735 aircraft.[10] British intelligence reports were giving firm indications of the scale of German expansion by the first weeks of 1918. As early as 28 November 1917, RFC Headquarters instructed brigade and wing commanders to husband their resources 'in order to place us in a strong position to deal with the enemy's aviation, which he is making strenuous efforts to improve and increase, at the commencement of the spring campaign'. By maintaining only 10 operational aircraft in each squadron, Trenchard argued, it would be possible to increase overall strength by 300 to 350 aircraft during the winter months.[11]

A study of British aircraft wastage gives some indication of the decline in activity occasioned by mutual attempts at conserving resources. The average number of aircraft destroyed or severely damaged, both in accidents and in action, fell from a monthly figure of 440 between September and November to 236 between December and February. In January alone, the number of new aircraft received from Britain exceeded the total lost or retired by 170.[12] Due to poor weather, the winter months always brought a drop in the output of new pilots – by January the figure had fallen by 35 per cent from the highest monthly figure of 1917 (689 in September) to 451.[13] Nevertheless, the general savings instituted by RFC Headquarters resulted in a substantial increase in the size of the British air contingent at the front.

When the RFC had taken the offensive at Cambrai on 20 November 1917, total British aircraft strength on the Western Front had been 961 machines. When the Corps began its defensive stand along the Third and Fifth Army fronts on 21 March 1918, it fielded 1,232 machines.[14] The RFC as a whole was also better equipped than it had been at the end of the 1917 campaign. In the months following Cambrai the remainder of the Corps's obsolete aircraft had been replaced by more modern machines. All fighter squadrons were equipped or equipping with Camel, Dolphin and S.E.5a aircraft, and all day bomber squadrons with the D.H.4, all types which would remain in service until the end of the war. In addition, there were five squadrons of the excellent Bristol F.2b two-seater fighter/reconnaissance machine, whose service life would extend a decade into peacetime. The only relic of an earlier era, the F.E.2b pusher, was employed solely as a night bomber.

From the autumn of 1916 to the end of 1917 British equipment had been generally inferior to that of the Germans. With the modernization of the RFC, this situation changed. A new generation of German fighter aircraft had been delayed by official complacency following the easy successes of early 1917. As a result, the *Jagdstaffeln* fought the battles of early 1918 with equipment only marginally superior to that of a year earlier. The relative qualitative decline of the German fighter force was accelerated by the *Amerika* programme. In order to increase the number of *Jagdstaffeln* from 41 to 81, the Germans were forced to withdraw a large number of experienced personnel from established units to form cadres for new squadrons. Training establishments in Germany were unequal to the task of producing sufficient new pilots to keep all units up to strength. As a result, the average establishment of front-line *Jagdstaffeln* decreased by between one third and one half, with corresponding declines in general combat efficiency. Thus when the German fighter force went over to the offensive, a function for which it was unsuited, either by doctrine or tradition, it found itself operating for the first time in one and a half years at a qualitative disadvantage to its opponents.[15]

The removal of Trenchard from the field command before the battle did not have the adverse effect on the RFC's fighting capability which Haig at least had feared. Although Salmond was only 36 when he arrived at RFC Headquarters in January 1918, and although he lacked recent operational experience, he was to prove a worthy successor, not least in his adherence to Trenchard's advice to 'remember in your dealings with the War Office that we are part of the Army and that we are not trying to run a separate show at the expense of the Army'.[16] Salmond's replacement of Trenchard did not constitute any break in continuity in administrative or operational practice. Despite the change in nomenclature on 1 April 1918, the air contingent in the field continued to act as the handmaiden of the BEF, surviving the upheavals in London and the German assault without serious interruption to its organizational well-being.

Salmond was given two clear months to prepare his new command for the expected assault. By February he had grasped the point that 'when the blow came it would be tremendous, that our lines would break under the enormous strain and the air methods developed to suit static warfare ... would be swept aside'. His solution was developed in the light of British experience with large-scale ground attack operations at Cambrai in the previous November:

The answer was to bear such a concentration of low-bombing

aircraft on the front of the advancing infantry and back areas of the attack that the impetus must inevitably slacken and consequently relieve the extreme pressure on our own troops.[17]

At a meeting with Trenchard in February, Salmond persuaded his chief to increase the motorized transport assigned to front-line squadrons so as to make them more mobile.[18] In order to facilitate further rapid redeployment of forces in the face of a breakthrough, efforts were made to reconnoitre and prepare new aerodromes behind existing installations. Army co-operation forces on the threatened Fifth Army front were reinforced, and brigade commanders were instructed to prepare for extensive low-level attacks against the attacking enemy.[19]

On 21 March 1918 the German attack began along the Third and Fifth Army fronts. In the north the British lines generally held firm, but in the Fifth Army area in the Somme region Gough's troops gave way almost immediately. For the first time since 1914, the British army was forced to conduct a fighting retreat. During the opening hours of the battle air participation was limited by adverse weather conditions, but thereafter the RFC was committed to just the sort of large-scale ground attack operations Salmond had foreseen. By denuding the French front of all but essential air support, the Germans had succeeded in achieving an unprecedented aerial concentration behind Ludendorff's attacking divisions. Along the whole British front, just over 1,000 German aircraft faced 1,200 British, but on the crucial sector south of the River Scarpe, XVII, II and XVIII *Armee* air contingents actually outnumbered those of the Third and Fifth Armies by 750 to 580.[20] It was the first time in the war that the British had actually found themselves significantly outnumbered on a battle front. In the event, the German numerical preponderance was to prove short-lived: within days of the battle beginning, reinforcements from other sectors and the superior British ability to replace losses more than restored the balance.

Salmond's contingency plans for a German breakthrough worked very well. No units were actually put out of action, and new aerodromes were occupied as the enemy overran existing installations with little disruption of operations. The aerial fighting of the last ten days of March was some of the fiercest of the entire war, both sides experiencing heavy losses, not only as a result of air combat, but also due to heavy ground fire over the battlefield and the difficulties of operating from temporary airfields. RFC losses between 21 and 31 March totalled 478 aircraft, more than in January and February combined.[21]

In 1916–17 aircraft production and pilot training facilities had experienced severe difficulty in keeping up with losses during periods of intensive activity. In 1918 the British were able to maintain the flow of replacements despite the general increase in aerial activity. During March

790 aircraft were struck off by the RFC in the Field, and a further 95 sent home as 'time expired'. To balance this, 743 new aircraft were received from Britain, and another 11 from the French, while 113 re-entered service after being reconstructed at the air depots under Salmond's command.[22] The output of new pilots was also equal to the demands placed on it, and throughout the battle Salmond was generally able to replace casualties as they occurred, without pulling units out of action. Indeed, such was the progress made in the training programme, now augmented by wings in Canada and the United States, that the British were never again to experience anything but the briefest personnel shortages.[23]

In the first four days of the battle alone, the RFC fired almost 200,000 rounds and dropped just over 100 tons of bombs on targets on the ground.[24] British and German sources are unanimous as to the effect these had on the German advance. While British airpower did not possess the destructive power to inflict heavy casualties on German infantry, artillery and transport, it succeeded in bringing considerable confusion to all three. It is impossible to measure the exact dimensions of the delay the RFC caused, but the disruption of countless local attacks, the harassment of artillery batteries and the interdiction of supply lines certainly contributed to the general loss of momentum of the attacking forces.[25] By the end of the month the German offensive was faltering before new lines of defence just east of the crucial communications centre of Amiens. While the British air forces had suffered heavy casualties, and lost many of their original bases, their fighting efficiency had not been seriously impaired. Their German counterparts, although suffering no more severely, had failed to make a significant impact on ground operations after the first few days of the battle, and were not able to replace losses quickly enough to maintain full operational strength.[26]

Even before the attack around Amiens had died out, the Germans launched a new offensive just south of the Ypres battlefield of 1917. A large proportion of the air strengths of both sides were transferred north to resume the struggle. While air operations in the north covered a smaller battlefield than they had in the south, they were just as intense. Once again, the emphasis was on low-level work, with the RAF utilizing its superior ground attack capability to counter German breakthroughs. In one three-day period, 11–13 April, 146 British aircraft were destroyed; in a similar period later in the month, 20–22 April, another 117 were lost. German losses, however, were heavy as well, and the British continued to enjoy the advantage both in the replacement of casualties and in the support of ground forces.[27]

When the failure of its attacks on the British sector became obvious at the end of April, the German high command shifted its attention south to the French. In order to help force a new breakthrough south of the

Somme, a large part of the aerial concentration opposite the British was broken up and redeployed behind the Aisne and Chemin des Dames sectors. As a result, the RAF found itself enjoying a pronounced numerical advantage.

Despite the reduction of German air strength, fighting north of the Somme remained heavy all through the summer of 1918. While the pressing need for anti-infantry and anti-artillery attacks had passed with the termination of the German offensive on the Lys, such operations remained an integral part of British air policy. Fighter squadrons which had spent most of 1917 flying offensive patrols above the enemy's rear areas now found themselves committed to low-level work on a regular basis. The casualties incurred on such missions were as high as they had promised to be when first instituted at Cambrai in the previous November. Some units, flying almost exclusively in the ground attack role, suffered average monthly personnel losses of 75 per cent over the last year of the war.[28]

That portion of the British fighter force engaged in regular encounters with the depleted *Jagdstaffeln* at higher altitudes also continued to suffer heavy losses. The intensity of the air war was heightened by the growth of the British day bombing effort. By June 1918 there were 11 squadrons of day bombers flying with the RAF in France. The daily raids flown by this force were significant as much because they forced the commitment of German fighter strength to battle, as because of the damage they inflicted on the aerodromes, lines of communication and supply centres which were their usual targets. The overall result of the maintenance of intensive air operations was that the casualty rate on the British sector did not fall significantly below the high level established in March.[29]

The RAF's Corps squadrons, charged with the provision of artillery observation, infantry contact and reconnaissance facilities at the very heart of the army–air co-operation programme, derived great benefit from the intensified tactical offensive. Since the summer of 1917, the air service had generally been successful in providing sufficient indirect protection for the Corps squadrons to allow them to carry out their duties without serious loss or interruption. In the confused, low-level fighting of March and April 1918, losses in these units had increased to more than a quarter of total casualties. Under the more stable conditions of the summer, the Corps squadrons found themselves operating in safer circumstances than ever before. Only 11 Corps aircraft were destroyed by enemy action in May, 10 in June and 16 in July.[30]

At the end of July, the RAF was in a better position than at any time in the preceding two years. Casualties remained heavy, but the relative immunity of army co-operation aircraft and the apparent weakening of enemy air strength promised well for the future. Having survived the German assault of the spring in better conditions than many would have dared hope, the RAF was ready to play a greater part than ever in the allied offensive of the autumn.

John Terraine has laboured hard over the past two decades to rescue the British victories on the Western Front in the last three months of the war from undeserved obscurity.[31] The activities of the RAF in the Field, which lent Haig's attacking armies a degree of air support unparalleled in the entire war, are not in need of similar treatment. Histories of the British air effort have given full play to the achievements of Salmond's squadrons over the retreating German ground forces. It remains, however, to come to a proper estimation of the part played by airpower in Haig's triumphs, and to assess the claim that the RAF finally managed to achieve aerial supremacy over its opponents in the final months of the conflict.[32]

Air operations remained relatively intense on the British sector of the Western Front even after the last German hopes of a breakthrough in the north flickered out around Mount Kemmel at the end of April. The RAF's casualty rate dropped only slightly through the late spring and early summer, but after May the service never again faced the bulk of the *Luftstreitkräfte*. Following the German offensive on the Rheims sector in the middle of that month, offensive action by one side or the other was almost continuous on the southern half of the Western Front. Forced to fight all along the front, the German air service was no longer able to achieve local parity. With the exception of a few weeks on the Somme sector in August, when a temporary concentration of *Jagdstaffeln* brought the Germans close to equal strength, the RAF enjoyed a pronounced numerical advantage.

The RAF's first major chance to press home its advantage came with Rawlinson's attack on the German salient opposite Amiens in early August. Slessor has justly criticized the air command for failing to concentrate more than 47 per cent of its bombers and fighters in direct support of the attack.[33] The old RFC policy of remaining strong all along the front regardless of local changes in operational circumstances was maintained through the system of linking one air brigade, composed of a balanced mix of available aircraft types, with each army headquarters. None the less, squadrons stationed in adjacent sectors did tend to be drawn into the fight, and in the crucial early days of the engagement the British enjoyed a significant superiority in numbers over the defending air contingent of II *Armee*.[34] British plans for the offensive drew heavily on the experience of ground attack duties gained in earlier operations. All of the fighter squadrons of V Brigade, the subordinate air formation of Rawlinson's Fourth Army, were assigned directly to low-level work, with general air superiority duties left to the units of IX (Headquarters) Brigade. The RAF also planned a major bombing effort against German lines of communication and supply behind the salient aimed at isolating the outnumbered and surprised divisions of II *Armee* in their forward positions.[35]

The Battle of Amiens was to prove one of the greatest British feats of arms of the war. While the initial breakthrough was eventually sealed off, the Germans were set inexorably off on that series of withdrawals which ended with them reeling back towards their own border at the armistice. For the RAF, however, Amiens proved as much an illustration of the aircraft's limitations as of its offensive potency.

The very surprise achieved by Rawlinson's attacking troops indicated that bad weather and the lack of anything but routine reconnaissance activity on the part of the enemy could still lead to ground forces remaining unappraised of even major offensive preparations against them. In the later stages of the battle British reconnaissance techniques were themselves found inadequate. The RAF's failure to assign more than a handful of aircraft to long-range surveillance flights left the army unaware of the arrival of large German reinforcements, and thus allowed the enemy to seal off the gap in his lines more easily than he might otherwise have done.[36]

The most obvious failure of British aviation, however, was its inability to disrupt German communications behind the salient. These latter were peculiarly vulnerable, depending almost entirely on eleven road and rail bridges across the Somme well within the range of British aircraft. Had these bridges been destroyed, the retreating II *Armee* would have been completely cut off. The bombers of the RAF brigades concerned launched almost continuous attacks on the bridges during the first few days of the battle, but failed to destroy even one. Such was the limited destructive capacity of the bombs of the day that stone bridges were invulnerable to anything but repeated direct hits – hits that the British bombers, repeatedly assailed by large formations of enemy fighters, were unable to attain.[37]

The renewal of intensive offensive operations pushed RAF losses even higher than they had been throughout the summer. Over the entire month of August, 847 British aircraft were either wrecked or lost to the enemy. On 8 August, the first day of the battle, 100 aircraft were destroyed, the highest daily total of the war. In the first four days of the offensive, losses totalled 243 aircraft.[38] The official RAF historian was later to claim that the air battles of early August, particularly those in defence of the Somme bridges, broke the back of the German fighter force.[39] An evaluation of available German records does not fully support this point of view. The German air commander in the II *Armee* area where almost all of the air fighting took place reported only 28 airmen killed, wounded or missing during the week of 8 to 14 August.[40] German aircraft losses were undoubtedly more severe, but the low state of operational readiness of some units at the end of the campaign was more a product of supply problems brought on by the general running down of war industry than of casualties suffered over the Amiens salient.[41] The severity of air fighting on the British sector in the remaining three months of the war was to prove beyond any doubt that the *Luftstreitkräfte*, and in particular its fighter contingent, was still a force to be reckoned with.

It would appear that the Germans managed to repair some of the damage done to the *Jagdstaffeln* by the *Amerika* programme and the offensive battles of the spring. The superb new fighter aircraft, the Fokker DVII, was finally becoming available in sufficient quantities to re-equip most frontline formations. By the end of August there were over 800 such aircraft at the front. German fighter units were frequently understrength, but the hard cutting edge of elite formations such as the three mobile *Jagdgeschwadern* remained capable of inflicting massive damage on attacking formations.

The *Luftstreitkräfte*, none the less, was extremely vulnerable. By the second half of 1918 the crumbling German industrial complex could no long sustain the heavy attrition on the Western Front. The aviation service was suffering severely from shortages of petrol and other such essentials as lubricants and rubber. While the industry behind it was still expanding, it had failed to keep pace with growth in its French and British rivals.[42] Heavy losses, such as might be incurred when a squadron was caught on the ground during an attack on its aerdrome, could not quickly be made good. When, for example, one fighter unit lost its entire complement of fighter aircraft in a British bombing raid in the middle of August, it was not able to return to full operational status until the end of the first week in September.[43]

Evidence suggests conclusively that aerodromes, protected neither by heavy automatic weapons nor by a dependable early warning system, were peculiarly vulnerable to attack.[44] The RAF, with its profound numerical superiority, was capable of launching such attacks on a regular basis. Some were indeed carried out with excellent results. Had they been repeated the German air service must have been bled dry by the autumn. Salmond's operational policy, however, continued to revolve around routine offensive patrols, low-level missions against well-protected front-line positions, and bombing attacks against such objectives as the Somme bridges which were not easily knocked out. As a result, the German defenders, though hard pressed, were generally able to engage intruding RAF formations under reasonable conditions. British aircraft losses remained heavy until the very end of the war, while the Germans continued to provide their ground forces with at least some degree of air support.

A study of British air casualties on the Western Front between August and the end of the war makes it clear why the RAF was never able to mobilize sufficient resources to mount a fully-fledged strategic bombing campaign. Aircraft losses from 1 August to 11 November, excluding even those machines sent home as unfit for further active service, totalled 2,692. Over the same period, 2,647 new aircraft were sent to the RAF in the Field from Britain. Heavy losses continued to be incurred even in the last days of hostilities. On 4 November, for example, 24 aircraft were wrecked and 39 lost behind enemy lines.[45] British commanders at the Front remained concerned about the strength of German air resistance even when the German infantry in the trenches were beginning to give way. Their fears were aggravated by the appearance of a new generation of German fighter aircraft. In August, one officer at RAF Headquarters was worried enough to tell a colleague at the Air Ministry: 'I am afraid the outlook is serious and that unless we really take off our coats and get down to it at once, we shall have a recurrence of 1915, when there was a good deal of talk of Fokker fodder with reference to our machines.'[46]

Although the RAF might have missed its chance to overpower its opponent in the air, it did continue to offer the army a comprehensive range of tactical support services. Haig's successful attacks on the heavily fortified German defence lines were characterized by a degree of careful planning and tight control hitherto lacking in British ground operations. In carrying out intensive reconnaissances of German positions, observing artillery fire and maintaining contact with advanced elements of the army, the RAF's Corps squadrons played an important part in the uninterrupted string of ground victories. Corps machine losses rose slightly above the low levels of the early summer (18 per cent of total losses in action in August, and 20 per cent in September), and some of the long-range reconnaissance work made necessary by the speed of the advance was seriously interfered with by German fighters, but overall British fighters continued to offer reasonable protection to army co-operation services.[47]

The German air force had not been driven from the skies by November 1918, but with the pressure upon it increasing steadily, and its training and supply services running behind those of its opponents, it is difficult to see how it could have survived much longer. While the other allied air services had played a more important role in the last year of the war, much of the damage had been inflicted by the RAF, which can at least be granted credit for bringing victory in the air near at the time of the armistice. The British air service's main contribution to victory, however, had come through its participation in the ground war. Haig's armies were certainly the best supported land formations on either side. Whether this achievement would resound to the long-term benefit of the RAF as an independent organization was unfortunately far from clear.

Notes

1   PRO, AIR 1/162/15/124/1.
2   Synopsis of British air effort throughout the war, 1 January 1919, Sykes Papers, RAF, MFC 77/13/62; Air Ministry publication D.A.1, no. 5, Results of air raids on Germany carried out by the 8th Brigade and the Independent Force, RAF, January 1st – November 11th, 1918, 1 January, 1920, PRO, AIR 1/2104/207/36.
3   Weir to Lloyd George, 29 October 1918, LG Papers, F/47/3/12.
4   Report of the aircraft bombing committee appointed by the Air Ministry to inquire into the effects of bombing in Belgium and the defensive measures taken by the enemy against it, March 1919, PRO, AIR 1/2115/207/56/1.
5   The Italians, in fact, deployed over 500 aircraft in the final battles of the war, the British substantially less than 100. For a general account of British air operations on the Italian front see N. Macmillan, *Offensive Patrol: the Story of the RNAS, RFC and RAF in Italy* (London: Jarrolds, 1973), *passim*.
6   PRO, AIR 1/153/15/122/1; G.T. 5862, 3 October 1918, CAB 24/65.
7   PRO, AIR 1/2267/209/70/41; IWM, Misc. Box 34, item 616.
8   *WIA*, Vol. 6, p. 402.
9   IWM, Misc. Box 34, item 616.
10 Frontbestand an Flugzeugen, Grosz collection.
11 Trenchard to RFC brigades, 28 November 1917, PRO, AIR 1/522/16/12/5.
12 PRO, AIR 1/850–3; IWM, Misc. Box 34, item 616.
13 PRO, AIR 1/2423/305/18/39.
14 *WIA*, Vol. 4, pp. 426–30, 446–51.
15 Morrow, *German Air Power in World War I*, pp. 91–2.
16 Trenchard to Salmond, 12 October 1917, Trenchard Papers, MFC 76/1/90.
17 Draft autobiography, Salmond Papers, RAF, AC 71/14.
18 ibid.
19 PRO, AIR 1/920/204/5/884.
20 Wise, *Canadian Airmen and the First World War*, p. 488; PRO, AIR 1/2267/209/70/41.
21 IWM, Misc. Box 34, item 616.
22 ibid.
23 Trenchard to Salmond, 25 March 1918, Trenchard Papers, MFC 76/1/92; PRO, AIR 1/2423/305/18/36.
24 PRO, AIR 1/2385/228/10.
25 PRO, AIR 1/2140–1; AIR 1/2385/228/10; Blake (ed.), *The Private Papers of Douglas Haig*, p. 296.
26 E. von Hoeppner, *Deutschlands Krieg in der Luft: Ein Rueckblick auf die Entwicklung und die Leistungen unserer Heeres-Luftstreitkraefte im Weltkrieg* (Leipzig: von Hase & Koehler Verlag, 1921), p. 156.
27 IWM, Misc. Box 34, item 616.
28 Slessor, *Air Power and Armies*, p. 100.
29 PRO, AIR 9/3, Folio 2; AIR 1/853–7.
30 PRO, AIR 1/853–7.
31 J. Terraine, *Douglas Haig: The Educated Soldier* (London: Hutchinson, 1963) and *To Win a War, 1918: The Year of Victory* (London: Sidgwick & Jackson, 1978).
32 Wise, *Canadian Airmen and the First World War*, pp. 542–76.
33 Slessor, *Air Power and Armies*, p. 184.
34 *WIA*, Vol. 6, pp. 435–6.
35 PRO, AIR 1/677/21/13/1887.

36 Slessor, *Air Power and Armies*, pp. 169–75.
37 PRO, AIR 1/677/21/13/1887.
38 IWM, Misc. Box 34, item 616; PRO, AIR 1/858/204/5/415–6.
39 *WIA*, Vol. 6, p. 444.
40 Kofl.2 Wochenberichte, 8 to 14.8.18, Kilduff collection.
41 A. Imrie, *Pictorial History of the German Army Air Service, 1914–1918* (London: Ian Allan, 1971), pp. 57–9.
42 Morrow, *German Air Power in World War I*, pp. 189–93.
43 W. R. Puglisi (ed.), 'Raesch of Jasta 43', *Cross and Cockade Journal*, vol. 8, no. 4 (1967), p. 322.
44 *WIA*, Vol. 6, pp. 158–61.
45 IWM, Misc. Box 34, item 616; PRO, AIR 1/858/204/5/415–8; AIR 1/859/204/5/419–20.
46 Brooke-Popham to Higgins, 17 August 1918, PRO, AIR 1/1/4/11.
47 PRO, AIR 1/858–9; AIR 1/711/27/13/2214.

Conclusion

When the armistice came into effect on 11 November 1918, the RAF was arguably the most effective air service in the world. From July 1916 on, it and its predecessors had claimed 7,054 enemy aircraft, dropped 6,942 tons of bombs, flown over 900,000 operational hours and fired over 10½ million rounds at targets on the ground.[1] Its contribution to victory, however, was largely ancillary. Attempts to influence the course of the war through the direct use of airpower against tactical or strategic objectives had brought little return. Long-distance bombing of industrial targets in Germany and such military targets as the docks at Ostend and Zeebrugge caused little damage or dislocation. Even when the German army began to retreat, British aircraft were unable to cause serious confusion in its ranks. The RAF's major contribution was to assist Haig to break through the Hindenburg Line by providing the same reconnaissance and observation facilities which had first brought the air service to prominence in the early years of the war.

The problems limiting the aircraft's direct intervention, either on or behind the battlefield, were largely technological. The major difficulty was simply that machines armed only with two machine-guns and a few hundred pounds of bombs could make little impact on most targets. Beyond this, air to ground communications were in an early stage of development, and the co-ordination of aircraft and ground forces was thus all but impossible. Efforts had been made to engineer co-operation between the RAF and the Tank Corps, but the tank itself was still a crude weapons system, and the ever present communications problems prevented more than isolated, local successes.[2]

Beyond these technical shortcomings, Britain's air forces were relegated to a secondary role by a lack of clear tactical doctrine. Offensive air operations had first evolved as a result of the campaign to provide assistance for infantry and artillery operations. The British use of the fighter to gain air superiority had rapidly gained a momentum of its own, and in the heyday of Trenchard's reign at RFC Headquarters the offensive policy had become a blunt instrument used to batter the enemy without thought to the balance of losses. In the last year of the war, the offensive had broadened to include intensive attacks on German ground targets, both by fighter aircraft against front-line installations, and by conventional bombers against the supply and communications network behind the trenches. It is difficult to detect a coherent policy behind these attacks. Low-level attacks were of obvious value in the confused, semi-mobile conditions prevailing during the German spring offensive. They made less sense when continued against established enemy positions later in the year, exposing the attackers to continuous loss without achieving more than nuisance effect. Similarly, the bombing squadrons of Salmond's command scattered their cargoes over the German rear areas without consistent regard to target priorities or potential enemy weak points, rendering themselves little more than an irritant to the mass army below.

Throughout the First World War, airpower's potential for direct intervention in the ground war remained limited. Aircraft were too small, and their capabilities too dimly understood, to impede the operations of millions of armed men. The air attacks which might have seemed decisive were carried out away from the main arena of hostilities against troops already beaten and in headlong retreat. That the German army was able to maintain its cohesion throughout the withdrawals of the last three months of the war, despite a great increase in Allied air activity, was final proof of the impotence of contemporary aircraft.

Immediately after the armistice, the RAF underwent a massive reduction which saw it shrink from almost 200 front-line squadrons to 33. Outstanding contracts were cancelled, huge quantities of equipment destroyed, and only a small percentage of trained pilots offered permanent peacetime commissions. All of Britain's services experienced a painful period of transition in 1919–20, but the army and navy could at least revert to the relative security of established peacetime roles. The RAF, unproven as a strategic instrument in its own right, and overwhelmingly committed at the armistice to roles which must disappear with the onset of peace, faced a less certain future.

The resignation of Weir from the Air Ministry at the end of 1918 and his replacement by Churchill, who simultaneously held the War Office portfolio, seemed to indicate that the air service must soon lose its independence.[3] The removal of Sykes from his post as Chief of the Air Staff after a period of less than a year pointed in the same direction. Almost alone among the senior officers of the RAF, Sykes had emerged as a strong proponent of a strategic air strike force, and the fact that no place could be found either for him or for staff officers like P. R. C. Groves who echoed his sentiments did not augur well for the maintenance of a separate service. His successor Trenchard, whatever his later achievements, could scarcely have been numbered among the most devoted adherents of the new force in 1919. Indeed, so convinced was the latter of the poor prospects of the RAF that only a few months before his elevation to the supreme command he was actively canvassing the possibilities of an appointment to a colonial governorship.[4]

The emasculation of the RAF and the attacks on its independence which were to follow were not simply the products of rapid demobilization and naval and military fears that their needs would not be provided for by a separate air force. The postwar trials of the RAF were also the inevitable result of its uneven development during the war years. The service had evolved largely as an ancillary to the army and navy, and no serious case could have been made for its strategic operations having contributed in any substantial manner to the allied victory. Independence itself had been granted largely as a result of perceived wartime difficulties with divided military-naval control. If some men in high places had seen the German air threat of 1917 as a harbinger of a new age in warfare, this vision had dissipated almost as quickly as the threat itself.

Only the most hindbound soldiers, sailors and politicians still believed in 1919 that the aircraft had no important role to play in the prosecution of war or the maintenance of peace. The majority, however, based their assumptions with regard to air policy on perceptions of the dominant trends in aviation during the recently concluded war. These latter were almost entirely concerned with the evolution of the aircraft as a tactical adjunct to the army and navy. Even after the creation of the RAF, air decisions had been taken with reference to the established services, and with the diminished need for air support of peacetime garrisons and naval bases there was little obvious need for a separate air administration. The spectre of attack on British cities did not entirely disappear, but only the re-emergence of German aerial might under Hitler could invest the Zeppelins and Gothas of 1914–18 with lasting significance. In the immediate aftermath of the First World War, Britain's defence needs were not generally evaluated in terms of the dawning of an air age. The RAF, though widely seen as a necessary wartime expedient, seemed an expensive administrative luxury in time of peace.

There is no place in this study for a detailed analysis of the RAF's ultimately successful struggle for survival in the 1920s. It is useful nonetheless to underline some of the connections between that struggle and the period of genesis during the First World War. At the dawn of the interwar period the RAF's position was weakened by a combination of three factors: the subsidiary role played by airpower in the war, the lack of any general perception of a more important future role, and the consequentially vague position of the air service within the defence community. With all of the services having to prove their viability to earn an adequate share of a reduced budget, it was natural that the navy should want back its carrier and coastal patrol aircraft and the army should be anxious to develop its own artillery observation and infantry co-operation machines. The air force, with little else to offer in 1919–20, needed both to hold on to these aircraft and to find other roles less susceptible to military/naval presumption, or at the very least more appealing to economy conscious ministers.

In the immediate postwar period, when the other services were attempting to re-establish themselves in traditional peacetime roles, the future of airpower was easily confused with the future of the independent air service. The leaders of the latter body became convinced that naval and military attacks upon the RAF actually constituted a serious threat to the development of the aircraft as a weapon. This belief finally transformed Trenchard and the remainder of the ex-RFC hierarchy from air-minded soldiers to fervent believers in their new service. At the armistice, most of these officers would have been quite happy to see their aircraft returned to the army. Within a few years, however, even the most conservative considered such a course to be a recipe for national disaster.

Unfortunately, there was little in the RAF's wartime record to give it the right to peacetime independence. Its search for legitimacy therefore drove it away from its established areas of expertise in army and navy co-operation, first to imperial policing and then to strategic bombing. The result of this process was an air force wedded to a poorly thought-out doctrine, and partially isolated from the remainder of the defence community. In one sense, premature independence was the father of Bomber Command; in another it was behind the fact that Britain, which in 1918 had possessed the best tactical air force in the world, was in 1939 forced to make do with a poor second.

Notes

1 Synopsis of British air effort throughout the war, 1 January 1919, Sykes Papers, RAF, MFC 77/13/62.
2 PRO, AIR 1/725/97/10.
3 M. Gilbert, *Winston S. Churchill, 1917–1922* (London: Heinemann, 1975), pp. 197–218; Smith, *British Air Strategy between the Wars*, pp. 21–2; Sykes, *From Many Angles*, pp. 260–79.
4 Trenchard to Lawrence, 12 and 17 January 1919, Lawrence Papers, India Office Records, Eur. F. 143/103.

Bibliography

MANUSCRIPT SOURCES

(i) *Government Records (Public Record Office, London)*

Admiralty Records	– ADM 1
	ADM 116
Air Ministry Records	– AIR 1
	AIR 2
	AIR 6
	AIR 8
	AIR 9
Cabinet Office Records	– CAB 14
	CAB 21
	CAB 23
	CAB 24
	CAB 37
	CAB 38
	CAB 42
	CAB 45
Ministry of Munitions Records	– MUN 4
PRO (Kitchener Papers)	– PRO 30/57
War Office Records	– WO 158

(ii) *Other Records*

Bodleian Library, Oxford	– Addison Papers
	Asquith Papers
	Milner Papers
	Simon Papers
Cambridge University Library	– Smuts Papers
Churchill College, Cambridge	– Weir Papers
House of Lords Record Office	– Bonar Law Papers
	Lloyd George Papers
Imperial War Museum, London	– Brancker Papers
	Garland Papers
	Groves Papers
	Read Papers

	Misc. Air Documents
	Sound Records Archive
India Office Records, London	– Curzon Papers
	Lawrence Papers
Liddell Hart Centre, London	– Brooke-Popham Papers
	Capper Papers
	Groves Papers
	Montagu of Beaulieu Papers
Liverpool Record Office	– Derby Papers
Royal Air Force Museum, London	– Henderson Papers
	Newall Papers
	Salmond Papers
	Sykes Papers
	Trenchard Papers
Science Museum Library, London	– Pearson Papers
Other Collections	– Bayerische Hauptstaatsarchiv-Kriegsarchiv, München (weekly reports of the Commander of Flying Troops, VI *Armee*)

Bundesarchiv-Militärarchiv, Freiburg (list of production orders, German air service)

Deutsches Museum, München (Nebel Papers)

Duiven, R., private collection (war diary of *Jagdstaffel* 35b)

Grosz, P., private collection (monthly returns of German air strength)

Hoover Institution, Stanford University (German air service intelligence summaries, 1918)

Kilduff, P., private collection (weekly reports of the Commanders of Flying Troops, II *Armee* and IV *Armee*)

Sykes, B., private collection (family papers)

University of Western Ontario, Hitchins Collection (German air service intelligence summaries, 1917)

Williams, G., private collection (weekly reports of the Commander of Flying Troops, *Armee-Abteilung* C)

PRINTED SOURCES

(i) *Serial Publications*

The *Daily Mail*
Parliamentary Debates (Hansard)
The Times
The *Westminster Gazette*

(ii) *Printed Documents, Diaries, Correspondence, etc.*

Barnes, J. and Nicholson, D. (eds), *The Leo Amery Diaries*, Vol. 1 (London: Hutchinson, 1980).
Blake, R. (ed.), *The Private Papers of Douglas Haig, 1914–1919* (London: Eyre & Spottiswoode, 1952).
Brock, M. and E. (eds), *H. H. Asquith. Letters to Venetia Stanley* (Oxford: Oxford University Press, 1982).
Churchill, R. S. (ed.), *Winston S. Churchill*, Companion Vol. 2 (London: Heinemann, 1969).
David, E. (ed.), *Inside Asquith's Cabinet. From the Diaries of Charles Hobhouse* (London: John Murray, 1977).
Gilbert, M. (ed.), *Winston S. Churchill*, Companion Vols 3 and 4 (London: Heinemann, 1972 and 1977).
Hancock, W. K. and Van Der Poel, J. (eds), *Selections from the Smuts Papers*, Vol. 3 (Cambridge: Cambridge University Press, 1966).
Lee, A. G., *No Parachute. A Fighter Pilot in World War I* (London: Jarrolds, 1968).
Puglisi, W. R. (ed.), 'Raesch of Jasta 43', *Cross and Cockade Journal*, vol. 8, no. 4 (1967), pp. 307–35.
Roskill, S. W. (ed.), *Documents Relating to the Naval Air Service, 1908–1918*, (London: Navy Records Society, 1969).

(iii) *Memoirs*

Baring, M., *RFC. HQ* (London: Bell, 1920).
Bartlett, C. P. O., *Bomber Pilot, 1916–1918* (London: Ian Allan, 1974).
Callwell, Sir C. E., *Experiences of a Dug-Out* (London: Constable, 1920).
Collishaw, R., *Air Command. A Fighter Pilot's Story* (London: Kimber, 1973).
Douglas, S., *Years of Combat* (London: Collins, 1963).
Hankey, Lord M., *The Supreme Command, 1914–1918*, 2 vols (London: Allen & Unwin, 1961).
Insall, A. J., *Observer. Memoirs of the R.F.C.* (London: Kimber, 1970).
Joubert de la Ferté, Sir P., *The Fated Sky. An Autobiography* (London: Hutchinson, 1952).
Lee, A. G., *Open Cockpit. A Pilot of the Royal Flying Corps* (London: Jarrolds, 1969).
Lewis, C., *Sagittarius Rising* (London: Peter Davies, 1936).
Livingstone, G., *Hot Air in Cold Blood* (London: Selwyn & Blount, 1933).
Longmore, Sir A., *From Sea to Sky, 1910–1945* (London: Geoffrey Blas, 1946).
Lloyd George, D., *War Memoirs of David Lloyd George*, 6 vols (London: Nicholson & Watson, 1933–6).
Macmillan, N. (ed.), *Sir Sefton Brancker* (London: Heinemann, 1935).

Robertson, Sir W., *Soldiers and Statesman, 1914–1918*, 2 vols (London: Cassell, 1926).

Stewart, O., *Words and Music for a Mechanical Man* (London: Faber, 1967).

Strange, L. A., *Recollections of an Airman* (London: Hamilton 1933).

Sueter, M. F., *Airmen or Noahs: Fair Play for our Airmen* (New York: Putnam, 1928).

Sydenham of Combe, Lord, *My Working Life* (London: Murray, 1927).

Sykes, Sir F., *From Many Angles. An Autobiography* (London: Harrap, 1942).

Taylor, Sir G., *Sopwith Scout 7309* (London: Cassell, 1968).

(iv) *Official Histories*

Edmonds, J. E., *Military Operations of the British Army in the Western Theatre of War in 1914–1918*, 16 vols (London: HMSO, 1922–49).

Ministry of Munitions, *History of the Ministry of Munitions*, 8 vols. (London: HMSO, 1922).

Postan, M. M. *et al.*, *Design and Development of Weapons. Studies in Government and Industrial Organization* (London: HMSO, 1964).

Raleigh, Sir W. and Jones, H. A., *The War in the Air. Being the Story of the Part Played in the Great War by the Royal Air Force*, 6 vols (Oxford: Clarendon Press, 1922–37).

Webster, Sir C. and Frankland, N., *The Strategic Air Offensive Against Germany*, Vol. 1 (London: HMSO, 1961).

Wise, S. F., *Canadian Airmen and the First World War. The Official History of the Royal Canadian Air Force*, Vol. 1 (Toronto: University of Toronto Press, 1980).

(v) *Other Printed Sources*

Adams, R. J. Q., *Arms and the Wizard. Lloyd George and the Ministry of Munitions, 1915–1916* (London: Cassell, 1978).

Anders, G., *History of the German Night Fighting Force, 1917–1945* (London: Jane's, 1979).

Ashmore, E. B., *Air Defence. An Account of Air Defence in England, 1914–1918* (London: Longman, 1929).

Barnett, C., *The Swordbearers. Studies in Supreme Command in the First World War* (London: Eyre & Spottiswoode, 1963).

Barnett, C., *The Collapse of British Power* (London: Eyre Methuen, 1972).

Beaverbrook, Lord, *Politicians and the War, 1914–1916*, 2 vols. (London: Thornton Butterworth, 1928).

Beaverbrook, Lord, *Men and Power, 1917–1918* (London: Hutchinson, 1956).

Best, G., *Humanity in Warfare. The Modern History of the International Law of Armed Conflicts* (London: Weidenfeld & Nicolson, 1980).

Bialer, U., *The Shadow of the Bomber. The Fear of Air Attack and British Politics* (London: Royal Historical Society, 1980).

Bidwell, S. and Graham, D., *Fire-Power. British Army Weapons and Theories of War, 1904–1945* (London: Allen & Unwin, 1982).

Bodenschatz, K., *Jagd in Flanderns Himmel* (Munich: Verlag Knorr & Hirth, 1938).

Boyle, A., *Trenchard* (London: Collins, 1962).

Broke-Smith, P. W. L., *The History of Early British Military Aeronautics* (Bath: Library Association, 1968).

Burge, C. G., *The Annals of 100 Squadron* (London: Herbert Reach, 1919).

Burk, K. (ed.), *War and the State. The Transformation of British Government, 1914–1919* (London: Allen & Unwin, 1982).

Charlton, L. E. O., *War from the Air. Past, Present, Future* (London: Nelson, 1935).

Churchill, R. S., *Lord Derby, King of Lancashire. The Official Life of Edward, Seventeenth Earl of Derby* (London: Heinemann, 1959).

Churchill, R. S., *Winston S. Churchill*, Vol. 2 (London: Heinemann, 1967).

Cole, C. and Cheeseman, E. F., *The Air Defence of Britain, 1914–1918* (London: Putnam, 1984).

Collier, B., *Leader of the Few. The Authorised Biography of Air Chief Marshal the Lord Dowding of Bentley Priory* (London: Jarrolds, 1957).

Collier, B., *Heavenly Adventurer. Sefton Brancker and the Dawn of British Aviation* (London: Secker & Warburg, 1959).

Cooper, M., 'A house divided. Policy, rivalry and administration in Britain's military air command, 1914–1918', *The Journal of Strategic Studies*, vol. 3, no. 2 (1980), pp. 178–201.

Cooper, M., 'The development of air policy and doctrine on the Western Front, 1914–1918', *Aerospace Historian*, vol. 28, no. 1 (1981), pp. 38–51.

Cooper, M., 'British flying operations on the Western Front, July 1917. A case study of Trenchard's offensive policy in action', *Cross and Cockade Journal*, vol. 23, no. 4 (1982), pp. 354–70.

Dean, Sir M., *The Royal Air Force and Two World Wars* (London: Cassell, 1979).

Divine, D., *The Broken Wing. A Study in the British Exercise of Air Power* (London: Hutchinson, 1966).

Ferko, A. E., *Fliegertruppe, 1914–1918* (Salem, Ohio: privately published, 1980).

Ferris, P., *The House of Northcliffe. The Harmsworths of Fleet Street* (London: Weidenfeld & Nicolson, 1971).

Fredette, R. H., *The Sky on Fire. The First Battle of Britain, 1917–1918 and the Birth of the Royal Air Force* (London: Cassell, 1966).

French, D., *British Economic and Strategic Planning, 1905–1915* (London: Allen & Unwin, 1982).

Gamble, C. F. S., *The Air Weapon. Being some Account of the Growth of British Military Aeronautics* (London: Oxford University Press, 1931).

Gibbs-Smith, C. H., *The Rebirth of European Aviation. A Study of the Wright Brothers' Influence* (London: HMSO, 1974).

Gilbert, M., *Winston S. Churchill*, Vols 3 and 4 (London: Heinemann, 1971 and 1975).

Gollin, A., 'The mystery of Lord Haldane and early British aviation', *Albion*, vol. 11, no. 1 (1979), pp. 46–65.

Gollin, A., 'The Wright brothers and the British authorities, 1902–1909', *English Historical Review*, vol. 95, no. 375 (1980), pp. 293–320.

Gollin, A., 'England is no longer an island. The phantom airship scare of 1909', 'Albion, vol. 13, no. 1 (1981), pp. 43–57.

Gollin, A., *No Longer an Island. Britain and the Wright Brothers, 1902–1909* (London: Heinemann, 1984).

Gooch, J., *The Plans of War. The General Staff and British Military Strategy, c. 1900–1916* (London: Routledge & Kegan Paul, 1974).

Gooch, J. (ed.), *The Prospect of War. Studies in British Defence Policy, 1847–1942* (London: Cass, 1981).

Goodhall, M., 'Royal Naval Air Service. Order of battle, Aug. 2 1914', *Cross and Cockade Great Britain Journal*, vol. 3, no. 4 (1972), pp. 137–46.

Grey, C. G., *A History of the Air Ministry* (London: Allen & Unwin, 1940).

Groves, P. R. C., *Behind the Smoke Screen* (London: Faber, 1934).

Guinn, P., *British Strategy and Politics, 1914 to 1918* (Oxford: Clarendon Press, 1965).
Hancock, W. K., *Smuts. The Sanguine Years, 1870–1919* (Cambridge: Cambridge University Press, 1962).
van Hauté, A., *Pictorial History of the French Air Force*, Vol. 1 (London: Ian Allan, 1974).
Hazelhurst, C., *Politicians at War, July 1914 to May 1915. A Prologue to the Triumph of Lloyd George* (London: Cape, 1971).
Higham, R., *The British Rigid Airship, 1908–1931. A Study in Weapons Policy* (London: Foulis, 1961).
Higham, R., *The Military Intellectuals in Britain, 1918–1939* (New Brunswick, NJ: Rutgers University Press, 1966).
Higham, R., *Air Power. A Concise History* (London: Macdonald, 1972).
von Hoeppner, E., *Deutschlands Krieg in der Luft* (Leipzig: von Hase & Koehler Verlag, 1921).
Hogg, I. V., *Anti-Aircraft. A History of Air Defence* (London: Macdonald & Jane's, 1978).
Holley, I. B., *Ideas and Weapons. Exploitation of the Aerial Weapon by the United States during World War I* (New Haven, Conn.: Yale University Press, 1953).
Holmes, R., *The Little Field Marshal. Sir John French* (London: Cape, 1981).
Hudson, J. J., *Hostile Skies. A Combat History of the American Air Service in World War I* (Syracuse, NY: Syracuse University Press, 1968).
Hunt, B. and Preston, A. (eds), *War Aims and Strategic Policy in the Great War, 1914–1918* (London: Croom Helm, 1977).
Imrie, A., *Pictorial History of the German Army Air Service, 1914–1918* (London: Ian Allan, 1971).
Imrie, A., *German Fighter Units, 1914–May 1917* (London: Osprey, 1978).
Imrie, A., *German Fighter Units, June 1917–1918* (London: Osprey, 1978).
Jones, H. A., 'Sir David Henderson, father of the Royal Air Force', *The Journal of the Royal Air Force College*, vol. 11, no. 1 (1931), pp. 6–12.
Jones, N., *The Origins of Strategic Bombing. A Study of the Development of British Air Strategic Thought and Practice up to 1918* (London: Kimber, 1973).
Joubert de la Ferté, Sir P., *The Third Service. The Story behind the Royal Air Force* (London: Thames & Hudson, 1958).
Kuropka, J., 'Die britische Luftkriegskonzeption gegen Deutschland im Ersten Weltkrieg', *Militär-geschichtliche Mitteilungen*, no. 1 (1980), pp. 7–24.
Laffin, J., *Swifter than Eagles. The Biography of Marshal of the Royal Air Force Sir John Maitland Salmond* (Edinburgh: Blackwood, 1964).
Lanchester, F. W., *Aircraft in Warfare. The Dawn of the Fourth Arm* (London: Constable, 1916).
Laux, J. M., 'Gnôme et Rhône – an aviation engine firm in the First World War', *Aerospace Historian*, vol. 27, no. 1 (1980), pp. 17–26.
Lewis, P., *The British Fighter since 1914. Sixty-Seven Years of Design and Development* (London: Putnam, 1979).
Macmillan, N., *Offensive Patrol: the Story of the RNAS, RFC and RAF in Italy* (London: Jarrolds, 1973).
Marder, A., *From the Dreadnought to Scapa Flow. The Royal Navy in the Fisher Era, 1904–1919*, 5 vols (London: Oxford University Press, 1961–70).
Marwick, A., *The Deluge. British Society and the First World War* (London: Bodley Head, 1965).
Mead, P., *The Eye in the Air. History of Air Observation and Reconnaissance for the Army, 1785–1945* (London: HMSO, 1983).

Montgomery Hyde, H., *British Air Policy between the Wars, 1918–1939* (London: Heinemann, 1976).

Morrow, J. H., *Building German Airpower, 1909–1914* (Knoxville, Tenn.: University of Tennessee Press, 1976).

Morrow, J. H., *German Air Power in World War I* (Lincoln, Nebr.: University of Nebraska Press, 1982).

Mosley, L., *Curzon. The End of an Epoch* (London: Longman, 1960).

Norris, G., *The Royal Flying Corps. A History* (London: Muller, 1965).

Nowarra, H. J., *Eisernes Kruez und Balkenkruez. Die Markierungen der deutschen Flugzeuge, 1914–1918* (Mainz: Verlag Dieter Hoffmann, 1968).

Pattinson, L. A., *History of 99 Squadron, Independent Force, Royal Air Force, March 1918–November 1918* (Cambridge: Heffer, 1920).

Pearsall, R., 'Aero engines of the First World War', *The Royal Air Force Quarterly*, vol. 12, no. 3 (1972), pp. 199–201.

Penrose, H., *British Aviation. The Pioneer Years, 1903–1914* (London: Putnam, 1967).

Penrose, H., *British Aviation. The Great War and Armistice, 1915–1919* (London: Putnam, 1969).

Pound, R. and Harmsworth, G., *Northcliffe* (London: Cassell, 1959).

Powers, B. D., *Strategy without Slide-Rule. British Air Strategy, 1914–1939* (London: Croom Helm, 1976).

Reader, W. J., *Architect of Air Power. The Life of the First Viscount Weir of Eastwood, 1877–1959* (London: Collins, 1968).

Rimell, R. L., *Zeppelin! A Battle for Air Supremacy in World War I* (London: Conway, 1984).

Robinson, D. H., *The Zeppelin in Combat. A History of the German Naval Airship Division, 1912–1918*, 3rd edn (London: Foulis, 1971).

Ronaldshay, Earl of, *The Life of Lord Curzon. Being the Authorized Biography of George Nathaniel, Marquess of Kedleston, K. G.*, 3 vols (London: Benn, 1928).

Roskill, S., *Hankey. Man of Secrets.* Vol. 1 (London: Collins, 1970).

Roskill, S., *Admiral of the Fleet Earl Beatty. The Last Naval Hero. An Intimate Biography* (New York: Atheneum, 1981).

Rowland, P., *Lloyd George* (London: Barrie & Jenkins, 1975).

Sanders, M. and Taylor, P. M., *British Propaganda during the First World War, 1914–1918* (London: Macmillan, 1982).

Scott, J. D., *Vickers. A History* (London: Weidenfeld & Nicolson, 1962).

Slessor, J. C., *Air Power and Armies* (London: Oxford University Press, 1936).

Smith, M., *British Air Strategy between the Wars* (Oxford: Clarendon Press, 1984).

Spender, J. A., *Weetman Pearson, First Viscount Cowdray, 1856–1927* (London: Cassell, 1930).

Stewart, O., 'Air forces in the Great War. Some strategical lessons', *Journal of the Royal United Service Institution*, vol. 79, no. 514 (1934), pp. 289–93.

Stonehouse, R., 'The Daimler Company of Coventry', *Cross and Cockade Great Britain Journal*, vol. 5, no. 1 (1974), pp. 29–39.

Sweetman, J., 'The Smuts report of 1917: Merely political window-dressing?', *The Journal of Strategic Studies*, vol. 4, no. 2 (1981), pp. 152–74.

Terraine, J., *Douglas Haig: The Educated Soldier* (London: Hutchinson, 1963).

Terraine, J., *To Win a War, 1918: The Year of Victory* (London: Sidgwick & Jackson, 1978).

Till, G., *Air Power and the Royal Navy, 1914–1945. A Historical Survey* (London: Jane's, 1979).

Troubridge, L. and Marshall, A., *John Lord Montagu of Beaulieu. A Memoir* (London: Macmillan, 1930).

Walker, P. B., *Early Aviation at Farnborough. The History of the Royal Aircraft Establishment*, 2 vols (London: Macdonald, 1974).

Winter, J. M. (ed.), *War and Economic Development. Essays in Memory of David Joslin* (Cambridge: Cambridge University Press, 1975).

Woodward, D. R., *Lloyd George and the Generals* (Newark, Del.: University of Delaware Press, 1983).

Young, D., *Member for Mexico. A Biography of Weetman Pearson, First Viscount Cowdray* (London: Cassell, 1966).

Index